'Digital media emerge, evolve and are remediated in ways that reflect our own paths through the life course. This volume examines how media can, and should, evolve along with us as our course through life is paved through imbricated layers of digital and non-digital moments. Unique, sophisticated, and original, this is a must read for those interested in the role digital media can play in constructing a life course out of a collection of "nows".'

Zizi Papacharissi, University of Illinois at Chicago, USA

'This impressive collection shows us how digital media have become embedded in nearly every aspect of society, and how people engage with these technologies at different stages of life. These lively and interesting studies reveal how engagement with ICTs is shaping the way we live and die, give birth, establish social relationships, handle mental health issues, deal with aging, and conduct politics. This is a valuable sourcebook for the field.'

Lance Bennett, University of Washington, Seattle, USA

Digital Media Usage Across the Life Course

New York Times columnist, Thomas Friedman declared the modern age in which we live as the 'age of distraction' in 2006. The basis of his argument was that technology has changed the ways in which our minds function and our capacity to dedicate ourselves to any particular task. Others assert that our attention spans and ability to learn have been changed and that the use of media devices has become essential to many people's daily lives and indeed the impulse to use technology is harder to resist than unwanted urges for eating, alcohol or sex.

This book seeks to portray the see-saw like relationship that we have with technology and how that relationship impacts upon our lived lives. Drawing on a range of theoretical perspectives that cross traditional subject boundaries, this volume examines the ways in which we both react to and are, to an extent, shaped by the technologies we interact with and how we construct the relationships with others that we facilitate via the use of Information Communication Technologies (ICTs) be it as discreet online only relationships or the blending of ICTs enabled communication with real life co-present interactions.

Paul G. Nixon is Principal Lecturer and Head of Research in European Studies, Faculty of Management and Organisation, The Hague University of Applied Sciences, The Netherlands. He has contributed chapters to many edited collections on the use of ICTs particularly in the fields of political parties, electronic democracy, and social welfare. He has co-edited five previous collections for Routledge: *Politics and the Internet in Comparative Context: Views from the Cloud* (with Rajash Rawal and Dan Mercea), *Understanding E-Government in Europe: Issues and Challenges* (with Vassiliki Koutrakou and Rajash Rawal 2010), *E-Government in Europe: Re-booting the State* (with Vassiliki Koutrakou 2007), *Political Parties and the Internet: Net Gain?* (with Steve Ward and Rachel Gibson 2003) and *Cyberprotest: New Media, Citizens and Social Movements* (with Wim van der Donk, Brian Loader and Dieter Rucht 2004). He has also published in the fields of culture and literature including editing a collection entitled *Representations of Education in Literature* (2000).

Rajash Rawal is Faculty Director, Faculty of Management and Organisation, The Hague University of Applied Sciences, The Netherlands. He is a visiting lecturer at the Fachhochschule, Eisenstadt, Austria and the Department of European Studies, Budapest Business School, Hungary. He has co-edited two previous collections for Routledge: *Politics and the Internet in Comparative Context: Views from the Cloud* (with Paul G. Nixon and Dan Mercea) and *Understanding E-Government in Europe: Issues and Challenges* (with Vassiliki Koutrakou and Paul G. Nixon 2010). He specializes in the impact of media on political agents in the modern era and has written a number of papers around this theme.

Andreas Funk is Lecturer in European Studies, Faculty of Management and Organisation, The Hague University of Applied Sciences, The Netherlands. His field of interests cover studies on social movements and their usage of social media platforms but also political philosophy, in particular problems in moral philosophy. He is currently undertaking research in 'reasonable pluralism and virtue'.

Routledge Key Themes in Health and Society

Available titles include:

Turning Troubles into Problems
Clientization in human services
Edited by Jaber F. Gubrium and Margaretha Järvinen

Compassionate Communities
Case studies from Britain and Europe
Edited by Klaus Wegleitner, Katharina Heimerl and Allan Kellehear

Exploring Evidence-based Practice
Debates and challenges in nursing
Edited by Martin Lipscomb

On the Politics of Ignorance in Nursing and Healthcare
Knowing ignorance
Amélie Perron and Trudy Rudge

Empowerment
A critique
Kenneth McLaughlin

The Story of Nursing in British Mental Hospitals
Echoes from the corridors
Niall McCrae and Peter Nolan

Living with Mental Disorder
Insights from qualitative research
Jacqueline Corcoran

A New Ethic of 'Older'
Subjectivity, Surgery and Self-stylization
Bridget Garnham

Forthcoming titles include:

Social Theory and Nursing
Edited by Martin Lipscomb

Identity, Ageing and Cultural Adaptation
Understanding longevity in crossdisciplinary perspective
Simon Biggs

Digital Media Usage Across the Life Course

Edited by
Paul G. Nixon, Rajash Rawal,
and Andreas Funk

Routledge
Taylor & Francis Group

LONDON AND NEW YORK

First published 2016
by Routledge
2 Park Square, Milton Park, Abingdon, Oxon OX14 4RN

and by Routledge
711 Third Avenue, New York, NY 10017

First issued in paperback 2017

Routledge is an imprint of the Taylor & Francis Group, an informa business

British Library Cataloguing in Publication Data
A catalogue record for this book is available from the British Library

Library of Congress Cataloging-in-Publication Data
Names: Nixon, Paul G., editor. | Rawal, Rajash, editor. | Funk, Andreas, editor.
Title: Digital media usage across the life course / [edited] by Paul G.
  Nixon, Rajash Rawal and Andreas Funk.
Description: Burlington : Ashgate, 2016. | Includes bibliographical
  references and index.
Identifiers: LCCN 2015041489 (print) | LCCN 2016011494 (ebook) |
  ISBN 9781472455802 (hardback : alk. paper)
Subjects: LCSH: Social media. | Internet—Social aspects. | Information
  technology—Social aspects.
Classification: LCC HM742 .D5424 2016 (print) | LCC HM742 (ebook) |
  DDC 302.23/1—dc23
LC record available at http://lccn.loc.gov/2015041489

ISBN 13: 978-1-138-49437-4 (pbk)
ISBN 13: 978-1-4724-5580-2 (hbk)

Typeset in Times New Roman
by Apex CoVantage, LLC

To Ingrid & Patrick
Paul G. Nixon

I'd like to thank Andrés, Claudia, and Laura. Without them none of this would be possible, or even worthwhile.
Rajash Rawal

Contents

x   *Contents*

Figures and tables

Figures

Tables

Contributors

Editors

Paul G. Nixon is a Principal Lecturer in Political Science and Head of Research at the European Studies, The Hague University of Applied Sciences, The Netherlands. He has contributed chapters to many edited collections on the use of ICTs, particularly in the fields of political parties, electronic democracy and social welfare. He has co-edited five previous collections for Routledge: *Politics and the Internet in Comparative Context: Views From the Cloud* (with Rajash Rawal & Dan Mercea), *Understanding E Government in Europe: Issues and Challenges* (with Vassiliki Koutrakou and Rajash Rawal 2010), *E-Government in Europe* (with Vassiliki Koutrakou 2007), *Political Parties and the Internet* (with Steve Ward & Rachel Gibson 2003) and *Cyberprotest* (with Wim van der Donk, Brian Loader & Dieter Rucht 2004). He has also published in the fields of culture and literature, including editing a collection titled *Representations of Education in Literature* (Edwin Mellen Press 2000).

Rajash Rawal is a Principal Lecturer in Political Science and Faculty Director at the European Studies, The Hague University of Applied Sciences, The Netherlands. He is a visiting lecturer at the Fachochschule, Eisenstadt, Austria and the Department of European Studies, Budapest Business School. He has co-edited two previous collections for Routledge: *Politics and the Internet in Comparative Context: Views From the Cloud* (with Paul G. Nixon & Dan Mercea) and *Understanding E Government in Europe: Issues and Challenges* (with Paul G. Nixon & Vassiliki Koutrakou 2010). He specializes in the impact of media on political agents in the modern era and has written a number of papers around this theme.

Andreas Funk is a Lecturer at the European Studies, The Hague University of Applied Sciences, The Netherlands. His fields of interest cover studies on social movements and their usage of social media platforms but also political philosophy, in particular problems in moral philosophy. He is currently undertaking research in 'reasonable pluralism and virtue'.

Contributors

Ronald W. Berkowsky is a graduate student in the Department of Sociology at the University of Alabama at Birmingham whose work has been published in *Journal of Applied Gerontology, Information, Communication & Society*, and *Educational Gerontology* and whose work has been presented at the annual meetings of the American Sociological Association and Gerontological Society of America, among others. His research focuses on examining the impacts of information and communication technologies on stress and health, particularly among those in the workforce and among older adults.

Catherine F. Brooks, PhD, University of California, is an Assistant Professor of Information and Communication at the University of Arizona. She studies online communities, internationalizing pedagogy, distance education, and interdisciplinarity. Her current work as the Director of Undergraduate Studies in Information involves the creation and maintenance of a new interdisciplinary eSociety degree program. She is also developing and will direct the new Center for eSociety, Information, and Data Studies at the University of Arizona.

Shelia R. Cotten is a Professor in the Department of Telecommunication, Information Studies, and Media (TISM) at Michigan State University. She studies technology use across the life course and the health, educational, and social impacts of this use for various populations. Other research interests include digital inequalities, multitasking, and online health activities. Her research has been published in *Social Science & Medicine, Journal of Applied Gerontology, Journal of Health Communication, Information, Communication, & Society, Computers in Human Behavior*, and *Computers & Education*, among others. She currently has funding from the National Science Foundation and the National Institute on Aging to support her research. Prior to moving to Michigan State, she was a Professor at the University of Alabama at Birmingham.

Vanessa P. Dennen is an Associate Professor of Educational Psychology and Learning Systems at Florida State University. She teaches courses on instructional design for ICTs, technology integration, and learning theory. Her research focuses on the use of computer-mediated discourse, social media, and mobile technologies to support learning in both formal and informal settings.

William H. Dutton is the Quello Professor of Media and Information Policy and Director of the James and Mary Quello Center at Michigan State University. An editor of *iCS* since its founding, Bill was Professor of Internet Studies at the University of Oxford and a Fellow of Balliol College, where he was the Founding Director of the Oxford Internet Institute and was the Principal Investigator of the Oxford Internet Survey from 2002–2013. Among his recent publications on the social aspects of information and communication technologies are *Society on the Line* (Oxford University Press 1999), *Digital Academe*, edited with

Brian Loader (Routledge 2003), *Social Transformation in the Information Society* (Paris: UNESCO for the WSIS Series 2004), which is available free online, *Transforming Enterprise*, edited by Dutton, Brian Kahin, Ramon O'Callaghan, and Andrew W. Wyckoff (MIT Press 2005), *The Oxford Handbook of Internet Studies* (OUP 2013), and *Society and the Internet*, edited with Mark Graham (OUP 2014).

Stine Gotved is Associate Professor at the IT University of Copenhagen, Denmark. She received her PhD in Cyber Sociology in 2000, and the research interests span variations in online social life and digital manifestations of physical death. In 2012, she initiated the Death Online Research Network, an international and multi-disciplinary network within the field of digital death, online grief, and connected legal matters. Currently, Stine is heading a small research project on QR codes on gravestones.

Natalie Pennington (MA, Kansas State University) is currently a PhD candidate at the University of Kansas in the Communication Studies department. Natalie's research focuses primarily on social media, impression management, and relational maintenance. Her work has previously been published in *New Media & Society*, *Computers in Human Behavior*, *Death Studies*, and *HUMOR: International Journal of Humor Research*.

Abigail Phillips is a fourth year doctoral student in the School of Information at Florida State University. Her research interests include social media, young adults, cyberbullying, digital citizenship, libraries, and librarianship. Abigail is currently working on her dissertation, which focuses on how rural librarians can be a source of support for rural cyberbullied young adults. Before entering the doctoral program, Abigail worked as a public librarian in a small, rural public library system in Southwest Georgia in the United States. She can be found by email alp07@my.fsu.edu, on her blog www.abigailleighphillips.com, or on twitter @abigailleigh.

Kelly Quinn (PhD, University of Illinois at Chicago) has an interdisciplinary research focus on new media and how it intersects with such diverse areas as the life course, social capital, friendship and privacy. Quinn's recent work has centered on midlife and older adults and their use of Internet communication technologies in their relationships. Her publications have been included in *Information, Communication & Society*, the *International Journal of Emerging Technologies and Society* and in several edited volumes.

Bianca C. Reisdorf is a Postdoctoral Researcher at the Quello Center, Department of Media and Information at Michigan State University with a focus in Digital Media and Methods in Communication Research. Bianca received her DPhil in Information, Communication and the Social Sciences from the Oxford Internet Institute, University of Oxford, in 2013, where she was involved in the Oxford Internet Surveys (OxIS) as a research assistant. Previous to her position at the Quello Center, Bianca worked as a Lecturer at the University of

Leicester and an Adjunct Assistant Professor at the University of Cincinnati. Her research interests include digital inequalities, Internet use among vulnerable groups, and cross-national comparative studies that apply both qualitative and quantitative methods.

Yukari Seko obtained a PhD in Communication and Culture at York University Canada, with a focus on digital narratives of mental health and qualitative Internet research. Approaching the intersection between communication studies and health research, she completed her postdoctoral fellowship in Social Aetiology of Mental Illness (SAMI) Training Program at the Centre for Addiction and Mental Health (CAMH) in Toronto, Canada. Her research interests include suicide, self-injury, therapeutic use of digital media, visual and art-based research, eHealth, youth and adolescent mental health, and Internet research ethics.

Katrin Tiidenberg is working on her PhD in Tallinn University, Institute of International and Social Studies, while lecturing in Sociology, Internet Studies and Research Methods. Her dissertation focuses on self-identity and the role online experiences play in its construction, with an emphasis on sexuality and embodiment, based on an ethnography with Tumblr, bloggers and self-shooters.

Vicki Winstead is a PhD candidate in Medical Sociology at the University of Alabama in Birmingham. She studies the effect of technology on older adults in continuing-care communities. She is currently completing her dissertation that examines the experience of older adults in assisted-living communities who have learned to use the computer and the Internet. Her work has been published in the *Journal of Applied Gerontology* and *Educational Gerontology*. Other research interests include dementia and neighborhood disadvantage.

Elizabeth Yost is a Visiting Assistant Professor at the College of William and Mary. She earned her PhD from the University of Alabama at Birmingham in Medical Sociology. Her research interests focus on the impact of technology on health and well-being outcomes among aging populations. Her work is published in *Educational Gerontology* and the *Journal of Applied Gerontology*. She teaches Medical Sociology, Health and Technology, and Global Health Issues.

Preface

Bringing together a collection like this takes time, effort, no little patience and, perhaps most of all, perseverance. What began as a germ of an idea at the AoIR conference in Denver in 2013 gestated into this collection. The editors would like to thank all the contributors for their inputs, efforts and forbearance. As so often in life, there is strength through unity, and we think that the contributions tell a thought-provoking story and that the divergence of the contributions from a series of excellent academics, at various stages of their careers, make this an interesting and intriguing collection to read. We hope you will agree.

We would also like to express our thanks to all the staff at Routledge who have aided us along our journey to completing this collection. They have made it a relatively painless experience and have been a pleasure to work with.

Of course we thank those close to us, friends and family members, who have tolerated our grumpiness, put up with our absences in the name of writing or editing and still provided us with tea and, when needed, sympathy.

Introduction

Digital Media Usage Across the Life Course

Paul G. Nixon, Rajash Rawal, and Andreas Funk

This book seeks to portray the seesaw-like relationship that we have with technology and how that relationship impacts our lived lives. It is a snapshot of the developing relationships we have with new technology and the way in which digital devices and the data that they produce are impacting our lives and having effects on the social norms and practices that we adopt to live our lives by. Drawing on a range of theoretical perspectives that cross traditional subject boundaries, this volume examines the ways in which we both react to and are, to an extent, shaped by the technologies we interact with and how we construct the relationships with others that we facilitate via the use of Information Communication Technologies (ICTs) be it as discreet online only relationships or the blending of ICTs enabled communication with real life co-present interactions.

The book is of interest to readers drawn from differing sections of society. We see it being of interest to academics in that the book will appeal to the growing number of academics with an interest in the effects of ICTs upon the way we interact with each other and the ways in which we live our lives today. As such it can be a text on the reading lists of media studies, sociologists and academics, particularly for those looking for thematic studies on the topic of the collection. It follows from this that it should also be of interest to students, and the collection provides a valuable and much-needed text for courses aimed at both undergraduate and postgraduate students. The collection is also a valuable resource for practitioners. It is likely to be of considerable interest to political actors from or interested in representing the needs of the various groupings as depicted in the content. It will also interest policy makers and those (within governmental organizations, social movements as well as non-profit organizations) who seek to have influence on political organizations and to seek to understand how they communicate with their publics and how ICT–enhanced social change is altering interactions in many spheres of life. The book will also help satisfy the ever-increasing demand from the public at large for good-quality material addressing the emerging issues associated with ICT adoption, how this impacts people at differing life stages and the Information Age lives we are now engaged in.

The chapter will briefly outline the ideas of life courses. It will go on to review the notions of social generations that have experienced or lived through, broadly, the same social and historical events, including experiencing technological changes and developments. Some scholars (e.g. Prensky, 2001, in his work on 'digital natives') have argued that this leads certain generations to have distinct technological competencies and capabilities that enable enhanced interaction with certain technologies, creating a generational digital divide, whilst others such as Lenhart and Horrigan (2003) see it being more of a spectrum where competencies are not found only in certain generations but are spread across people from all generations. Even the supposed 'digital natives' do not, in fact, have the range of competencies and abilities often, mistakenly, ascribed to them. It will then draw together these concepts and describe the perceptions that will flow through the contributions and lead into the substantive chapters. This introduction will then be followed by a brief description of the individual chapters from the contributors, their relevance and resonance, and how the chapters contribute to meeting the aims of the book. Thematic linkages will be foregrounded, and the flow of the life course, as described by the individual contributions, will be presented.

New York Times columnist Thomas Friedman declared the modern age in which we live the 'age of distraction' in 2006. The basis of his argument was that technology has changed the ways in which our minds function and our capacity to dedicate ourselves to any particular task. This claim further is reified by Carr (2010) in his book *The Shallows*, who asserts that our attention spans and ability to learn have been changed. Moreover, some researchers suggest that the use of media devices has become essential to many people's daily lives, and indeed the impulse to use technology is harder to resist than unwanted urges for eating, alcohol, or sex.

One interesting facet of the book is that it seeks to stretch the conceptions of 'life' to show how new technologies are influencing perceptions of life both at the prenatal and postmortem stages, thus examining digital media's influence over a life as a whole. The contributors to this collection weave a tapestry of empirical evidence together with relevant theory to give the reader a snapshot of digital media use. We do not claim this to be an all-encompassing glossary of all activities influenced by such technologies but rather a selection of the major changes that are noticeable within an ever-changing field.

Aims and objectives for the collection

This collection will:

- Provide the reader with a comprehensive portrait of the ways in which the Internet and associated digital technologies afford a space for engagement of and between individuals, organizations, and ad hoc collectives, illustrating how our life patterns have changed and involve a much more complicated structure in which information plays a more obvious and explicit role.
- Examine the differing scope and pace of changes in use, practice, and context shift through stages of the life course within a hybrid social environment.
- Encompass theoretical underpinnings and elaborate upon practical empirical research. Focusing upon means, tools, and strategies employed at varying points

through the life course. Question the stereotypes associated with the usage of digital media by persons of certain age groupings. Pinpoint differences and similarities and attempt to account for the seemingly differing interplays in progress.

- Bring together and showcase the work of experienced and internationally renowned scholars as well as some fresh young voices.

What we hope to engender through the research presented in this book is a more profound understanding of the need for research on Internet and ICT use which implies not an episodic approach but a longitudinal one and charts the ways in which we interact with technologies and new developments throughout our lifetimes and if the life-stage approach to this may have a resonance. It is also important to focus not only on the individual or even on the cohort but also upon the context, location, and life domains (family, work, institutions) we may study those actions in, as they are the contextualizing factors in which events take place.

Our lives and actions are a mix of individual and collective contexts in which decisions are taken, and Mayer (2009) notes the recognition of this as being an integral part in understanding and interpreting those lives. Mayer charts the rise of life course sociology demonstrating how it has evolved to include the concept of age differentiation as a structural category, showing how a "close link between psychological, social-psychological, social and historical perspectives remained a major focus in the extensive work of Elder and his associates" (Mayer, 2009, p. 2).

In one of his many major works contributing to the field, Elder (1994), whose work (including that done with many of his associates) is underpinned by an emphasis upon "the social forces that shape the life course and its developmental consequences" (p. 4), argued that life course trajectories could be observed as the experiencing and timing of various events which were affected by four themes that he determined to be:

a   Historical time, which Elder saw as the recognition that as a cohort we are born into "different historical worlds with their constraints and options" (Elder, 1994, p. 5). Each cohort will experience the same events differently dependent upon their age and development at the time of the said event. For example a 12-year-old will be much more vividly impacted in a war situation than a 2-year-old.

b   The timing of lives implies that there is social meaning attached to the notion of age, and later actions and experiences can be determined by how events are experienced in relation to other subsequent events.

c   Linked lives, which identifies that our life experiences are inextricably linked to those of others, most often though not exclusively within family or kinship relationships. Those linkages are reformed and added to through various events in our lives, starting to work at a new workplace, or the acquisition of a new set of relatives through marriage. The events that also affect those to whom we have close bonds in social and/or labour market situations impact our own life experiences. This can be particularly true in smaller, closerknit communities, which experience severe labour market disruptions due to

   industrial and economic decisions leading to social change. An example of
   this could be the 1984/5 miners' strike in the UK.
d   Human agency, whereby individuals shape their own futures related to the
   situational context in which decisions are taken, with the context of those
   decisions being, at least in part, contextualized by previous events and decisions. Expectations and goals can thus be fuelled or tempered by lived experiences of the individuals and those in similar situations. In later work (Elder &
   Shanahan, 2006) he added another theme, that of lifetime development, recognizing that development and ageing are life-long processes.

As the notions of childhood and what is or can be expected of children are
socially constructed, so the responsibilities and attitudes that those children experience are part of the shaping of their trajectories into other life stages (Green,
2010, p. 73). These contexts are not of course mutually exclusive. If one thinks of
an individual child one thinks of them being socialized in a number of contexts
via interactions in the family, with friends at school, and so forth. The family is
the predominant focus with parents and others attempting to shape the child's
development, in terms of providing both resources and protection in an environment in which the child can best meet the goals or aspirations that they set for
that child. Such protection may also add to the child's resilience or ability to
be able to absorb 'shocks' or disadvantages in later life stages. However, this
household context is, as Bronfenbrenner (1979) pointed out, shaped by social
contexts such as the economy, the environment (both in a broad sense and also in
the more physical aspects of the child's upbringing), social norms, and expectations. One can also add the role of government or other policy agencies to this.
Certain policy programmes can also play a part in modifying child development
and thus decreasing or magnifying inequality that may arise as a consequence of
their family situation. Leisering and Leibfried (1999) posit modern social policy
as "life-course policy," and as Cook and McWhirther (2011, p. 20) note, "can be
thought of as primarily working by affecting the timing and experience of various
life-course transitions."

Schulenberg and Maslowsky (2015) put forward two models for how someone may develop over the life course. The first is the 'shot out of a cannon'
model, whereby a person's trajectory is mainly seen as being constrained by pre-
determined, rigid characteristics such as birth, class, economic circumstances,
and family expectations and what Schulenberg and Maslowsky term "the aim
of the cannon" (p. 320). The second model they describe is the 'contact sport'
model, whereby a person's lifelong trajectory is determined by the interaction
"between an active self-constructing individual on the one hand and a powerful
changing context on the other hand" (p. 320). This model implies more responsibility to the individual to play a part in determining their life choices and
development through the life course, mirroring notions of social mobility and
meritocracy that are prevalent in society today. Certainly one might imagine the
broadly equalizing tendencies inherent in ICT use to contribute to this diminution
of pre-determinism, although it should not be overstressed.

Policy interventions can also have a direct impact on later life experiences in terms of health interventions that may allow that child to be more active or in better condition than its parents were at a similar age, as they did not experience the same interventions at an early life stage. The length of time spent in education has also changed, with children starting earlier than their parents or grandparents would have done and extending that education beyond school into college or university or even into embracing the notion of life-long learning. Muennig (2015) shows how interventions undertaken in early childhood can impact higher attainment in education, increased social connections, and fewer behavioral problems. We can also see how certain social policy interventions such as pension policy can help institutionalize certain life-course patterns (Kohli, 1986).

Those collective contexts may be both longstanding (e.g. church, family, or trades union) or more transient (friends, relationships, employment). This mélange of longstanding and transient collective contexts together with prior life histories are important in that they can impact actions or in this case ICT usage, and the shifts of perspective and emphasis within them facilitate new relationships and use of and engagement with technology. Notions of gender, racial, and class differences in the timing of various events, such as marriage and childbearing, can be identified, and there is little doubt that these impact the individual in later life, affecting life course trajectories. As Moen and Han (2001) suggest, women's transitions in the domains of family and work are different to men's and impact their life opportunities. There are worries that the power inequalities identifiable in the wider world will be replicated in the online world, leading to a reinforcement of existing gender power inequalities in a range of power arenas such as work and/or home amongst others (Loader, 1998). Helsper (2010) notes that women tend to be more equal in terms of access opportunities when they are students, unemployed, or retired rather than when they are employed. She goes on to note the gendered usage of online spaces, with women being predominant in spaces centered on health issues and men being predominant in areas of gaming and sex. As societal attitudes toward sex change, particularly but not exclusively, in relation to a challenging of the hetero-normative agenda and the breaking down of stereotypes and taboos spread through the life course. Will we see an acceptance and acknowledgement of the reality that people other than men are also interested in and wish to have a voice on sexual issues? Will we see an increasing push towards online equality?

The flow of the collection

In short the collection commences with three chapters which deal with some of the overarching themes that stretch across the contributions and which, to some extent, impinge upon or inform the lives that we lead. In Chapter 1 William H. Dutton and Bianca C. Reisdorf show how age has been one of the most dominant factors related to patterns of access and use of the Internet. In Chapter 2, Rajash Rawal and Paul G. Nixon engage with the ways in which technology and its development shape our lives. In Chapter 3 Andreas Funk postulates on how those changes are affecting democracy and our attempts to provide ourselves with a more modern notion of citizenship. The collection then takes us on a journey through life stages ranging from pre-birth to postmortem in which we see how much lives are being changed in ways that are positive but also have potential negative consequences.

Let us now examine the chapters in a little more depth in order to give the reader a more cogent path through the book. Chapter 1 by William H. Dutton and Bianca C. Reisdorf illustrates how age has been one of the most dominant factors related to patterns of access and use of the Internet. Drawing on the research literature and analysis of survey data in Britain and other nations, this chapter describes the empirical findings underpinning this generalization and explores three dominant explanations for the strong relationship between age and Internet use: (1) age as an indicator of 'aging,' such as physiological changes over time in such factors as vision or finger dexterity; (2) 'cohort,' with age cohorts growing up adapting to different technologies dominant among their age group; and (3) life-stages, which create different sets of needs and demands on users who are students versus employees versus retirees. As patterns of use feed into the experiences of different age groups with the Internet, trust in the Internet as an experience technology tends to reinforce and maintain early patterns of use. While it is practically impossible to disentangle the relative significance of these alternative explanations, given that they are so closely interrelated, it is useful to conceptualize these factors as additive and complementary rather than alternative explanations and therefore helpful in explaining why age has been and is continuing to be so strongly related to use. For all of these reasons, age is likely to remain an important factor shaping the use of the Internet.

However, the relationship has changed in some important respects, suggesting more changes ahead. For example, age is less of a determinant in some nations, such as the United States, than in others, such as Britain. Moreover, the Internet itself is changing over time, such as with the development of social media and mobile Internet applications that might embed the Internet in everyday life and work in ways that are easier to use and more 'intuitive' and accordingly less affected by aging and cohort effects. As a consequence, it is important to view age and the Internet as a dynamic relationship rather than a static one, in which both people and the Internet are co-evolving. It is clear that further research will need to continually track these relationships and not assume the role of age is socially or technologically determined rather than shaped by the interactions of technical and social change.

In the second chapter Rajash Rawal and Paul G. Nixon will examine the impact of technology on our daily lives and attempt to assess what this has done to our existence. As highlighted by Nicolas Carr in his work *The Shallows*, people's patterns of thinking, acting, and doing have changed tremendously in the Internet era. This has moved even further in the so called 'post–PC' era. Mobile devices, both phones and tablets, have led to the development of various applications that aid us to remember when to eat, exercise, or sleep. Moreover, this technology has become 'wearable' with the advent of smart watches and fuel bands. The question here is what impact will this have on future development? Does this aid our mental health or hinder it? Is it right that all humans need to eat, move, or sleep in tune to the beck and call of an application?

In Chapter 3 Andreas Funk investigates the ways in which the public sphere may be being reshaped and how virtual life is impacting notions of democracy. The emergence of new forms of democracy is tied to novel conceptions of both the citizens and the public space in which these citizens engage in political affairs. Have the technological advancements that characterize what we term the 'information society' altered political relationships? Citizens in the Athenian polis received information, deliberated, and influenced decision making at the marketplace. Contrasting to this ancient form of democracy, contemporary models such as deliberative democracy are seen to be linked to a less physical sort of public space, the public sphere. As the concept of e-democracy has emerged we can identify new ideas around the way in which we should govern and in which we are governed. As part of the public sphere has become located in the virtual world new possibilities and potentialities have emerged. In particular new technologies have facilitated those who hope that the Internet can be the locus to display a public space that enables more participatory and dialogic politics. Certainly we can see the impacts of social media usage challenging traditional discourses and expanding the fora in which democratic discourses take place and widening participation within those discourses. Such widening of access has not always enriched the quality of the discourse engaged in, though on the whole one would argue that on balance the positive gains outweigh the negatives.

The gap between such initial optimism about the potential of e-democracy and the problems which have been experienced in terms of its realization are often explained by a supposedly idealistic conception of the virtual public sphere overlooking its exclusionary and fragmented nature. What has been less discussed than the notion of the virtual public sphere, however, is the meaning of citizenship linked to the idea of e-democracy and how this may or may not fluctuate over differing life stages. This chapter will include a re-drafting of a conception of digital citizens with regard to e-democracy. More precisely, it will examine to what extent e-democracy raises new challenges and requires distinct political virtues from digital citizens and postulates how this may change over differing life stages.

Yukari Seko and Katrin Tiidenberg in Chapter 4 address the emergent phenomenon of prenatal 'digital birth,' in which the unborn baby is (re)configured as an ultrasound image that signifies social life of both the baby and their parents. The examples that they draw, taken from everyday digital media (blogs, zines, online prenatal communities, social network sites, and photo/video-sharing sites), signal ways in which the unborn is animated, materialized, and anthropomorphized through visual technologies and later via online sharing platforms. This is also a theme that will find resonance in other contributions, particularly that of Dennen in Chapter 5. By analyzing the increasingly common act of treating a medical image as a cultural artifact, Seko and Tiidenberg describe how new meaning is attached to the making of sonogram scans, an activity hitherto confined to the realm of scientific positivism which is now taking place in everyday online life.

Today a child's digital life may well commence prior to their actual birth occurrence. A 2010 survey with 2,200 mothers from 10 countries revealed that 23 per cent of participants gave 'digital birth' to their children by posting sonogram scans on the Internet (AVG Technologies, 2010). Prenatal life online appears intriguing in three respects. First, this phenomenon symbolizes the increasing integration of medical images into popular conceptions of pregnancy. In a hospital setting, foetal ultrasonography is primarily a diagnostic means to look through maternal bodies primarily for the detection of foetal abnormalities and to allow any subsequent intervention that may be deemed necessary for the health of the mother and/or foetus. Through this visualization process, a foetus is virtually removed from the mother's uterus and reconstructed as the 'unborn patient' (Casper, 1998) who deserves intensive medical treatment. The digital birth implies that the ultrasound image is now seen as an iconic representation of a real foetus and thus adored like a born baby. Newer technologies of three-dimensional and four-dimensional sonogram are seen as useful to please parents eager to have more life-like, 'crisp' images of their baby, although they have no diagnostic advantages over conventional ultrasonography (Mask, 2013). Virtually constructed via visual technologies, the animated foetus no longer connotes something unreal. Rather, the image marks a Deleuzian concept of virtual as a movement of actualization, a yet-unrealized potential of becoming rather than a simulacrum (Grosz, 2005). The way expectant parents use sonogram images also illustrates the fact that the lay use of medical photography is, despite the visual turn and the consequent scholarly acceptance of images as socially constructed (Pink, 2005), still governed by the regime of truth (Foucault, 1977). The regime of truth is carried by an assumption the photographed artifacts have finite, fixed symbolic meanings (Pink, 2005).

Second, the digital birth of a child is inseparably linked to digital 'birth' of parenthood. Viewing the image of the foetus may be of particular significance for the fathers-to-be, as the visual access to the foetus goes some way towards potentially equalizing their positions with their partners (Draper, 2002). And once uploaded online, the image – just like any other private photographs – renders private affairs to public viewing, operating as a form of social currency (van Dijek, 2008). The image solicits comments from friends, families, or other expectant parents regarding their ongoing transition to parenthood. This virtual baby shower develops the first digital footprint for the child, and simultaneously, leads the expectant parents to publicly announce and acknowledge their new roles to the wider world. The ultrasound image, in this vein, symbolizes a changing social status of the parents who, along with their baby, would socially grow up online. Thus, in this case, the sonogram image could be viewed as a declarative, communicative act of announcing the pregnancy and soliciting acknowledgement for one's changing social and role-identity from peers.

Finally, the sonogram image, while often referred to as a first selfie of the baby, is also a selfie of the parents. In the budding selfie-scholarship, selfies are often conceptualized as forms of "self-narration and representation" (Richter & Schadler, 2009, p. 171) thus an important aspect of self-identity. This is inextricably linked with questions of agency. Writing about foetal ultrasound images,

Sally Han (2009) starts her chapter by quoting her informant, Josie, who links showing printed out sonogram images to being a 'good' mother, and performing her excitement about her transition to motherhood. In the case of prenatal images, the foetus is unable to refuse to have its picture taken or posted. Then when does life online really begin? Does the practice of online sharing blur the boundary between mother and the foetus constructed via visual technology? In line with Holloway et al. (2013) who warn parents to be aware that "their children's online dossiers are likely to be with them for the rest of their lives" (p. 24), this chapter concludes by exploring potential ethical, moral and legal implications of digital birth on the children.

Chapter 5 has Vanessa P. Dennen outlining how children grow into their own digital footprint and how different today's child's connections with technology are in comparison to those experienced by their parents in their own childhood. Today's children are born into a world where cameras, screens, and social sharing are fairly ubiquitous. Pregnancies are announced by posting ultrasound photos, and mothers document their pregnancy journeys online. Before birth, some children already have domain names, email addresses, and Facebook accounts reserved in their names. Their births are tweeted and posted, as are many of their early moments. These are the acts of proud, loving parents. As these children become increasingly aware of their surroundings, including the various technologies in their home and used by their caregivers, they develop their own understanding of technology and the role that it plays in everyday life. For each generation, a new set of technologies and new types of life documentation and interactions are accepted as the norm.

This chapter documents the various ways in which the information and communication technologies (ICTs) intersect the lives of young (preschool) children, both in terms of how they develop a personal understanding of and relationship with ICTs as well as the tensions that emerge as they begin to develop a consciousness of how their lives are being documented by these ICTs. In a fascinating mix of academic research and social observation of her own child's experiences as she has grown and how her daughters interactions with technologies that Dennen herself has had to 'learn' to use is shaping her daughter's view of what to expect in later life, Dennen examines the omnipresent means of life documentation and sharing of photos and videos – the development of virtual relationships (e.g. Skyping with distant family members). She notes the intuitive use of technology by children and the ongoing implications of early ICT use for these children in school and the privilege it may afford them over those who have not had such access.

In Chapter 6 Abigail Phillips carries on our journey from childhood into the often difficult teenage years. She first presents an overview of the digital lives of teens. Following this, the key roles that digital media and online communication play in the lives of teens are examined. It is interesting to note the ubiquitous nature that ICT use has in the lives of modern teens. Then the darker side of digital media will be assessed. This includes negative online behaviors such as cyberbullying, trolling, cyberstalking, and cyberdating violence. Because cyber violence and abuse are unfortunate realities, it is necessary to study these behaviors from both a researcher and practitioner lens. Finally, this chapter will close with a discussion of the implications for schools, libraries, parents, and community agencies, as well as suggest directions for future research. As role models for teens, these adult figures serve an important ancillary role as 'media mentors,' creating opportunities for teens to develop media skills and to incorporate them into the fullness of their lives. Phillips asks the questions around how those needs might be nurtured and encouraged in a safe environment and how we might embrace the concept of connected learning both in the classroom and also in the wider society.

Our next contributor, Natalie Pennington, examines the use of social media by the 20- to 30-year-olds of today. In Chapter 7 her piece "Living Social: Comparing Social Media Use in Your 20s and 30s," she starts by reviewing past literature that exists surrounding the use of social media by Millennials (i.e. 20- to 30-year-olds) today. The focus is placed upon interpersonal communication through social networking sites, drawing on research regarding both impression management and relational development and maintenance. In addition to reviewing past work that is key to the discipline, this chapter shares new data comparing the use of Facebook for a variety of communicative and relational purposes by individuals in their 20s and their 30s. While Millennials range from those born in the early 1980s to the 2000s, the behavioral patterns within that group have the potential to range as well. The majority of past research on social media samples almost exclusively college students in their late teens/early 20s, making this new survey data on those in the late 20s/30s important for considering the full context of use today. The context of their usage is far more heterogeneous than that studied in earlier works, giving a much more rounded picture of the usage. The chapter rounds off by offering reflections on where social media use may well be headed for this particular life stage, and Pennington offers suggestions for how individuals at this point in their life can most benefit from engaging through social media.

In Chapter 8, in the first of her two contributions to this collection, Kelly Quinn investigates the use of social media platforms in midlife stages. How do we engage with those technologies at a time of transition in our own lives, with different roles, expectations, and perspectives adding to our search for self-identity? Social media platforms enable us to maintain connection with a larger number of weak relationships than more traditional communication technologies have, providing additional opportunities to develop and maintain social capital and preserve distant ties. Use of these platforms in this way, however, often results in 'context collapse,' as disparate social circles and relations merge into a single social space. At midlife, complex relational contexts and the simultaneous fulfillment of contrasting roles are common, resulting from a peak in familial and personal responsibilities, the melding of present and past identities, and the performance of a succession of occupational positions. The blending of audiences and relational contexts which characterizes social media use therefore presents conflicts and challenges at midlife that are unlike those at other, especially earlier, life stages. This chapter presents results of a study of 23 midlife adults, between the ages of 45 and 65 years, that examined the behaviors and attitudes related to the use of social media. It explores how careful curation of content and the use of social strategies, such as selectivity in making connections, are used in combination as mechanisms of boundary regulation, thereby preserving privacy and maintaining social borders. Reflective of Bourdieu's conception of *habitus*, the practices and dispositions resulting from accumulated life experiences differentiate social media use at midlife from that of youth and young adults, more well-studied groups, and provide a snapshot of how these platforms might be utilized differently at various points in life.

Chapter 9 sees Catherine Brooks comment upon retrospective narratives about life with anxiety across the life course. Staking the United States as her case study she notes that millions of people in the United States suffer from anxiety and anxiety-related disorders. Documenting a growing mental health crisis that has been under represented in terms of subject for examination by social scientists studying e-health or the Internet, she seeks to examine how those suffering from mental illness and anxiety engage the Internet across the life course. Brooks sees a life course approach as particularly valuable for understanding the role of the Internet relative to mental health suffering because many sufferers experience heightened illness effects during certain periods or around events tied to particular life stages. Such events may occur at any life stage (e.g. abuse) or indeed span several stages, and other events may often be directly anchored within a particular life period (e.g. military involvement) – though these events may happen differentially across time periods, they have the potential to have an acute impact on mental health outcomes (Allen et al., 2008, Gothelf et al., 2004). She shows how child labour is an experience that is particularly tied to a certain life stage and has been clearly linked to some illnesses related to anxiety in the sufferer (Vasconcelos et al., 2007). Brooks then views any focus on the life course and the role of the Internet for support across periods of that life course as particularly germane to furthering our understanding of mental health issues and the role of the Internet in anxiety's evolution over time.

The Internet has facilitated a variety of shifts in health care. With changing foci on how people find health information, how they access support and support services as patients or caregivers, how they engage as members of online health communities, or how people navigate new data-management tools and plans, e-health as Brooks shows is an important concern for us all.

In Chapter 10 Kelly Quinn's second contribution to this collection focuses on older adults often known as silver surfers. She shows how social media use by adults over age 65 has accelerated markedly in recent years, underscoring its relevance and importance to everyday living. Despite these increases, wide disparities in adoption levels persist between younger and older users, and the usage patterns and adoption rates of specific social media platforms vary widely. Perhaps because of these differences, research on the use of social media at older ages is an emerging and important field of study. This chapter presents a review of the important questions that have been the focus of academic research on social media use at older ages to date and the principal theoretical frameworks that have guided this research. It draws attention to three areas of older adult social media practice that predominate scholarly thinking: the nonuse of social media by older adults, generational differences between social media users, and the beneficial aspects of social media use. While these prevailing approaches have provided a foundation to understand the functional and operative considerations surrounding social media engagement by older adults, Quinn argues that they do not aid our understanding of the valued place of these media in the everyday lives of older adults, nor have they provided answers about how use of these platforms might develop with life experience. The chapter concludes with important next steps for scholars to consider based on existing research limitations and the emergence of recent findings and makes evident the substantial opportunities for evolution and progress in this developing area of study.

Chapter 11 is a second chapter looking at older adults. In it Elizabeth Yost, Vicki Winstead, Ronald W. Berkowsky, and Shelia R. Cotten examine how technology can improve health and well-being in aging populations and how you are never too old to learn. Older adults are at increased risk for social isolation, loneliness, depression, and lower overall quality of life. Many of these declines are related to the loss of social ties, increasing health concerns, and changes in living environments as people progress through older age. Using (ICTs) has shown to be effective in negating some of these declines in older adults.

Individuals often move into assisted and independent living communities (AICs) when their health begins to decline, when they need assistance with activities of daily living, and when their spouse/partner dies and they cannot maintain their independence. In many respects, individuals in these communities are frailer than those who live independently in their homes. The research presented here in this chapter details results of a randomized controlled trial designed to teach older adults in 19 assisted and independent living communities to use computers and the Internet and assesses the impacts on their quality of life over time. Data for this project include multiple surveys over the course of a 1-year period, focus group notes, observational files, and field notes from training activities. A total of 314 older adults participated in the project. Key outcomes assessed included attitudes towards technology, technology use, depression, loneliness, social isolation, social capital, mattering, life satisfaction, and social connectedness.

As the chapter shows, results of this study suggest that older adults can learn to use ICTs and overcome the digital divide, even those in assisted and independent living communities. In teaching ICT courses to AIC residents, special attention was given to developing a training manual that was easily accessible for participants. In addition to class lectures, hands-on training was provided for each individual participant so that skills were reinforced in class. Our findings suggest that use of this specially designed manual, along with the other accommodations made in the ICT classes to cater to the special needs of the AIC residents, helped improve positive attitudes towards computers and successfully decreased perceived limitations the residents faced in handling the computer and Internet technologies.

In Chapter 12 Stine Gotved takes us on a journey to an area of Internet activity that we often shy away from and prefer not to engage in, that of dealing with death online. As the physical life is intrinsically connected with online services and digital social networks, so is the physical death. This chapter describes the last journey, from the reluctant planning to the digital manifestations afterwards. Using a simple time line of antemortem, perimortem, and postmortem (before, just around, and after the physical death of an individual), the digital possibilities in the different stages are presented. They range from the need for being prepared for one's demise in a digital context to the intricate questions of digital assets and inheritance, from the service of online undertakers to the shared memorials on social network sites and the notions of digital legacies. The truly cross-disciplinary research into death online is in the process of assembling as a field; thus this chapter presents the diverse and dynamic activity surrounding physical death in the digital age.

Chapter 13 explores the suicidecam phenomenon (live streaming of one's suicide via webcam) as Yukari Seko investigates one of the emerging forms of autobiographical narrative transmitted through the social medium of the webcam. Though relatively rare in number, public suicides are ubiquitous. Unlike many isolationists who take their lives alone, some choose public settings – by jumping off buildings or bridges, for instance – perhaps hoping to engrave their last moment in the minds of witnesses. A 20-year-old University of Guelph student who attempted suicide on December 2, 2013, also set up a stage for people to bear witness to his last moments. What made his attempt unique was the fact that his intended witnesses were not physically standing beneath him. Two hundred witnesses who observed the suicide attempt were behind their computers watching him light his dorm room on fire and crawl into bed. This suicide attempt was not the first in which a webcam-broadcast suicide was seen on the Internet. The first well-known suicide on webcam dates back to 2007, in which a 42-year-old British man hung himself to death in front of a live-streaming webcam (Ungoed-Thomas, 2007). In August 2008, a young man from Utah shot himself in the chest with a hunting rifle while his ex-girlfriend was watching via webcam.

What does this online broadcasting of private suicides, or what may be called the 'suicidecam' phenomenon, indicate? What should be recognized instead is that emerging cyberculture, along with its new equipment for documentation and its new ways of relating to the possibilities, introduces a new practice of self-expression whose outcome is to be instantly shared, circulated, and consumed by (sometimes anonymous) audiences within the virtual network. Specifically, as Lev Manovich (2008) articulately points out, the explosion of user-generated media network, or so-called social media since the turn of the 21st century, has given a birth to a 'new media universe' in which every single moment of life, literally from the cradle to the grave, becomes viewable and sharable to the public.

So now it falls to you, the reader, to interrogate the contributions and to discover whether they reflect the lived realities of your life. It is clear that the use of new technologies will change the ways in which we interact with each other and even, potentially, our life chances. There is also little doubt that those in different age cohorts will have differing relationships with ICTs and their uses as they progress through the life course. Due to technological advancements in such fields as robotics and artificial intelligence over the next 60 years, the experience of a

20-year-old today will be markedly different from that of today's 80-year-old. The one certainty is that, barring a natural catastrophe, we will all be more dependent and socially embedded in a society ever more driven by, information, social networking, and technological aids. As history has shown us as social change occurs, this will have effects upon and consequences for people's lives and affect their life course in as yet unimagined ways.

References

AVG Technologies. (2010). Digital Diaries 2010. Retrieved from http://www.avg.com/digitaldiaries/2010 (accessed September 1, 2014).

Bronfenbrenner, U. (1979). *The Ecology of Human Development: Experiments by Nature and Design.* Cambridge, MA: Harvard University Press.

Carr, N. (2010). *The Shallows, What the Internet Is Doing to Our Brains.* New York: W. W. Norton & Company.

Casper, M. (1998). *The Making of the Unborn Patient: A Social Anatomy of Fetal Surgery.* New Brunswick: Rutgers University Press.

Cooke, M., & McWhirter, J. (2011). "Public policy and aboriginal peoples in Canada: Taking a life-course perspective." *Canadian Public Policy*, 37, Supplement, April/avril 2011, 15–31.

Draper, J. (2002). "'It was a real good show': The ultrasound scan, fathers and the power of visual knowledge." *Sociology of Health & Illness*, 24(6), 771–795.

Elder, G. H. (ed.). (1974). *Children of the Great Depression.* Chicago: University of Chicago Press.

Elder, G. H., Jr. (1994). "Time, human agency, and social change: Perspectives on the life course." *Social Psychology Quarterly*, 57, 4–15.

Elder G. H., Jr., & Shanahan M. J. (2006). "The life course and human development." In: Damon, W. and Lerner, R. M. (eds), *Handbook of Child Psychology. Vol. 1. Theoretical Models of Human Development*, 6th ed., New York: John Wiley & Sons, pp. 665–715.

Foucault, M. (1977). *Discipline and Punish: The Birth of a Prison.* London: Penguin Books.

Green, L. (2010). *Understanding the Life Course, Sociological and Psychological Perspectives.* Cambridge: Polity Press.

Grosz, E. (2005). *Time Travels: Feminism, Nature, Power.* Durham, NC and London: Duke University Press.

Han, S. (2009). "Seeing like a family: Fetal ultrasound images and imaginings of kin." In: Sasson, V. R. and Law, J. M. (eds), *Law, Imaginings of the Fetus, the Unborn in Myth, Religion and Culture.* Oxford: Oxford University Press, pp. 275–290.

Helsper, E. (2010). "Gendered Internet use across generations and life stages." *Communication Research*, 37(3), pp. 352–374.

Holloway, D., Green, L., & Livingstone, S. (2013). *Zero to Eight. Young Children and Their Internet Use.* LSE, London: EU Kids Online.

Kohli, M. 1986. "The world we forgot: A historical review of the life course." In: Marshall, V. W. (ed.), *Later Life: The Social Psychology of Aging.* London: Sage, pp. 271–303.

Leisering, L., & Leibfried, S. 1999. *Time and Poverty in Western Welfare States: United Germany in Perspective.* Cambridge: Cambridge University Press.

Lenhart, A., & Horrigan J. B. (2003) "Re-visualising the digital divide as a digital spectrum." *IT & Society*, 1(5), 23–29.

Loader, B. (1998). "Cyberspace divide: Equality, agency, and policy in the information society." In: Loader, B. (ed.), *Cyberspace Divide: Equality, Agency, and Policy in the Information Society.* New York: Routledge, pp. 3–18.

Manovich, Lev. (2008). Software Takes Command. Retrieved from http://www.software studies.com (accessed April 3, 2014).

Mask, M. (February 15, 2013). 3-D Ultrasounds give expectant parents crisp images of unborn baby. *Wral.com.* Retrieved from http://www.wral.com/3d-ultrasounds-give-expectant-parents-crisp-images-of-unborn-baby/12114445/ (accessed April 3, 2014).

Mayer, K. U. (2009). *New Directions in Life Course Research.* Mannheimer Zentrum für Europäische Sozialforschung; Arbeitspapiere – 122, Mannheim Mannheimer Zentrum für Europäische Sozialforschung.

Moen, P., & Han, S. K. (2001). "Rethinking careers: Work, family, and gender." In: Marshall, V. W., Heinz, W. R., Krüger, H., and Verma, A. (eds), *Restructuring Work and the Life Course.* Toronto: University of Toronto Press, pp. 84–106.

Muennig, P. (2015). "Can universal pre-kindergarten programs improve population health and longevity? Mechanisms, evidence, and policy implications." *Social Science & Medicine*, 127, 116–123.

Pink, S. (2005). *Doing Visual Ethnography.* London: Sage.

Prensky, M. (2001, October). "Digital natives, digital immigrants." *On the Horizon* (MCB University Press), 9(5), 1–6.

Richter, R., & Schadler, C. (2009). "See my virtual self: Dissemination as a characteristic of digital photography – the example of Flickr.com." *Visual Studies*, 24(2), 169–177.

Schulenberg, J., & Maslowsky, J. (2015). "Contribution of adolescence to the life course: What matters most in the long run?" *Research in Human Development*, 12(3–4), 319–326.

Ungoed-Thomas, J. (March 25, 2007). Police hunt chatroom users over web suicide 'goading.' *Sunday Times.* Retrieved from http://www.thesundaytimes.co.uk/sto/news/uk_news/article62066.ece (accessed September 27, 2014).

van Dijck, J. (2008). "Digital photography: Communication, identity, memory." *Visual Communication*, 7(1), 57–76.

Vasconcelos, M. S., Sampaio, A. S., Hounie, A. G., Akkerman, F., Curi, M., Lopes, A. C., & Miguel, E. C. (2007). "Prenatal, perinatal, and postnatal risk factors in obsessive–compulsive disorder." *Biological Psychiatry*, 61, 301–307.

1   The Internet through the ages

William H. Dutton and Bianca C. Reisdorf[1]

Introduction

In the 21st century, the Internet has become nearly ubiquitous in highly advanced societies, such as North America or Western Europe, where the majority of individuals and households are online. However, not all online connectivity is equal, and studies have shown repeatedly that uptake rates and how much people use the Internet once they are online are highly dependent on a number of social and economic factors, with one of the most important being the age of the individual (Blank and Dutton 2012; Reisdorf 2011; Van Deursen and Van Dijk 2014; Zillien and Hargittai 2009). For this reason, a large number of studies in the field have focused on how different age groups – especially younger and older age groups – are using the Internet in different ways (Hargittai and Hsieh 2013; Livingstone and Helsper 2007; Van Deursen and Helsper 2015). The terms 'digital natives' (Helsper and Eynon 2010; Palfrey and Gasser 2013; Prensky 2001) and 'digital immigrants' (Prensky 2001, 2009) have been frequently used to denote the degree to which young people, who grew up surrounded by ICTs such as the Internet, are more well versed with their use than those who are older and who learned how to use the Internet later in their lives. Only recently, a so-called Internet meme[2] spread widely on social media that was aimed at reminding young Internet users (i.e. 'digital natives') to be patient with their parents (i.e. 'digital immigrants') when they ask questions about how to use technologies, since the parents taught their children 'how to use a spoon' (Pinterest 2015).

However, a growing number of studies have shown that such generalizations are overly simplified. While a larger proportion of older people are offline compared to younger people, there are dramatic variations within the younger and older age groups. Not all young people are well versed in using the Internet (Eynon and Geniets 2012), and not all older people are slow in their take-up of new Internet technologies, software, and gadgets (Dutton and Blank 2012). Other aspects often, though not always, related to age, such as income, education, and urban–rural location, also need to be considered (Farrington et al. 2015). Moreover, age itself is an indicator of multiple aspects of one's life, such as a stage of life as well as an age cohort.

Outline of this chapter

In this chapter, we will first describe the influence of age on access to and use of the Internet, drawing on descriptive and multivariate analyses from surveys conducted in Britain mainly through the results of the Oxford Internet Surveys (OxIS),[3] and in the United States, primarily through the findings of the Pew Internet & American Life Project.[4] We then examine the intersections of various aspects of age, including physiological ageing, age cohorts, and life stage, asking which of these factors is predominantly driving the importance of age in Internet use.

We argue that all dimensions of age are additive and therefore need to be jointly considered to draw a complete picture of why age and Internet use are so closely intertwined. We then move to a discussion of the inherent dynamics of age and the Internet. Will the 'digital natives' of 2015 be on the leading edge of Internet use in 2025? Probably not. In addition, the Internet and related information and communication technologies (ICTs) are also rapidly and constantly evolving, with new gadgets and applications being invented at a pace that is difficult for any individual user to keep up with. The co-evolving changes of individual users and the Internet create a dynamic interaction that is likely to alter over time. So while many people perceive a clear and settled relationship between age and Internet use, we argue that this relationship is likely to shift in the coming years and decades in ways that will make contemporary stereotypes of the 'born digital' generation an anachronism.

Age and Internet use: millennials, silver surfers, and refusniks

A growing body of social research has shown that age is a strong factor in describing both access to and patterns of use of the Internet. Age has emerged as a major aspect of digital divides research regarding access to the Internet and related factors, such as skills in using the Internet, that creates inequalities across individuals in society (Hargittai and Hsieh 2013). These digital inequalities are important because they often follow and reinforce other socio-economic inequalities, such as income and education. This makes them socially and economically significant, and not just a difference in whether someone decides to use a particular technology. It is sometimes a 'choice', but one that is socially shaped and which has social and economic consequences, as will be discussed further in the sections that follow.

The basic finding of most studies is that being older is one of the major factors related to being less likely to use the Internet. Study after study has found a strong correlation between being older and not using the Internet at all, that is someone who has never been online (Blank and Dutton 2012; Helsper and Reisdorf 2013). In Britain and the United States, when controlling for all other standard socio-demographic factors, such as education, income, or having children in the household, age is one of the strongest predictors of who is online and who is not

(Blank and Dutton 2012; Zickuhr and Madden 2012). For instance, in Britain in 2013, nearly every person in school or of school age was online, while only about 60 per cent of those retired or at the age of retirement were online (Dutton and Blank 2013, p. 19).

However, this is not a constant. While a lower proportion of older people are online in many nations, they are also among the groups that are growing in their proportion of Internet users. In the United States, for example, Pew has shown a steady increase in Internet users among all age groups, including older adults and seniors (Zickuhr and Madden 2012, p. 4). Nevertheless, this growth in older Internet users does not erase the vast difference between proportions of users between age groups, with seniors still lagging behind in most nations. In 2012, Pew reported that 'for the first time, half of adults ages 65 and older are online' (Zickuhr and Madden 2012, p. 2). Between 2000 and 2012, the percentage of senior Internet users increased from less than 15 per cent to 53 per cent, while the proportion of Internet users aged 50 to 64 increased from 45 per cent to 77 per cent (p. 4). All other age groups had reached numbers higher than 90 per cent by 2012.

According to the latest data from the Pew surveys, 59 per cent of American citizens aged 65 years and older were online in 2013, but the proportion of Internet users decreased sharply by the age of 75 (Pew Research Center 2014). In addition, uptake of broadband access was considerably lower among adults who were 65 years of age or older, with only 47 per cent using broadband Internet services versus 70 per cent among the general adult population (pp. 1–2). These numbers dropped sharply as well with increasing age. For example, 74 per cent of 65- to 69-year-olds were online in 2013 (68 per cent among ages 70–74), and 65 per cent of them had broadband access at home (55 per cent among ages 70–74). However, these numbers decreased markedly to 47 per cent (Internet use) and 34 per cent (broadband) in the age group 75 to 79, and 37 per cent and 21 per cent respectively for US citizens aged 80 years or older (Pew Research Center 2014, p. 2).

Research in Britain arrived at similar findings, indicating a sharp drop-off in Internet use in the age group of 65 years and older (Dutton and Blank 2011, 2013). In 2013, only 39 per cent of this age group described themselves as Internet users, only 12 percentage points more than in 2005 and 14 percentage points fewer than in the United States during the same period (Dutton and Blank 2013, p. 19). In short, while older individuals are catching up with younger people in adopting the Internet and – although significantly less so – broadband access at home, they still lag behind, especially in contrast to those under the age of 30, who display the highest Internet usage rates, based on findings in both the United States and Britain.

Research has provided many explanations for the lower proportions of Internet users in the higher age groups. According to Helsper and Reisdorf (2013), older respondents were significantly less likely to mention access and the cost of Internet connections, equipment, and gadgets as reasons for not using the Internet, but instead, the older people were, the more likely they were to express a lack of interest in the Internet. More generally, a lack of interest and general attitudes towards the Internet could be major factors. In many of the most developed nations, nearly everyone who wants to be online is online (Dutton and Blank 2013). We have referred to the phenomenon of people simply choosing not to go online as 'digital choice' (Dutton et al. 2007).

The existence of a 'digital choice' does not imply that such choices are random but that attitudes towards the Internet are very significant and that these can be shaped by such factors as age and education in ways that could perpetuate or diminish general socio-economic divides. In fact, our research on what we have called 'cultures of the Internet' has shown that the attitudes of users are more important than demographic factors in explaining adoption and use of the Internet (Dutton and Blank 2015). Of course, these attitudes, which are in turn influencing interest in the Internet, are shaped by demographic and socio-economic factors, such as age, but attitudes are not determined by these factors, leaving room for initiatives that might shape the values and attitudes of people to adopt and use the Internet in positive ways. Looking specifically at Internet- and technology-related attitudes of Internet users and non-users, for example, Reisdorf and Groselj (forthcoming) found that strong negative or positive attitudes played as strong a role in predicting who was offline and who was online as the strongest socio-economic factors, such as education or age, which are best viewed as background factors shaping attitudes and behaviour related to the Internet.

Older people also face some more unique challenges that come with ageing. Researchers at the Pew Research Center (2014, p. 2) have not only noted barriers for older people, such as scepticism, as discussed, but also physical challenges. Clearly, as people age they might have physical limitations, such as weaker eyesight, or might find it harder to learn new things. Over the years, for example, individuals who report having disabilities are less likely to be online (Dutton and Blank 2013).

However, many seniors are online and sophisticated Internet users. Moreover, even seniors who move online at a later age find the Internet becoming a more integral part of their lives, such as becoming part of their daily routine, with many of them going online every day (Dutton and Blank 2013; Pew Research Center 2014).

But this does not negate the potential for older people to be on the wrong side of the digital divide and face the consequences of the digital inequalities that emerge across age groups. Research on digital inequalities argues that the older so-called 'silver surfers' tend to engage in fewer activities and stay online for shorter periods of time relative to younger Internet users (Helsper 2010). This may lead to older users missing out on many opportunities online, or what Zillien and Hargittai (2009) describe as capital-enhancing uses of the Internet, that is, activities that allow Internet users to gain economic, cultural, or social capital. Ironically, older people are among the groups most likely to benefit from online activities, such as online shopping or banking or access to governmental, health, and medical information and services, but they often fail to recognize and seize these potential advantages. Moreover, these gaps are self-reinforcing when industry tends to focus its marketing and initiatives on the younger and heavier users.

Unravelling the age explanations

Because a strong relationship is found between age and Internet use, researchers have offered up a virtual 'dog's breakfast' of miscellaneous explanations and often conflate very different kinds of explanatory factors. The main problem is that age is highly correlated with many things. Social scientists often discuss this as 'block-booking' from the tradition of movie theatres, which had to purchase a set of films even if they only wanted to show a particular subset. The films could not be separated, as they were 'block-booked' by the production and distribution companies.

Likewise, it is impossible to entirely disaggregate all the changes that come with age, but there are at least four distinct but general explanations for a relationship between age and the use of ICTs, such as the Internet, which are closely related to studies of ageing more generally (Hsu, Lew-Ting and Wu 2001; Palmore 1978; Riley 1971; Szeto 2005). These will be referenced here as ageing, cohort, life stage, and design explanations.[5]

1   Ageing, focused on physical or physiological changes that come with ageing, such as diminished eyesight or finger agility, which is useful, for example, for texting;
2   Cohort effects, referring to the technology that was dominant when one was growing up and beginning to use media, whether one grew up with radio, television, a personal computer, the Internet, or smartphones;
3   Life stage effects, shaped by the demands placed on individuals at different stages of their lives, from being a child to a student to having a particular career or being in retirement.
4   Design, relating to the way technologies are designed that might disadvantage older individuals or be targeted towards the young.

Given these different aspects of ageing, it is not very useful to say that being older per se is *the* key factor influencing Internet engagement. As Czaja and Lee (2007, p. 344) put it: '[O]ne cannot draw conclusions on age-technology interaction on the basis of chronological age alone'. What is it about ageing that shapes Internet use?

Physical changes with age

Physical ageing, as one aspect of age, has an influence on a number of cognitive skills, including an increasing difficulty in learning new skills and remembering and recalling new information related to these new skills (Czaja and Lee 2007). This may include seemingly simple tasks, such as using a web browser or logging into an email account, and remembering passwords, and it will include learning how to handle new software, such as social media, smartphone applications, and others. In addition, physical barriers, such as deteriorating vision or problems with arthritis and other diseases affecting finger dexterity, may play a role in preventing older people from using the Internet at the same intensity or agility as younger people, such as in multi-tasking.

However, newer technologies, such as tablets, may be an opportunity to address some of these issues, as we are moving towards more 'intuitive' touchscreen technologies, which allow setting bigger icons on these screens, and the use of fickle gadgets, such as physical keyboards and a mouse, may become obsolete in the future (Ofcom 2014). In fact, Pew's latest report on seniors and their use of technologies showed that older respondents were more likely to own tablets than smartphones, possibly as tablets are bigger and easier to handle than the small smartphone screens (Pew Research Center 2014). Nonetheless, all Internet-enabled gadgets have a lower uptake rate among older age groups than younger age groups (Zickuhr and Madden 2012), which may be related in large part to their attitudes towards the Internet and technologies in general (Blank and Dutton 2012).

Age cohorts

As noted, most discussion of age and the Internet evokes discussion of the 'born digital' generation, which is an explanation based on a cohort effect. Specific attitudes and perceptions can be related to growing up in a certain era and belonging to a certain generation, and the socialization that occurs during one's youth and continues throughout life with one's cohort, depending in part on the media and technologies that were available during that time, whether that was newspapers or computers (Meyer 1985; Peiser 2000).

Young adults in the 1980s and 1990s were likely to be exposed to the use of personal computers and bulletin boards, and from the 2000s onwards, young adults grew up with the Internet. In line with this early technology- and Internet-heavy socialization, so-called Millennials (born between 1977 and 1993) are more immersed in social media and are more likely than any other generation to access the Internet through wireless and mobile gadgets (Zickuhr 2010). For instance, 32 per cent of Internet users are on Twitter among 18- to 29-year-olds, compared with only 6 per cent of Internet users 65 years of age and older (Duggan et al. 2014).

Millennials are also more likely to be Internet users in contrast to all other age cohorts, with 95 per cent of American Millennials online in 2010, but only 86 per cent of Gen X (born 1965–1976), and much lower numbers across all other generations (Zickuhr 2010, p. 5). However, breadth of use is narrower among Millennials than among Gen X (Zickuhr 2010), which is interesting considering that Millennials are often regarded as the 'masters' of the Internet who are able to do anything online. Actually, they may have been raised with simpler and less general-purpose technologies that could make them less tech savvy than earlier generations.

Recently, a number of publications have claimed that the elderly are catching up with Internet and social media use faster than any other age group (Hart, Chaparro and Halcomb 2008; Madden 2010; University of Wisconsin Extension – Learning for Life 2003). However, most of these studies fail to acknowledge that although individuals remain part of the same *generation* for their whole lives, they do not remain part of the same *age group*, which is often the factor considered in research projects, rather than generations. This means that those who were part of a certain age group 10 years ago – for example 45- to 54-year-olds – are now part of a different age group – for example 55- to 64-year-olds. However, we cannot simply claim that older people are getting more interested in the Internet, as cohorts keep moving. Accordingly, we cannot say that a certain cohort's attitudes have changed: instead a cohort simply moved from one age group into the next – possibly without changing.

However, as people gain experience with the Internet, they tend to develop a greater familiarity and trust in the technology. This led us to speak of the Internet as an 'experience technology', since experience led to greater trust and positive patterns of use (Blank and Dutton 2012; Dutton and Shepherd 2006). But these experiences with a technology at one point in time can have a braking effect on the use of newer technologies, serving to reinforce and maintain early patterns of use. For example, early Internet users gained experience with desktop computers, email, and the Web, but they were not as comfortable with social media and were slow to take it up. As younger users have moved on to many new social media, some older Internet users have started taking up social media, such as Facebook. To users who grew to know the Internet by using email and the Web, the move to social media has been a major one – the equivalent of a shift from being a non-user of the Internet to adopting it. There are different kinds of Internet use, and each has different patterns of adoption and diffusion over time. New developments around Internet television, the Internet of Things, such as the Internet of Toys, will also have unique patterns of uptake. The Internet is not one thing.

Age cohorts also affect Internet use: for example some cohorts have had the opportunity to come across ICTs and the Internet in an institutional setting, such as school or work. Younger generations are largely considered to be well versed in using the Internet due to the high likelihood that they were introduced to it at an earlier stage in life – especially Millennials who, as we have said, are often considered to be 'digital natives' (Prensky 2001) and who are likely to have come across ICTs and the Internet in school and university. Gen X can also be considered a cohort that has come across the Internet in an institutional setting, mainly in their working environment. The chance of 'forced' or contextually imposed engagement with the Internet in these settings is lower for older generations, especially those who were already close to retirement when the Internet started spreading widely among the population.

Stages of life

A third factor of ageing is that it is strongly related to, and sometimes impossible to disentangle from, age cohorts, and physical age is a life stage, that is, whether someone is a student, employed, unemployed, looking after children, or retired. Helsper (2010, p. 355) defines life stages as 'the traditional points in a person's life where daily rhythm and routine alter drastically due to a change in a person's role in society', and she includes three different factors in this life-stage approach: occupational status, marital status, and having children living in the household.

Although these different stages of life are closely related to physical age, many people move in and out of these life stages fluidly, such as mature students or early retirees, individuals seeking employment straight after school and finishing their studies at a later stage in life, individuals getting married and getting divorced or becoming widowed, children being born and moving out, and so on. Mature students, for example, would be forced to make regular use of the Internet for accessing readings, submitting assignments, getting in touch with their tutors, and the like. While being online and keeping their skills up to date is a necessity for students of all ages, this would be less relevant for, say, retirees, who often do not perceive a need to use the Internet in their everyday lives. Changes in life stages can drive changes in Internet use. For example, one common reason for people dropping off the Internet is that they have experienced a change in their living circumstances, such as leaving school or losing a job (Dutton and Blank 2013; Eynon and Geniets 2012).

In this context, Selwyn (2004) refers to an issue of 'life fit' and argues that not everyone needs to be online. Hence, life stage and the according differences in life fit may have a profound impact on attitudes towards the Internet, as well as on the general interest in using new technologies.

In her study of the impact of life stage on being online versus offline, Helsper (2010) confirmed that both physical age and life stages were strong factors predicting Internet use in general. However, measuring differences in gender and Internet use, Helsper found that physical age was not a significant factor – all age groups of men and women displayed similar levels of general Internet uptake. However, life stage had a strong and significant influence on both Internet use and what kinds of activities men and women were engaging in once they were online. For example, '[w]omen looked more frequently for health information than men, independent of the life stage or generation group they were in. Employed people were also more likely to search for health information than the other occupational groups' (Helsper 2010, p. 364).

Data from OxIS also demonstrate a strong impact of life stage on being an Internet user in the United Kingdom (Dutton and Blank 2014). Between 2003 and 2013, the percentage of Internet users among students increased from an already high 96 per cent to 100 per cent, while the number of Internet users among those who were in employment soared from 76 per cent to 93 per cent during the same timespan (Dutton and Blank 2013, p. 22). However, those in retirement were still lagging behind, with 22 per cent of retirees online in 2003 and 45 per cent in 2013 (Dutton and Blank 2013, p. 22). Although this means that the proportion of retirees who are online has doubled in 10 years, this group is still lagging behind in Internet uptake as compared to other groups.

Another factor closely related to life stage is whether someone lives with children in the household. This factor has had a strong impact on whether a household has Internet access, with the presence of children tending to increase interest in the Internet as a means of learning, education, and entertainment (Dutton and

Blank 2013). Parents want to introduce children to new technology. However, Reisdorf and Groselj (forthcoming) compared regression models that contained only socio-economic factors, including physical age, life stage, and children in the household, with regression models that also included attitudinal variables. They found that once they controlled for attitudes towards technologies and the Internet, the effect of children living in the household on the likelihood of being an Internet (non-)user became insignificant, demonstrating the strong inter-vening role of attitudes, which in turn are shaped by factors such as age and life stage. This points towards the key problem researchers have in distinguish-ing which age-related variable has the strongest impact on Internet use, as they seem impossible to disentangle in a genuine way, because they are bundled in everyday life.

Design

Finally, but closely related to ageing, is the issue of whether the present design of computer systems and/or services is not focused on the elderly (Hart et al. 2008). The elderly are unlikely to be the strongest market for the Internet industry, lead-ing design considerations to focus on youth or the high-tech information worker rather than the ageing population. Content, applications, and websites are often designed for youth rather than the elderly, since they represent a more significant market for the industry.

In sum, these explanations for possible relationships between age and Internet use are very understandable but not distinct. They are interwoven and overlap-ping, making it difficult to untangle them empirically without longitudinal data that would be virtually impossible to gather over the time periods required.

Spurious or additive effects

Having explored these four key factors we identified as being part of the 'age' variable, it becomes not only clear that it is virtually impossible to disentangle the relative significance of these alternative explanations but also that such an exer-cise might be unrealistic. Instead, we argue that all these factors – physical age, age cohorts, life stage, and design – are important factors that have an additive effect. It is by wrapping these explanations together in an ensemble of comple-mentary explanations that it is possible to understand why age has such a strong relationship with Internet use.

For example, a retired senior who lives alone and grew up during the Sec-ond World War will be affected in their cognitive and physical skills due to their greater age. They will also be affected in their attitudes towards the Internet by socialization as well as by being in retirement and not having an immediate need or requirement to use the Internet. However, if the same senior decided to keep working or going back to school instead of going into retirement, the 'life fit' of using the Internet (Selwyn 2004) would be a lot higher, and the likelihood of regu-lar engagement with the Internet would increase. Similarly, a recent retiree may be younger and have fewer physical barriers than our senior in the last scenario.

However, due to the lack of necessity to be online, the life fit of using the Internet may be limited, and the considerably younger but retired individual may see no need to use the Internet.

Given that physical age, age cohorts, and life stage are so closely interrelated, it is useful to conceptualize these factors as additive and complementary rather than alternative explanations. While each factor in itself is already strongly related to Internet use, regarding them as one larger component of the attributes of age is therefore helpful in explaining why age has been and is continuing to be so strongly related to use. For all of these reasons, age is likely to remain an important factor shaping the use of the Internet.

The ever-changing Internet and its ever-changing users

However, the relationship between age and Internet use has changed in some important respects, suggesting more changes ahead. For example, as we have seen in the data presented earlier, age is less of a determinant for Internet uptake in some nations, such as the United States, than in others, such as Britain. In addition, the Internet itself keeps changing over time, such as with the development of social media and mobile Internet applications that might embed the Internet in everyday life and work in ways that are easier to use, and design is continuously becoming more 'intuitive' and accordingly less affected by the effects of ageing and cohort. As a consequence, we believe that it is important to view age and the Internet as a dynamic rather than static relationship in which both people and the Internet are continuously co-evolving.

As described in the previous sections, we can see such changes unfolding in many ways. Tablets and smartphones are more user friendly and therefore helpful in bringing some older users online. Internet television is part of a technical array of technologies bringing entertainment back into the living room. These changes are likely to disrupt present relationships between the Internet and age in unpredictable ways.

Points of summary and conclusion

A common joke flowing from discussions of digital divides affecting older people is that the problem will 'die out' with the older generation. Not only is this 'joke' not that funny, but it is also not very likely, as it assumes that technology stands still and that individuals fail to move through many of the same problems and stages as the people who came before them.

The data and arguments presented in this chapter point toward a strong interrelation between a number of factors that are related to age, including physical age, age cohorts, life stage, and questions regarding the design of both hardware and software. While physical age, cohorts, and stage of life are closely interwoven, they can vary immensely among the population, and it would be wrong to claim that all seniors are the same when they in fact represent a very heterogeneous group with various reasons for (dis)engagement with Internet technologies (Van Deursen and Helsper 2015).

To determine how 'age' affects uptake and use of the Internet, we need to consider all age-related factors as additive in their effects instead of claiming that one may be more important than the others that are actually spurious. That is, if the major age-related variable is life stage, then the relationships between ageing and cohorts with Internet use could be an artefact of being associated with life stage. We argue that this is not the case. All three dimensions of age-related factors interact in ways that are shaping Internet use through the ages, and they are reinforced by the strategies of an industry seeking to appeal to the leading segments of the market.

In addition, research needs to look at the relationship between 'age' and the Internet from a dynamic standpoint. While it is almost a 'given' that technologies are developing at rapid speed, 'the elderly' are often regarded as a static group that does not change or, if so, only very slowly. However, while belonging to a certain generation may not change, as it is determined by year of birth, these generations keep 'moving' through the age groups that we consider in social research. In 30 years' time, many Millennials who are now considered to be 'digital natives' will be considered 'seniors' who have physically aged, and the life fit of Internet-enabled technologies may no longer be strong because of changes in life stage. Will this mean that they fall behind on new technologies and become new 'digital immigrants' later in life? Longer-term longitudinal research would be required to bring major new insight into these changes in life fit and the relevance of technologies, as well as changing attitudes and circumstances among Internet users and non-users. This would allow researchers to shed more light on the complicated and dynamic relationship among physical age, age cohorts and generations, and stages of life. This research is required in order to inform and devise useful interventions to address continuing digital divides and inequalities that will not be lessened by an industry focused on appealing to the major segments of the market across the ages.

Notes

1 The authors thank the editors and Barbara Ball for their input on this chapter.
2 A meme is often conveyed by a picture, mostly distributed on social networking sites and usually with a caption, which is changed and adapted by different users as it becomes more widely and rapidly spread online.
3 The OxIS is based on a multi-stage random sample of Britain, including England, Wales, and Scotland but not Northern Ireland. Details on the surveys and sample designs can be found online at: http://oxis.oii.ox.ac.uk/research/methodology/
4 Details on the methods and samples of the Pew Internet and American Life Project are available online at: http://www.pewinternet.org/
5 Martin Levine (2006), personal communication, 31 July.

References

Blank, G., and Dutton, W. H. (2012). Age and trust in the Internet: The centrality of experience and attitudes toward technology in Britain. *Social Science Computer Review*, *30*(2), 135–51.

Blank, G., and Groselj, D. (2014). Dimensions of Internet use: Amount, variety, and types. *Information, Communication & Society*, *17*(4), 417–35.

Czaja, S. J., and Lee, C. C. (2007). The impact of aging on access to technology. *Universal Access in the Information Society*, *5*(4), 341–9.

Dugan, M., Ellison, N. B., Lampe, C., Lenhart, A., and Madden, M. (2014). *Demographics of Key Social Networking Platforms*. Pew Research Center. Available online: <http://www.pewinternet.org/2015/01/09/demographics-of-key-social-networking-platforms-2/> (accessed 12/09/2015).

Dutton, W. H., and Blank, G. (2011). *Next Generation Users: The Internet in Britain*. Oxford: Oxford Internet Institute, University of Oxford.

Dutton, W. H., and Blank, G. (2013). *Cultures of the Internet: The Internet in Britain*. Oxford: Oxford Internet Institute, University of Oxford.

Dutton, W. H., and Blank, G. (2015). Cultural stratification on the Internet: Five clusters of values and beliefs among users in Britain, pp. 3–28 in Robinson, L., and Cotten, S. (eds), *New Media Cultures: Communication and Information Technologies Annual*, Vol. 11. Emerald Studies in Media and Communication. Bingley, UK: Emerald Group Publishing Limited.

Dutton, W. H., and Shepherd, A. (2006). Trust in the Internet as an experience technology. *Information, Communication & Society*, *9*(4), 433–51.

Dutton, W. H., Shepherd, A., and di Gennaro, C. (2007). Digital divides and choices Reconfiguring access: National and cross-national patterns of Internet diffusion and use, pp. 31–45 in Anderson, B., Brynin, M., Gershuny, J., and Raban, Y. (eds), *Information and Communications Technologies in Society*. London: Routledge.

Eynon, R., and Geniets, A. (2012). *On the Periphery? Understanding Low and Discontinued Internet Use amongst Young People in Britain*. Report for the Nominet Trust. Available online: <http://www.nominettrust.org.uk/sites/default/files/NT%20lapsed%20Internet%20users%20final.pdf> (accessed 01/09/2015).

Farrington, J., Philip, L., Cottrill, C., Abbott, P., Blank, G., and Dutton, W. (2015). *Two-Speed Britain: Rural Internet Use*. Aberdeen, UK: Aberdeen University Press.

Hargittai, E., and Hsieh, Y. P. (2013). Digital inequality, pp. 129–150 in Dutton, W. H. (ed.), *The Oxford Handbook of Internet Studies*. Oxford: Oxford University Press.

Hart, T. A., Chaparro, B. S., and Halcomb, C. G. (2008). Evaluating websites for older adults: Adherence to 'senior-friendly' guidelines and end-user performance. *Behaviour & Information Technology*, *27*(3), 191–9.

Helsper, E. J. (2010). Gendered Internet use across generations and life stages. *Communication Research*, *37*(3), 352–74.

Helsper, E. J., and Eynon, R. (2010). Digital natives: Where is the evidence? *British Educational Research Journal*, *36*(3), 503–20.

Helsper, E. J., and Reisdorf, B. C. (2013). A quantitative examination of explanations for reasons for Internet nonuse. *Cyberpsychology, Behavior, and Social Networking*, *16*(2), 94–9.

Hsu, H.-C., Lew-Ting, C.-Y., and Wu, S.-S. (2001). Age, period, and cohort effects on the attitude toward supporting parents in Taiwan. *The Gerontologist*, *41*(6), 742–50.

Livingstone, S., and Helsper, E. (2007). Gradations in digital inclusion: Children, young people and the digital divide. *New Media & Society*, *9*(4), 671–96.

Madden, M. (2010). *Older Adults and Social Media: Social Networking Use among Those Ages 50 and Older Nearly Doubled over the Past Year*. Pew Internet & American Life Project Report. Available online: <http://www.pewinternet.org/files/old-media//Files/Reports/2010/Pew%20Internet%20-%20Older%20Adults%20and%20Social%20Media.pdf> (accessed 07/09/15).

Meyer, P. (1985). *The Newspaper Survival Book*. Bloomington: Indiana University Press.

Ofcom (Office of Communications) (2014). *Adults' Media Use and Attitudes Report 2014*. London: Office of Communication. Available online: <http://stakeholders.ofcom. org.uk/market-data-research/other/research-publications/adults/adults-media-lit-14/> (accessed 07/09/15).

Palfrey, J., and Gasser, U. (2013). *Born Digital: Understanding the First Generation of Digital Natives*. New York: Basic Books.

Palmore, E. (1978). Are the aged a minority group? *Journal of the American Geriatrics Society, 26*, 214–7.

Peiser, W. (2000). Cohort trends in media use in the United States. *Mass Communication & Society*, 3(2&3), 185–205.

Pew Research Center (2014). *Older Adults and Technology Use*. Pew Research Report. Available online: <http://www.pewinternet.org/2014/04/03/older-adults-and-technology-use/> (accessed 02/09/15).

Pinterest (2015). *I Taught You How to Use a Spoon Meme*. Available online: https://www. pinterest.com/pin/140456082106278321/> (accessed 01/09/2015).

Prensky, M. (2001). Digital natives, digital immigrants part 1. *On the Horizon, 9*(5), 1–6.

Prensky, M. (2009). H. sapiens digital: From digital immigrants and digital natives to digital wisdom. *Innovate: Journal of Online Education, 5*(3), 1.

Reisdorf, B. C. (2011). Non-adoption of the Internet in Great Britain and Sweden: A cross-national comparison. *Information, Communication & Society, 14*(3), 400–20.

Reisdorf, B. C., and Groselj, D. (forthcoming). Internet (non-)use types and motivational access: Implications for digital inequalities research. *New Media and Society.*

Riley, M. W. (1971). Social gerontology and the age stratification of society. *Gerontologist, 11*, 79–87.

Selwyn, N. (2004). The information aged: A qualitative study of older adults' use of information and communications technology. *Journal of Aging Studies, 18*(4), 369–84.

Szeto, C. (2005). The impact of age, generation and life stage on use of mail and media. Pitney Bowes, Background Paper No. 11, 13 July.

University of Wisconsin Extension – Learning for Life (2003). *Older Adults Are Fastest Growing Internet Audience*. Available online: <http://www.uwex.edu/news/read. cfm?id=570> (accessed 07/09/15).

Van Deursen, A. J., and Helsper, E. J. (2015). A nuanced understanding of Internet use and non-use among the elderly. *European Journal of Communication, 30*(2), 171–87.

Van Deursen, A. J., and Van Dijk, J. A. G. M. (2014). The digital divide shifts to differences in usage. *New Media and Society, 16*(3), 507–26.

Zickuhr, K. (2010). *Generations 2010*. Pew Internet & American Life Project Report. Available online: <http://pewinternet.org/Reports/2010/Generations-2010.aspx> (accessed 04/09/15).

Zickuhr, K., and Madden, M. (2012). *Older Adults and Internet Use: For the First Time, Half of Adults Ages 65 and Older Are Online*. Pew Internet & American Life Project Report. Available online: <http://pewinternet.org/Reports/2012/Older-adults-and-internet-use.aspx> (accessed 02/09/15).

Zillien, N., and Hargittai, E. (2009). Digital distinction: Status-specific types of Internet usage. *Social Science Quarterly, 90*(2), 274–91.

2   Singularity

A double bind?

Rajash Rawal and Paul G. Nixon

This chapter will examine the impact of technology on our daily lives and attempt to assess how this has changed our daily lives and contributed to the existence and development of the human race. The move towards classifying society as an information society implies that where society is exposed to ICTs it is being fundamentally changed (Habermas, 1979, 1987a, 1987b). The technology is not socially deterministic but acts as 'a mediating factor in the complex matrix of interaction between social structures, social actors and their socially constructed tools' (Castells, 1999, p. 1). As highlighted by Nicolas Carr (2010) people's patterns of thinking, acting and doing all sorts of things in their lives have changed tremendously in the evolving Internet era. This development has intensified even further in the so-called 'post–PC' era. Market demand for desktops and laptops has slumped (Hamblen, 2012), and users are replacing PCs with mobile devices equipped with microprocessors which communicate via wireless networks (Stajano, 2002). Mobile devices, both phones and tablets, have led to the development of various applications that aid us to remember when to eat, exercise or sleep and even how to try to reduce one's waistline (Seo & Niu, 2015). Singularity is more than just a dot on a sci-fi horizon. The seamless joining of various devices and our reliance on them to aid us in our daily practices and habits has brought this concept closer to today than tomorrow.

For example, technology has become 'wearable' with the advent of smart watches and fuel bands (Park et al., 2014). Coupled with this is the rise of the Internet of Things (IoT) which gives us unparalleled opportunities to control and interact with systems and environments as never before. The number of connected devices, will increase exponentially which, whilst providing and myriad of improvements and enhancements to our daily lives may also have consequences such as increased energy usage. There may also be calls for standardization of technologies and devices to provide seamless connectivity and security which, whilst seeming benign, may give rise to fears of market domination and hegemonic power relationships.

If that wasn't bad enough there is the looming spectre of Singularity, the fear that one day artificial intelligence will come to the fore to create a world so complex as to be unfathomable to even the most intelligent human. Foregrounded in science fiction in such stories as Asimov's *I Robot* (1950) and widely forecast to happen within 40 years from now (Kurzweil, 2005), we can already see examples in our everyday lives where we are happy to let machines think for us. Calculators and computers such as the one on which this chapter is being typed are examples of how even at a relatively low level we allow artificial intelligence into our lives. As we shall see, this is changing the world around us and the values which we hold on issues such as education. Do we learn in the same ways as our grandparents did – and perhaps more aptly, should we learn in such ways?

The question here is what impact may these ICT advances have on our future development as societies? How will this impact and influence other social changes? Does this aid our individual and collective mental health or hinder it? Is it right that all humans need to eat, move or sleep in tune to the beck and call of an application? In relation to the adoption of ICTs, individuals need to be knowledgeable about the existence of such technologies and then given a reason or motivation to utilize them in their daily lives. When it can be demonstrated that ICTs are of value then, and only then, will individuals, particularly those who have a distrust of new technologies, become motivated enough to want to use them.

We can already observe that certain generations of individuals are thought to be disadvantaged in the information society that we live in. The so called Millennials or Net Generation, born in the 1980s are thought by some to differ from older generations in terms of their ability to engage with ICTs having different capabilities and cognitive styles (Tapscott, 1998; Howe & Strauss, 2000; Dutton & Blank, 2013). This is perhaps overplayed, and although one can observe some level of computer anxiety and technophobia in mature adults and especially seniors (Hogan, 2009) this is changing.

In 2006, *New York Times* columnist Thomas Friedman declared the modern age in which we live the 'age of distraction' (Carr, 2010). His claim is that technology has changed the ways in which our minds function and our capacity to dedicate ourselves to any particular task. This is further expounded by Carr (2010), who asserts that our attention spans and ability to learn have been changed. Moreover, some researchers suggest that the use of media devices has become essential to many people's daily lives, and indeed the impulse to use technology is harder to resist than unwanted urges for eating, alcohol or sex.

By exploring the pros and cons of technology and online presence we can test these ideas and ascertain whether we need to re-examine our behaviour and dependency. Moreover, Elder's works (1974, 1994, 2003) on the value of life course studies (as put forward in the Introduction) can be used to illustrate the dilemmas we face. However, it is not a simple question of right or wrong. Each new twist and turn enabled by technology and its application has many facets, each of which comes with a plethora of advantages and disadvantages which can become complicating factors obfuscating any weight conception of whether such developments are to be viewed as a boon or a hindrance to human kind.

As the reader will see this chapter poses more questions than it delivers answers and endeavours to take time out from the busy seemingly never ending ICT developments and allow us reflect on what is taking place and to ponder its ubiquity. For in our time-constrained, busy and hectic lives, reflection upon those lives and their intersections with the very technologies that are providing us with seemingly limitless distractions is the one form of activity that does not seem to be encouraged by those technologies.

The chapter will now look at various 'life areas' in which technology has played a key role in the developments.

Generational linkage

The advent of technological access has opened up many channels that were previously closed or only open to an exclusive few. In the not-so-distant past technology was often posited as the great divide between generations. Whether this was as true as some would have us believe is open to debate, but for these purposes we will accept the premise. Parents would watch their iPod-using children isolate themselves from the outside world, distracted from face-to-face real life interaction, under the cocoon of their headphones, their eyes and attention rigidly fixed on the data being disgorged from the device, whilst it was often the case that their grandparents could hardly turn on a computer, let alone FaceTime or Skype. Moore (1999) notes that the adoption of technology relates to the individual's perception of the value and attributes of technology. Thus it has been imperative to make technology relevant to the lives of all generations.

Separate research from Werner and Werner (2012) and Romero and Barbera (2012) noted how seniors found that compared with conventional PC technologies, mobile devices and particularly tablets were easier to use. They saw this as being due to such devices making use of touchscreen technology that was less complex and more intuitive to use, with the drag-and-drop navigation of tablets being preferred to using a mouse and keyboard for the same procedure on a standard PC. Thus technical barriers to use were reduced by the advent and subsequent ubiquity of mobile devices such as tablets. The fact that tablets also soon became cheaper than a fixed PC has helped seniors overcome socioeconomic barriers to engaging with new technology. Romero and Barbera (2012) also recognized the value that social interaction helped users build up confidence, digital competence and a sense of belonging to the learning community in their study. Facets of this also hold true for the acquisition of confidence through intergenerational engagement.

However, as time and accessibility have changed and technology has become simpler to use and more ubiquitous we are seeing formerly 'divisive' technologies connecting older and younger generations in ways never before thought possible. Look no further than mobile apps, social networks and games like Candy Crush, which are cross-generational successes (Bernström, 2013).

If we consider the famous motto of Marshall McLuhan, the "medium is still the message," then technology now sits at the hub of our conversations. It is not just the medium through which we communicate but an integral part of our lives. Freire (1972, 1974), in another context, argued that literacy was a crucial part of individual and community empowerment. We would argue that this argument also holds good for the empowerment of individuals in the multiple online communities in which they engage. Language and culture inform this literacy (Castells, 1999), and without it, it would be difficult to create online sociability or community, enhanced by the elimination of those earlier barriers of time and geographic space (Rheingold, 1994).

Nonaka (1994) argues that individuals acquire and transfer knowledge through four distinct patterns of conversion: (1) observation, interaction and the imitation of experts; (2) idea exchange via concepts, images and written documents; (3) use of ICTs, meetings and conversations and (4) individual and collective reflection to integrate knowledge into the individual's conceptions. Whilst Nonaka's ideas were formulated for work organizations the same can be said to hold true for familial inter-generational knowledge acquisition.

Generations around the world can now join together in the exchange of sentiments and ideas, and arguably innovations in communications have helped deepen and broaden family relationships and close the generational gap. However, we now live in a world where people not only want but demand immediate access to everything – and this extends to people, not just physical items. User-friendly interfaces have broad appeal to old and young alike, and the interconnectedness of devices and ubiquity of apps like Facebook or Whatsapp that allow you to reach contacts across smartphones, tablets or desktops have opened the door for us to be many 'places' at once, nearly always available in an instant. Software has created a major leap forward from traditional landline and even mobile phone calls, allowing for faster response times and more frequent connections. This has in turn also caused friction where attention to local family and friends may become secondary to contact with 'far-away' family and friends. Benedict Anderson's notion of transnationalism has become easier to visualize (Anderson, 2004).

However, the days of when a teenager's worst nightmare was getting a Facebook friend request from a parent are becoming a distant memory. For today's Generation X parents, being present on social networks is considered almost as essential as having an email address. Although there are deep concerns from some individuals (West et al., 2009) about exposing their private lives to their parents even though those private lives are published on a public site, it is no longer a surprise to see parents posting a link on their son or daughter's Facebook wall, or by the same token sending a LinkedIn request to connect or even a grandfather sharing a YouTube video from his favourite rock 'n roll band with his friends. Of course, the answer is to simply have a shadow site for parents, a sanitized version of the 'real' space, or to simply move one's conversation to another space/ platform, a space which parents are not aware of, and thus are unable to intrude into or to spy upon.

However, the younger generations retain the need for privacy – some apps and social networks like Snapchat, Instagram, Tumblr and instant messaging apps like Kik show that many younger social network users still want ways to socialize online without parental involvement as will be demonstrated later in this collection. This may also be due in part to the 'disapproval' or judgment that older generations may exercise on this activity. Nonetheless the fact remains that the presence of older generations on social networks is a trend that's here to stay and one that will continue to keep future generations better and more closely connected.

Unrestricted messaging and calling apps enhance communication

Thanks to advancements in VoIP and over-the-top (OTT) messaging and services, there are now many more ways for people to stay in touch aside from a traditional phone call, letter or email. The best part of all is that many of them are free, at least at the point of use, so calls are no longer conducted with the prevailing thought, "We should probably cut this call short – it's long distance, you know!" Skype has played a large part in the adoption of alternative communication tools thanks to its free video calling. Figures accurate at the time of writing (September 2015) show Skype's 230,000,000 users (Statista, 2015) among them making 1,879 calls every second (internetlivestats, 2015).

As the world has become more mobile, new services have emerged that have become popular with millions of international users. Services like WhatsApp make the problems and cost of staying in touch with distant relatives a thing of the past.

A recent report from Informa indicates that OTT messages sent by consumers would reach 41 billion per day by the end of 2013, more than doubling the output of SMS messages (19.5 billion) (Bernström, 2013). The additional bonus is that many of these services can be obtained for free, although there may be hidden costs such as data usage charges etc.), and they each offer clever ways to circumvent those expensive carrier charges for texting, roaming and long distance. Whereas technology may have initially driven us apart, recent advances are bringing us back together, bridging the distance between families and friends and making loved ones feel closer and better connected than ever before.

Education

Technology brings into the classroom more interesting and diverse materials than ever before possible. Multimedia technologies are progressing rapidly and promise to offer easy access to everything from historical documents to breaking news. Hundreds of libraries and museums have already recorded parts of their collections in digital form and distribute these resources through electronic media (Ravenwood et al., 2015). Much of this archived material is available for free. Science students are witnessing exciting astronomy discoveries as they unfold thanks to technologies that allow them to view images from the Hubble telescope. Computer-based tools have the possibility to allow students to learn in a deeper and more instantaneous fashion (Hawkins, 1997).

However, it is possible to conclude with relative certainty that the technological transformation or revolution we have experienced over the past 15 years has clear educational implications. Consider the way children – and older students – are assessed at school and university. They are, by and large, asked to memorize and repeat material. Although modern thinking tells us that learning model is in conflict with the way we learn, think and solve problems today as suggested if we apply the ideas of Elder (1994). If the most important form of knowledge today is knowing where to find knowledge (and how to assess it), then schools and universities should teach and assess just that. Many institutions now speak of developing 21st-century skills. However, it remains a difficult area to test and assess, thus making it a luxury item that many curricula claim to offer but by and large ignore.

Access to information and 'changing the world'

A good example of how access to information can impact the world is the social media revolutions that swept across the Middle East and North Africa (MENA) in the spring of 2011. Traditional Western media wondered with surprise and, to a certain degree, pride as the tools of the information superhighway liberated oppressed people from dictatorships that the west detested (Curtis, 2015). Democracy and the freedom of the Internet were heroes of the day. However, roll forward to the autumn of the same year, 2011, and the same tools were producing angst and fear amongst the very same Western governments in their own backyards. The global Occupy movements and the determination with which they took over prominent squares in cities throughout the Western world in order to make a statement against the handling of the financial crisis once again illustrated the speed of the social media word but this time sought to challenge the wrong leaders in Western eyes.

As Brooke (2011) states, modern technology has broken down traditional social barriers of status, class, power, wealth and geography – changing them with an ethos of collaboration and transparency. The rise in use of social media as a tool for organizing and coordinating activities has many advantages. Diani (2001) identifies four main reasons: technology is relatively inexpensive, it is fast, its impact is immediate and it is above all participatory. Alkalimat and Williams (2001) identified three types of 'cyber power' that emerged through individuals who create social capital, social groups who collect the individuals and organize their focus and ideas and policy being promoted through ideological groups. An example of this is 'indymedia', an anti-capitalist group. Moreover, network sociality personifies looseness and informality, bringing a sense of power back to the people and their roots. Indeed the Internet has allowed for a greater level of knowledge and participation in most areas of our lives, causing us to at least call into question, if not reconstruct, how we live our daily lives. The traditional political class has been reluctant to embrace this change, being somewhat skeptical of the impact a questioning/protesting public may have on truth, trust and power relationships (Brooke, 2011).

Milakovich furthered the idea of a shifting balance of power, suggesting the Internet has made it possible for new forms of participation in advanced societies (Milakovich, 2011), not least in the sense that the notion of citizen journalism via Internet and social networking sites such as Facebook, Twitter and the like was facilitating new challenges to the status quo and disturbing the often somewhat cosy equilibrium that had developed between the traditional media and the political classes. The uprising in MENA has shown us that it may not be just limited to those traditionally developed economies but may also be transferable to many if not all societies. It should be noted that with the rise of mobile technologies the Internet penetration rate via relatively expensive PC hardware is no longer a stumbling block to increased access and usage of net-based facilities, and thus the trend of increased usage is spreading.

However, the role of Twitter/Facebook has been overhyped. While no one can deny they were important tools, they could always be shut down – thus it was more the use of the technology that was key. Technology opens doors, and this frightens government, as it subsequently challenges power. Ironically, this is the essential element of a thriving democracy, but yet it petrifies freely elected governments and dictatorships alike. We are at a critical juncture; the global digital age has meant it is very hard to control what we know, and this disturbs traditional power mechanisms. The notion of e-protest challenging e-democracy seems to make logical sense, but we need to understand this better.

However, one must also consider that user-generated content is not always right – it is an opinion, a feeling, it may not be factually correct, and thus basing and entire movement on it is dangerous and may also undermine the notions of democracy that we hold dear. Yesteryear saw leaders manipulating citizenry by controlling information, but today it is nigh on impossible to control what people read, watch, hear or think. Technology has undone these shackles and united people to challenge authority or at least allow them to. The notion of 'surveillance' now co-exists with that of 'sousveillance', that is, the spied upon can now spy back. WikiLeaks opened the door, the #revolutions shoved it wide open and Edward Snowden with his leaking of huge amounts of classified information continued the trend. The genie is well and truly out of the bottle (Rawal & Nixon, 2012).

Real versus artificial intelligence

Life has become more complex, but this is camouflaged because technology has made the complexity simpler than ever. As identified by Chamoro Premuzic, some psychologists will explain this dichotomy in terms of two distinct aspects of human intellect, namely fluid and crystallized intelligence (after Raymond Cattell's 1940s model of IQ; Chamarro-Premuzic, 2013). Fluid intelligence refers to the ability to acquire and process information. In computers, this would be the processing speed and RAM capacity – the more you have, the faster and more effortlessly you can multi-task and the higher the quantity and complexity of stuff you can handle. If you consider a busy high street, to outsiders there's just a lot going on, but to locals that is just the standard level of data to process. Research suggests that – in humans – fluid intelligence has been increasing for decades. The average child from 1950 would be handicapped by today's standard IQ tests, and the average child today would be gifted by 1950s standards . . . but that is just in terms of their fluid intelligence or ability to process complex information quickly and effectively.

The second aspect of intellect – crystallized IQ – refers not to our ability to collect information but what we actually know; in other words, crystallized intelligence equals knowledge. Naturally, with all the knowledge of the world being now outsourced, crowdsourced and cloudsourced, the individual storage of information is minimal (at least in comparison). Funnily enough people today are like most of the gadgets we use – our ability to solve problems depends not on the knowledge we can store but on our ability to connect to a place where we can retrieve the answer to find a solution. This is what some consider being the 'hyper-link' economy (Chamarro-Premuzic, 2013): the only knowledge we need to have is the knowledge of where to find stuff. Notice that the traditional meaning of crystallized IQ referred to knowledge stored 'inside our head' (this probably peaked with Leonardo, Voltaire and the encyclopaedists). There is a suggestion that we are becoming more stupid from a crystallized IQ perspective . . . but one wonders whether we really need to see the research evidence. Indeed the less we train our brains, the less they are maximized. Perhaps a link can be made to the growing number of dementia sufferers (see official statistics of Alzheimer Disease International; Naish, 2015).

As for the way intelligence is defined, it may be time to consider people's willingness to solve complex problems as a key ingredient of IQ. Consider the following: technology will continue to evolve, and the gap between what can be solved with and without it will only increase. That is, we will become more and more dependent on technology, and the only intellectual disadvantage will be the inability (or unwillingness) to learn to use it. One could also imagine that this IT overload may prove too much for some – we may seek to 'non-exist' in terms of online presence, but that comes at a social cost.

To put it bluntly, people who are able to keep up with technology will outsmart those who aren't (even more than they do now). Therefore, all walks of life in society should try to foster an appetite for complexity, a curious and hungry mind, especially when it comes to paying attention to technological advances.

Distraction

There are many who believe that technology has had a detrimental effect on our capacity to focus and maintain attention. It is suggested that there is a growth in distraction (Klopper, 2015). There are two main ideas about why this is so. The first is material: it holds that our urbanized, high-tech society is designed to distract us. In 1903, the German sociologist Georg Simmel argued, in an influential essay called 'The Metropolis and Mental Life', that in the tech-saturated city "stimulations, interests, and the taking up of time and attention" turn life into "a stream which scarcely requires any individual efforts for its on-going" (quoted in Klopper, 2015). (In the countryside, you have to entertain yourself.) One way to understand the distraction boom, therefore, is in terms of the spread of city life: not only has the world grown more urban, but digital devices let us bring city-like experiences with us wherever we go.

We are now cocooned, Crawford argues, within centuries' worth of technology designed to insure our autonomy – the smartphone just represents the innermost layer. If you check Twitter from your tablet computer while watching *Game of Thrones* on demand or listen to Spotify while working on a something at your desk, then you are taking advantage of many technologies of autonomy at once. A central irony of modern life, Crawford writes, is that even within our cocoons the "cultural imperative of being autonomous" is as strong as ever. That imperative depends on the "identification of freedom with choice, where choice is understood as a pure flashing forth of the unconditioned will" (a click, a scroll, a tap; Crawford quoted in Klopper, 2015).

Sharing versus privacy

Another of the modern debates surrounds what we share and what we keep private. However, this discussion is made more complex when we consider what we 'knowingly' share and what we 'knowingly' keep private. As we previously noted there can be generational tensions over online presences (West et al., 2009). Thus, just as in the offline world, when we're online, there are things we can control and things we can't. For example, we can control the passwords we use and the platforms in which we say what we say in social media. However sometimes we are victims of other people's carelessness or malice, such as when a service provider, platform or retailer is hacked or a government employee loses a briefcase containing a laptop with people's unencrypted personal information. Then our control is broken into pieces, and our digital activity may be laid bare for all to see.

We are also confronted by other privacy breaches that result from deliberate policies of service providers and advertising networks to gather user information for a variety of purposes, ranging from targeting advertising to conducting market research. The use of beacons to help lure shoppers into stores by rewarding them with coupons and discounts is a clear example of how data can be gathered and sent via Bluetooth. A good example of this technology in action is Regent Street in London, UK (Perry, 2014).

When it comes to trying to protect ourselves from companies and agencies being hacked or losing data, we are compliant bystanders. We have to trust that the organizations that we are dealing with are doing all they can. However, there is not much we can do be to be safer, as the majority of the security measures are not in our hands. Clearly, it seems to makes sense to only provide personal information to trusted, reputable organizations, though when hacking victims include the likes of Sony Network, Target, Wal-Mart or Apple iCloud, there isn't a great deal we can do and even such status doesn't seem to offer much solace or protection. Government played a role in at least informing us of those breaches. California was one of the first states to require companies to disclose data breaches to anyone who might be affected (Magid, 2013).

While we can't prevent such attacks, we can protect ourselves to a degree. One precaution is to use strong passwords and make sure we don't use the same password for each of our accounts. There is software available that will even generate random passwords that are very hard to crack, although this is but another example of transferal of power to technology.

Another issue are marketing-related privacy invasions like tracking cookies or online profiles. Some are bothered by them, and others accept them as the price we pay for all these great 'free' services. I recently researched a trip to Lanzarote and keep seeing ads for trips and hotels there pop up in a variety of my online spaces. Google's Doubleclick and other ad networks that serve these ads insist that they're not collecting personal information. However, even though there most likely is not a printed list anywhere with my name and the word Lanzarote, it's clear that there are servers out there that know something about my recent travel.

Society is sharing increasing amounts of information about themselves on the Internet with their friends and families, but how much of that information is actually being shared with advertisers or strangers? Online privacy is an important topic of discussion in the age of social networks and geolocation services. A study conducted by researchers at the University of California, Berkeley, and the University of Pennsylvania suggested that more than 90 per cent of people believed that there should be a law that requires websites and advertising companies to delete all stored information about an individual. Almost 70 per cent said there should be a law that gives people the right to know everything that a website knows about them. Sites like Twitter, Facebook and Google are encouraging people to share their information with the world, making them part of the ever-expanding social web – where your online connections frame your everyday life (Magid, 2013). We are getting restless not knowing who knows what about us.

Consumers are finding it more and more difficult to understand the complicated privacy policies and are in many cases unaware that the information they thought they were sharing with their friends is actually being shared with anyone on the Internet who cares to take a peek.

The most obvious and effective way of keeping your information safe and free from prying eyes is to avoid joining social networks like Facebook and Twitter and to refrain from logging into sites like Google when you search. For most of us, this is simply not a practical option. For many, their lives are defined by their search history, updates, the photos they post, 'check-ins' to the visited locations, their long lists of likes and dislikes and their filtering and sharing of content they find on the web. If it's not on Facebook, there is a fear that it didn't happen, state the generation of Internet-savvy teens that have made the Internet such a big part of their lives they can't even go 24 hours without connecting.

The most important part of online privacy is being aware of what you are sharing with others. It is often a surprise to find out how much of your personal information is freely available on the web. An easy way to find out is by simply searching for your name in a search engine. Your digital footprint is often larger than you dreamt possible.

Social skills

For as long as the Internet has been around, there has been intense debate about its repercussions on social well-being. There are two groups involved in the debate about Internet use. The first group comprise those who claim that social media and the Internet have enabled people to cultivate richer social lives than before (Kremer, 2015). The second group are those who suggest that the increased time people spent active on the web has become to an increasing extent more excluded from others and are lacking in true human connections.

A study completed at the Stockholm School of Economics (Klopper) looked into the association between people's Internet use and their results on different measures of social well-being, such as their work–life balance and emotional health. The lead investigator of the study, Dr. Engleberg, discovered that people with high Internet use were markedly more lonesome and had a poorer work–life balance than those with low Internet use.

The results of research disclosed that individuals who are addicted to the Internet are exhausted, bored, lonely and depressed and suffer from social anxiety and have more social deprivation and seclusion. Individuals who use Internet most find it tough to keep friendships, spend less time with their relatives, experience more stress and feel more lonely and depression.

This strongly supports the viewpoint that the social media cannot take the place of true face-to-face interaction. It seems that no matter how much people interact through social media, they don't find the true human interactions that they desire. Moreover, it seems that excessive Internet use also prevents people from acquiring the skills they need to interact with others. Dr. Engelberg revealed that people who spent large amounts of time online scored lower on scales of emotional intelligence and social skills.

This leads to a catch-22 situation. Those that most need to learn how to interact with others are the ones spending the most time on their computers alone. Subconsciously, that makes sense: if people find it difficult to interact with others, they are less inclined to participate in social interaction. As a result they spend their time in solitary activities, such as surfing the web. However, in doing so, these people have no chance to improve their communication skills. They've entered a downhill slide, where they spend more and more time online and become more and more lonesome but never feel comfortable communicating with others.

To conclude, we can see the ubiquity of ICT entrenchment in our daily lives. Of course there are those who seek to resist, but for the vast majority in modern developed and developing economies, this is our lived reality. For those born in the last 20 years the idea of a life without ICTs is just simply unimaginable. The subsequent chapters in this collection show how those realities are being lived today and give glimpses of how the life course of an individual is impacted by the embrace of technology.

References

Alkalimat, A., and Williams, K. (2001). "Social capital and cyberpower in the African-American community," in: Keeble, L. and Loader, B. D. (eds), *Community Informatics: Shaping Computer Mediated Social Relations.* London: Routledge, p. 203.

Alzheimer Disease International. http://www.alz.co.uk/research/statistics.

Anderson, B. (2004). *Imagined Communities: Reflections on the Origin and Spread of Nationalism.* London: Verso.

Asimov, I. (1950). *I Robot.* New York: Gnome Press.

Bernström, A. (2013). How Technology Brings Generations Together Like Never Before. *Huffington Post Blog* 13/6/2013. http://www.huffingtonpost.com/andreas-bernstr/how-communications-techno_b_3435756.html.

Brooke, H. (2011). *The Revolution Will Be Digitised: Dispatches from the Information War*. London: Heinemann.

Carr, N. (2010). *The Shallows, What the Internet Is Doing to Our Brains*. New York: W. W. Norton & Company.

Castells, M. (1999). "The social implications of information and communication technologies," in: UNESCO (ed.), *World Social Science Report*. New York: UNESCO, pp. 236–245.

Chamarro-Premuzic, T. (2013). Is Technology Making Us Stupid (and Smarter)? How the Internet Makes Life More Complex – by Making Complex Things Simple. *Psychology Today*. https://www.psychologytoday.com/blog/mr-personality/201305/is-technology-making-us-stupid-and-smarter.

Curtis, A. R. (2015). From Arab Spring to Shahbag: The Role of Social Media in Terms of National Crisis. *Journal of Mass Communication Journalism*, *5*(241), 2. http://www.omicsgroup.org/journals/from-arab-spring-to-shahbag-the-role-of-social-media-in-terms-of-national-crisis-2165-7912-5-241.pdf.

Diani, M. (2001). "Social movement networks: Virtual and real," in: Webster, F. (ed.), *Culture and Politics in the Information Age*. London and New York: Routledge, pp. 117–128.

Dutton, W., & Blank, G. (2013). *Cultures of the Internet: The Internet in Britain*. Oxford Internet survey 2013 report. http://oxis.oii.ox.ac.uk/sites/oxis.oii.ox.ac.uk/files/content/files/publications/OxIS_2013.pdf.

Elder, G. H. (ed.) (1974). *Children of the Great Depression*. Chicago: University of Chicago Press.

Elder, G. H., Jr. (1994). Time, Human Agency, and Social Change: Perspectives on the Life Course. *Social Psychology Quarterly 57*, 4–15.

Elder, G. H. (2003). "The life course in time and place," in: Heinz, W. R. and Marshall, V. W. (eds), *Social Dynamics of the Life Course*. Weinheim: Deutscher Studien Verlag, pp. 57–71.

Elder, G. H., Jr., & Shanahan M. J. (2006). "The life course and human development," in: Damon, W. and Lerner, R. M. (eds), *Handbook of Child Psychology. Vol. 1. Theoretical Models of Human Development*, 6th ed. New York: John Wiley & Sons, pp. 665–715.

Freire, P. (1972). *Pedagogy of the Oppressed*. Harmondsworth: Penguin.

Freire, P. (1974). *Education for Critical Consciousness*. New York: Seabury Press.

Habermas, J. (1979). *Communication and the Evolution of Society*. Boston, MA: Beacon Press.

Habermas, J. (1987a). *The Theory of Communicative Action. Lifeworld and System: A Critique of Functionalist Reason* (T. McCarthy, Trans., Vol. 2). Boston, MA: Beacon.

Habermas, J. (1987b). *The Theory of Communicative Action: Reason and the Rationalization of Society* (T. McCarthy, Trans., Vol. 1). Boston, MA: Beacon.

Hamblen, M. (2012). *Smartphone Shipments Outpaced PCs in 2011 for First Time*. http://www.computerworld.com/s/article/9223956/Smartphone_shipments_outpaced_PCs_in_2011_for_first_time.

Hawkins, J. (1997). *The World at Your Fingertips: Education Technology Opens Doors*. Edutopia http://www.edutopia.org/world-your-fingertips.

Hogan, M. (2009). "Age differences in technophobia: An Irish study," in: Barry, C., Conboy, K., Lang, M., Wojtkowski, G. and Wojtkowski, W. (eds), *Information Systems Development: Challenges in Practice, Theory, and Education, Vol. 1*. New York: Springer, 117–130.

Howe, N., & Strauss, W. (2000). *Millennials Rising: The Next Great Generation*. New York: Vintage.

Internetlivestats (2015). http://www.internetlivestats.com/statistics/.

Klopper, N. (2015). The Negative Effects of the Internet on Social Skills. http://www.self growth.com/articles/the-negative-effects-of-the-internet-on-social-skills.

Kremer, W. (2015). Are Humans Getting Cleverer? http://www.bbc.com/news/magazine-31556802?utm_source=pocket&utm_medium=email&utm_campaign=pockethits.

Kurzweil, R. (2005). *The Singularity Is Near: When Humans Transcend Biology.* London: Penguin.

Magid, L. (2013). Online Privacy and Shared Responsibility: Government, Industry and You. *Forbes Online* http://www.forbes.com/sites/larrymagid/2013/02/12/online-privacy-and-security-is-a-shared-responsibility-government-industry-and-you/

Milakovich M. E. (2011) *Digital Governance: New Technologies for Improving Public Service and Participation.* Abingdon: Routledge.

Moore, G. A. (1999). *Crossing the Chasm: Marketing and Selling High-Tech Products to Mainstream Customers* (Rev. ed.). New York: HarperBusiness.

Naish, J. (2015). Is Sat Nav Harming Your Brain? *Mail Online* http://www.dailymail.co.uk/health/article-2976614/Is-satnav-harming-brain-Scientists-warn-use-modern-technology-linked-memory-loss-depression-later-life.html.

Nonaka, I. (1994). A Dynamic Theory of Organizational Knowledge Creation. *Organization Science 5*, pp. 14–37.

Park, S., Chung, K., & Jayaraman, S. (2014.). "Wearables: Fundamentals, advancements, and a roadmap for the future," in: Sazonov, E. and Neuman, M. R. (eds), *Wearable Sensors: Fundamentals, Implementation and Applications. Encyclopedia of Information Science and Technology.* San Diego, CA: Academic Press, pp. 1–24.

Perry, K. (2014). Regent Street to Deploy Beacon Technology in Shops. *The Telegraph Online* http://www.telegraph.co.uk/finance/newsbysector/retailandconsumer/10875969/Regent-Street-to-deploy-beacon-technology-in-shops.html.

Ravenwood, C., Muir, A., & Matthews, G. (2015). Stakeholders in the Selection of Digital Material for Preservation: Relationships, Responsibilities, and Influence. *Collection Management, 40*(2), 83–110.

Rawal, R., & Nixon, P. G. (2012). Re-Tweet to Democracy: The Social Media #Revolution in Perspective. ICEG Sant Cugat, June 2012.

Rheingold, H. (1994). *The Virtual Community.* London: Minerva.

Romero, M., & Barbera, E. (2012). *Technology Enhanced Learning for Creative Collaboration in Older Adults.* Paper presented at II Open Workshop A-C-M / BCN, Barcelona. http://blogs.uoc.edu/mireia/files/2012/10/Romero_Barbera.pdf

Seo, D. C., & Niu, J. (2015). Evaluation of Internet-Based Interventions on Waist Circumference Reduction: A Meta-Analysis. *Journal of Medical Internet Research 17*(7), e181. http://www.ncbi.nlm.nih.gov/pmc/articles/PMC4527011/.

Stajano, F. (2002). *Security for Ubiquitous Computing.* Chichester: John Wiley & Sons.

Statista (2015). http://www.statista.com/statistics/272014/global-social-networks-ranked-by-number-of-users/.

Tapscott, D. (1998). Growing Up Digital. The Rise of the Net Generation. *Education and Information Technologies 4*(2), 203–205.

Werner, F., & Werner, K. (2012). Enhancing the Social Inclusion of Seniors by Using Tablets as a Main Gateway to the World Wide Web. http://www.corp.at/archive/CORP2012_112.pdf.

West, A., Lewis, J., & Currie, P. (2009). Students' Facebook 'friends': Public and Private Spheres. *Journal of Youth Studies 12*(6), 615–627.

3 Citizenship in the virtual public sphere

Reasonableness as a modus vivendi for life online

Andreas Funk

The emergence of new models of democracy is tied to novel conceptions of both the citizen and the public space in which political life takes place. It is one prime task of political thought to bring together apt conceptions of both democratic models and the conceptions of the citizen. Simply speaking, there are competencies we need qua citizens, and these competencies precondition the very possibility of a particular model of democracy. The idea of a just polis seems to presuppose (some) sense of justice amongst (some) citizens (see Williams, 1973). Likewise, the idea of digital democracy and the virtual public sphere must be linked to a corresponding conception of digital citizens and their competencies. How precisely does such a changing model of democracy affect our attempts to provide ourselves with a more modern notion of citizenship? What kind of possibly new civic competencies are required with regard to the ideal of digital democracy and digital citizenship?

In recent years, questions revolving around political life online have become increasingly prominent in academic publications, mainly in the field of political communication. Scholars have pointed to an ongoing change in citizenship linked to the emergence of online environments (Bennett et al., 2011, Papacharissi, 2010). Contributions target the ability of individuals to access ICTs, being the means of digital democracy (Mercea, Lekakis, & Nixon, 2013), or the question of whether digital democracy should imply a citizen's right to access the Internet (Oyedemi, 2014). Others' writings center on new forms of citizenship, such as the notion of liquid citizenship (Papacharissi, 2010) or the distinction between a sort of actualizing citizen opposed to the traditional notion of a dutiful citizen (Bennett, Wells, & Rank, 2009). What is largely missing, as Bennett et al. point out (2011), is an inventory of civic competencies considering the specific requirements that stem from the notion of a political life online, a life as a digital citizen actively and effectively participating in the virtual public sphere.

The aim of this piece is to contribute to such an inventory of civic competencies for political life online. As opposed to existing accounts focusing on what is particularly new about digital citizenship, the main argument here focuses on a rather traditional competency, namely reasonableness. Concretely, it will be argued that (1) political life online can be enriched insofar as the virtual public sphere provides new potentials as a deliberative forum and that (2) reasonableness remains a prime competency for a political life online. As both propositions presuppose a sound understanding of digital democracy and its *playing field* – the virtual public sphere – the following section begins with some preliminary remarks on the former.

The virtual public sphere as a deliberative forum

The discourse on the virtual public sphere and more generally on digital democracy has as a central underpinning the idea that the advancements in information and communication technologies (ICTs) can bring about changes in terms of civic practices (Papacharissi, 2010). Whether these changes are desirable, provide added value and can be empirically observed is a matter of disagreement. Indeed, discourse on digital democracy is characterized by both high hopes as well as serious scepticism (see Bohman, 2004). Therefore it seems advisable to employ a neutral and modest approach according to which digital democracy must not necessarily be seen as a new model of democracy, but rather a variation – a variation that, thanks to the advanced technologies, can foster "deliberative, discursive, democratic forms" (Hague & Loader, 1999, p. 6). So, within the framework of this chapter, digital democracy is understood first and foremost as providing potential for democratic political deliberation.

Dahlberg (2011) also notes the importance of deliberation in the context of digital democracy but presents additional alternative understandings of the concept. For example, a liberal-individualist understanding would put emphasis on digital democracy's potential to allow citizens access to information for examining political positions and subsequently expressing their choices in the form of e-voting, petitions or the like (Dahlberg, 2011). According to this position, digital democracy is valued more for its facilitating of citizens pursuing their atomic self-interest than for its potential towards collective deliberation. Another common position on digital democracy and its value is one that emphasizes the prospects for it to serve as a vehicle for political protest. Here, Dahlberg (2011) points to the role of digital democracy for contestation and activism, where ICTs are used to organize, communicate and support political dissent (see also Malina in Hague & Loader, 1999). These understandings will be revisited when discussing the implications of reasonableness as a civic competency in the virtual public sphere. For now, however, we focus on digital democracy as providing deliberative potential.

We have seen that authors argue for a positive effect of digital democracy on political deliberation. We have not yet seen why this is supposedly the case. Here, the central claim is that digital democracy transforms the hitherto public sphere into a now *virtual* public sphere. This move supposedly enhances the already existing deliberative potential of the public sphere significantly. More precisely: following Habermas, the public sphere has been perceived as "institutional communicative spaces" with the purpose to "facilitate the formation of public opinion and political will-formation" (Dahlgren, 2006, p. 273). This shows that, first, the traditional public sphere serves as a forum for deliberation, as it has a clear end, namely the formation of a commonly agreeable public opinion and, eventually, a political will. This political will established in the public sphere is insofar democratically legitimate as during the process "speakers may express their views to others [. . .] who in turn respond to them and raise their own opinions and concerns", whilst everyone is free and equal (Bohman, 2004, p. 133). Why and how does digital democracy further enhance the potential for deliberation?

With the emergence of digital media, being the "tools of change" at the core of digital democracy (Bennett, 2008, p. 9), the aforementioned traditional notion of public sphere was revisited and transformed into the concept of the virtual public sphere. The virtual public sphere can also be seen as a communicative space with both the final end being the formation of a political will and the basic principle being equal participation of all citizens. The claim that the virtual public sphere carries even more deliberative potential than the traditional public sphere is best understood along the theoretical dimensions of space and time. In terms of time, the move from public sphere to virtual public sphere consists of an "increasing instantaneity and simultaneity", allowing citizens to communicate and act on several political issues with less effort (Ellison 2013, p. 58). More relevant for this piece, however, is the second theoretical dimension, namely space. In terms of spatial change, the virtual public sphere is no longer a (possibly even physical) space in which communication is confined to some territory, for instance national borders. Rather, computer-mediated communication does extend the spatial dimension of the virtual public sphere and enables citizens to engage in international affairs and issues regardless of state boundaries (Bohman, 2004, Papacharissi, 2010).

Thus, with the virtual public sphere one finds a space that, in theory, renders possible political deliberation amongst (most if not) all world citizens (Barlow in Loader, 2007, p. 11). Accordingly, it appears that the virtual public sphere is not fundamentally different from the public sphere but rather exceeds its deliberative potential by expanding previously existing limitations concerning time and space. As such, the virtual public sphere's appeal is that it might provide new possibilities for citizen engagement and political participation (Bohman, 2004).

Why reasonableness matters for political life online

So the increased deliberative potential appears to be a key appeal of digital democracy and political life online. Why then would reasonableness, as the second proposition of this piece states, be a prime civic competency? The answer lies in the hyper-pluralism a political life online inherently features. Regarding the public sphere, Habermas (2001) grasped the challenge of pluralism as follows:

> The sphere of questions that can be answered rationally from the moral point of view shrinks in the course of development toward multiculturalism within particular societies and toward a world society at the international level. But finding a solution to these few more sharply focused questions becomes all the more critical to coexistence, and even survival, in a more populous world.
>
> (p. 91)

Whilst the traditional public sphere might be characterized by value pluralism, the aforementioned expansion of time and space that comes with the virtual public sphere multiplies the diversity of citizens involved and hence potentially amplifies the degree of pluralism. In fact, what one can expect from a networked virtual public sphere without spatial boundaries is a multitude of citizens that hold diverse and different comprehensive doctrines – these can be political, religious or moral doctrines. The fact that such doctrines are at times incompatible or even diametrically opposed, for instance theism and atheism, posits a challenge. This is because, as previously stated, the goal of deliberation and the virtual public sphere, perceived as a deliberative forum, is to find common political conceptions, justifiable to citizens regardless of their comprehensive doctrines. In short, reasonableness as a civic competency is needed because it precisely allows citizens to deliberate effectively given the pluralistic environment of the virtual public sphere.

What then does reasonableness mean and how does it address the predicament of pluralism in the virtual public sphere? The most prominent advocate of reasonableness, Rawls (1993), promises that reasonable citizens bring about qualities that make possible a meaningful deliberation in a pluralistic regime. First, Rawls claims that reasonable citizens will not disagree about fundamentals concerning an abstractly formulated political will and therefore will be able to agree on a common final goal of deliberation (see Waldron, 1999). Concretely, reasonable citizens would, despite pluralism in the virtual public sphere, be able to formulate a common final goal, such as political stability or democratic reform.

Second, reasonableness implies the quality to deliberate so that citizens exercise public reason, meaning to "reason from premises which [. . .] all acknowledge" (Larmore, 2003, p. 380). "A reasonable citizen is equally capable of giving and receiving public reasons" (Garsten, 2006, p. 6), and this would ensure that deliberation in the virtual public sphere is one that is commonly agreeable. Hence, reasonableness as a civic competency would render possible a meaningful deliberation in the virtual public sphere, as it facilitates citizens' acknowledgement of a shared final goal of deliberation as well as equips citizens with the quality to deliberate using reasons that all can adopt.

To illustrate the proposition: The virtual public sphere, stretching the boundaries of time and space, would allow citizens worldwide to deliberate online on an international issue. Citizen *C1* and *C2* hold different and incommensurable comprehensive doctrines (e.g. atheism and theism). In case the issue in question touches on the citizens' doctrines – and in fact most significant issues do – deliberation would be practically impossible as long as both stick to their doctrines. As a consequence, the deliberative potential of the virtual public sphere would collapse. In case both citizens are reasonable in the aforementioned sense, they would first agree on the final goal of deliberation on the issue in question and therefore open space for a commonly agreeable political will. In fact, reasonable citizen *C1* would deliberate the issue using reasons that can also be understood from the viewpoint of citizen *C2*'s doctrine and vice versa. To simplify the matter, reasonableness can rescue the deliberative potential of the virtual public sphere despite its inherent pluralistic nature.

Concerning the prospect of digital democracy, reasonableness can thus be seen as an essential civic competency, as it enhances the deliberative potential of the virtual public sphere. But is it plausible to suggest that, in theory, all citizens can be reasonable? In other words, does reasonableness as a modus vivendi leave the option for universal participation? Here, empirical findings cast doubt: In fact, previous studies show that only a minority of citizens exercise deliberative reasonableness (Rosenberg, 2005). One reason could be that, as empirical literature points out, we do not know enough about the qualities needed to participate in deliberative reasonableness effectively (Delli Carpini et al., 2004, p. 328). Let us take a closer look at those qualities.

As reasonableness is mainly a deliberative competency, the corresponding qualities needed are first and foremost cognitive. Here, Rawls (1993) mentions exemplarily "the intellectual powers of judgement, thought, and inference" (p. 81). What appears more problematic than possessing the cognitive powers for reasonableness, however, is to have conclusive reasons, or even better the motivation, to deliberate in a reasonable fashion. The point is to find out what it is that makes us want to engage deliberative reasonableness. To have this sort of moral motivation is by no means obvious. In fact, it is most likely far less universal than the cognitive powers needed for reasonableness. As noted earlier, reasonable citizens must agree on a final goal or outcome. Second, reasonable citizens need to give and receive reasons towards this end. But reasonable citizens cannot just give any sort of reasons here. They are "expected to divorce their private and public beliefs and values to the extent required by [Rawls's] ideal of citizenship" (McCarthy, 1999, p. 328). In Rawls's (1993) words, "reasons given explicitly in terms of comprehensive doctrines are never to be introduced in public reason" (p. 247). What this means in practice is that to engage in deliberative reasonableness, citizens do not only need to agree on common final goals but also to deliberate on the basis of what one could call second-best reasons.

Imagine citizen $C1$ has a good reason V to argue for a certain course of action. In fact, V might be the best reason $C1$ can think of. If V derives from $C1$'s doctrine (say atheism), V (something like 'Because there is no god . . .') would not be in line with reasonableness. Why? Because reasonableness asks to use reasons that others can accept – a theist like $C2$ would, however, never accept a reasoning like 'Because there is no god'. $C1$ could come up with a second-best reason R that supports the preferred course of action, whilst R is unrelated to the doctrine of $C1$ (atheism). As a reasonable citizen in a Rawlsian sense, $C1$ must do so. But the question remains: What can be $C1$'s motivation to use the second-best reason R instead of V? What can be $C1$'s reasons to be reasonable? True, that we can find a second-best reason (like R) necessitates a cognitive quality. But that we want it, that we have reasons to be reasonable, is equally important and cannot derive from cognition only.

What sort of qualities then would provide reasons to be reasonable? As Williams (1981) shows, for a citizen to have reason to Φ (Φ may stand for any verb of action, in this case for deliberating in a reasonable manner), there must be some motive M that is part of this citizen's subjective motivational set S which consists of projects in the wider sense (Williams, 1981). Elements of such a motivational set could be desires ('$C1$ deliberates in a reasonable manner because $C1$ desires a stable regime'); further, some sort of disposition could provide motivation to be reasonable ('$C1$'s sense of justice provides reasons to be reasonable'); last, moral motivation to be reasonable can be a matter of loyalty ('$C1$ uses second-best reasons because it is for the good of the political community') (see Williams, 1981, p. 101). Hence, to render possible reasonableness in the virtual public sphere presupposes two things at least, namely to develop citizens' cognitive powers for deliberation and also to make sure citizens have the motivational set, desires or dispositions or loyalties that make them want to act in a reasonable manner.

Concluding remarks

It has been shown that one of the significant appeals of digital democracy is that it furnishes a virtual public sphere that exceeds the boundaries of the traditional public sphere. Thereby, the virtual public sphere increases the deliberative potential remarkably. In fact, as has been illustrated, the virtual public sphere potentially allows citizens worldwide to deliberate international issues largely disregarding earlier limitations of time and space.

To realize the full potential of the virtual public sphere as a deliberative forum, as has been argued, reasonableness seems to be a prime civic competency. Reasonableness can inform citizens' political life online insofar as it mitigates the differences that stem from the pluralistic nature of the virtual public sphere.

Whether reasonableness can be a feasible modus vivendi for the virtual public sphere depends on whether citizens have the cognitive powers to deliberate well and, more crucially, whether citizens have the desires, dispositions or loyalties that provide motivation to deliberate in a reasonable manner. Looking closer on the noted aspects that can provide motivation to act reasonable seems to set limits on universal participation (Wilhelm, 1999).

In the context of the virtual public sphere, we often speak of citizens that use the Internet to practice civic activities paired with the security and comfort of the – also physical – private sphere (see Papacharissi, 2010). The question is whether possible motivations to be reasonable ('desiring a stable regime', 'sense of justice', 'the good of the political community') are applicable in such environments or whether digital citizens rather enjoy the virtual public sphere for preserving personal autonomy, expressing their own possibly non-reasonable opinions and expressing political dissent (see also Papacharissi, 2010).

Further, it might be worthwhile to discuss whether reasonableness whilst enhancing the deliberative potential of digital democracy at the same time harms its prospect for contestation – the agreement on the common final goal deliberative reasonableness presupposes might contradict the political dissent at the core of an activist political life online.

References

Bennett, W. L. (ed.) (2008). *Civic Life Online: Learning How Digital Media Can Engage Youth.* London: The MIT Press.

Bennett, W. L., Wells, C., & Rank, A. (2009). Young Citizens and Civic Learning: Two Paradigms of Citizenship in the Digital Age. *Citizenship Studies*, 13 (2), pp. 105–120.

Bennett, W. L., Wells, C., & Freelon, D. (2011). Communicating Civic Engagement: Contrasting Models of Citizenship in the Youth Web Sphere. *Journal of Communication*, 61 (5), pp. 835–856.

Bohman, J. (2004). Expanding Dialogue: The Internet, the Public Sphere and Prospects for Transnational Democracy. *The Sociological Review*, 52 (Supplement), pp. 131–155.

Dahlberg, L. (2011). Re-constructing Digital Democracy: An Outline of Four 'Positions'. *New Media & Society*, 13 (6), pp. 855–872.

Dahlgren, P. (2006). Doing Citizenship: The Cultural Origins of Civic Agency in the Public Sphere. *European Journal of Cultural Studies*, 9 (3), pp. 267–286.

Delli Carpini, M. X., Cook, F. L., & Jacobs, L. R. (2004). Public Deliberation, Discursive Participation, and Citizen Engagement: A Review of Empirical Literature. *Annual Review of Political Science*, 7, pp. 315–344.

Ellison, N. (2013). Citizenship, Space and Time: Engagement, Identity and Belonging in a Connected World. *Thesis Eleven*, 118 (1), pp. 48–63.

Garsten, Bryan. (2006). *Saving Persuasion – A Defense of Rhetoric and Judgment.* London: Harvard University Press.

Habermas, J. (2001). *Justification and Application – Remarks on Discourse Ethics.* Cambridge: MIT Press.

Hague, B. H. & Loader, B. D. (eds) (1999). *Digital Democracy: Discourse and Decision Making in the Information Age.* London: Routledge.

Larmore, C. (2003). Public reason. In Freeman, S. (ed.), *The Cambridge Companion to Rawls* (pp. 368–393). Cambridge: Cambridge University Press.

Loader, B. D. (ed.) (2007). *Young Citizens in the Digital Age: Political Engagement, Young People and New Media.* London: Routledge.

McCarthy, T. (1999). Kantian constructivism and reconstructivism: Rawls and Habermas in dialogue. In Weithman, P. J. & Richardson, H. S. (eds), *The Philosophy of Rawls – A Collection of Essays* (pp. 320–340). Cambridge: Cambridge University Press.

Mercea, D., Lekakis, E., & Nixon, P. G. (2013). Taking stock: A meta-analysis of the virtual public sphere in communication journals. In Nixon, P. G., Rawal, R., & Mercea, D. (eds), *Politics and the Internet in Comparative Context: Views from the Cloud* (pp. 10–25). London: Routledge.

Oyedemi, T. (2014). Internet Access as Citizen's Right? Citizenship in the Digital Age. *Citizenship Studies*, 19 (3–4), pp. 450–464.

Papacharissi, Z. (2010). *A Private Sphere: Democracy in the Digital Age.* Malden, MA: Polity.

Rawls, J. (1993). *Political Liberalism.* New York: Columbia University Press.

Rosenberg, S. (2005). The Empirical Study of Deliberative Democracy: Setting a Research Agenda. *Acta Politica*, 40, 212–224.

Waldron, J. (1999). Disagreements about justice. In Weithman, P. J. & Richardson, H. S. (eds), *The Philosophy of Rawls – A Collection of Essays* (pp. 78–93). Cambridge: Cambridge University Press.

Wilhelm, A. G. (1999). Virtual sounding boards: How deliberative is online political discussion? In Hague, B. H. & Loader, B. D. (eds) (1999). *Digital Democracy: Discourse and Decision Making in the Information Age*. London: Routledge.

Williams, B. (1973). The analogy of city and soul in Plato's republic. In Lee, E. N. & Mourelatos, A. P. D. (eds) *Exegesis and Argument: Studies in Greek Philosophy* (pp. 196–206). New York: Humanities Press.

Williams, B. (1981). *Moral Luck*. Cambridge: Cambridge University Press.

4 Birth through the digital womb

Visualizing prenatal life online

Yukari Seko and Katrin Tiidenberg

Introduction

Nowadays, a child's digital life may start prior to their actual birth. On December 6, 2012, Gerard Piqué, a famous football player and boyfriend of then mother-to-be pop star Shakira, tweeted an ultrasound picture of their son-to-be. The black-and-white scan titled "His first pic! #excited #cute" on WhoSay.com soon went viral on social media, allowing thousands of viewers a sneak peek at the singer's unborn baby (Pearson 2012). Other celebrities jumped on the trend adding their own twist: Beyoncé showed off a sonogram of her unborn daughter in the trailer for her documentary *Life is But a Dream* (Ramsdale 2013), while TV actors Genevieve and Jared Padalecki announced their second pregnancy by tweeting a photo of their older son holding a sonogram of his "future sibling" (Frith 2013).

Shakira, Beyoncé and the Padaleckis are not alone in the emerging trend among expectant parents. Nowadays ultrasound pictures and videos are ubiquitous on everyday digital media including blogs, online prenatal communities, social network sites (SNSs) and photo/video-sharing sites, where expectant parents share excitement of starting a new phase in life. A 2010 survey with 2,200 mothers from 10 countries revealed that 23 per cent of children have had their sonogram scans posted on the Internet by their parents. The tendency was most conspicuous in North America, with 37 per cent of Canadian and 34 per cent of American parents admitting that they gave "digital birth" to their children prior to the actual birth (AVG Technologies 2010). According to Leaver (2014), a total of 11,320 images and videos hashtagged #ultrasound were posted on 3-month period from March to May 2014.

Despite the growing visibility of sonogram pictures online, there are as yet few critical explorations into how prenatal "digital birth" generates new ways of conceptualizing pregnancy, parenthood and (digital) life course of children. This chapter aims to contribute to this nascent area of inquiry by addressing some of the ways in which the foetus acquires social visibility first via ultrasonography, then via online sharing platforms. We aim to ignite a discussion on the implications of the growing – and seemingly uncritical – online circulation of sonogram pictures by parents-to-be, exploring how visual and social media technologies become an integral part of performing pregnancy and mothering. In what follows, we first offer an overview of literature on foetal ultrasound and delineate the increasing reconfiguration of medical technologies and cultural imagination into women's embodied knowledge. The crux of our first argument lies in the power of visuality that constructs the reality of pregnancy, blurs the boundaries between clinical and social meanings of "seeing the foetus," and transforms the imagined foetus into a tangible, "unborn baby." In doing so, we draw attention to the role medical experts play in translating a blurry black-and-white scan into a picture of a "cute" baby. Once constructed as such, the image serves as social currency on the Internet, through which expectant parents and their audiences engage in co-construction of being prenatal and parental. Through this co-enactment of imagined parenthood, we argue, ultrasound images become a complex hybrid of parental identity narratives (or their "selfies"), family photography and, most crucially, a public performance of "digitally engaged" parenthood. In line with critical discussions on the "digitally engaged patient" (Lupton 2013), we argue that performing pregnancy online is becoming yet another addition to the ever-expanding responsibilities of expectant mothers, who are expected to constantly monitor and discipline their bodies for the sake of the foetus. However, given that the foetus has no agency to resist parents posting its "first pic" online, the impacts the digital birth and accompanying digital footprints may have on children remain uncertain. This chapter concludes with a discussion on potential ethical implications and privacy dilemmas with respect to the digital birth.

Seeing the baby through ultrasound image

Ultrasonography found its way into the field of obstetrics in the late 1950s to 1960s. Developed initially as a warfare technology, then a diagnostic tool for screening tumours, ultrasound scanning has quickly extended to clinical obstetrics as a non-intrusive method for detecting foetal abnormalities (Woo 2002). Although the safety and medical value of ultrasound remains contested to date (Gammeltoft 2007), by the 1980s it became a routine part of prenatal care in many countries with developed healthcare services (Harris et al. 2004). While the recommended number of routine scans varies among countries depending on healthcare policies and funding systems, most national guidelines of Western European and North American countries recommend one or two routine scans per low-risk pregnancy (Harris et al. 2004). For instance, in Canada the Society of Obstetricians and Gynaecologists of Canada (SOGC) advises women without pregnancy complications to take at least one routine ultrasound examination in their second trimester[1] (between 18 and 22 weeks' gestation) for monitoring foetal growth and identifying the risk of foetal anomalies (Cargill & Morin 2009). In addition, recent clinical guidelines from the SOGC also recommend a dating scan in the first trimester (between 10 and 14 weeks) to assess gestational age (Butt & Lim 2014).

Since the 1980s, the penetration of ultrasonography into prenatal care has sparked vigorous critique from feminist and cultural thinkers. A number of feminist authors (e.g. Petchesky 1987; Terry 1989; Oakley 1984; Georges 1996) have raised concerns with the "technomedical takeover" of maternal bodies (Davis-Floyd & Sargent 1997), drawing attention to the way ultrasound presents the foetus as the "unborn patient" (Casper 1998) who deserves independent care and intervention. The framing of the foetus as an independent, precious and vulnerable patient has assigned women a passive role in pregnancy, wherein their pregnant bodies are evaluated in terms of their quality as "containers."[2] Some feminist writers have also criticized the use of ultrasonography for devaluing women's embodied experience in favour of masculine, objective knowledge (e.g. Oakley 1984; Rothman 1989; Davis-Floyd & Sargent 1997). For instance, in her study with child-bearing couples, Sandelowski (1994) concludes that foetal ultrasound empowers men more than women, because the technology places expectant fathers (as well as obstetricians, sonographers and other male observers) in a position more equal to that of the mothers. For men, ultrasonography serves as a sort of "prosthetic device" (p. 232) that technologically redresses the inequality in knowledge of the foetus, whereas the same technology may serve a "disabling mechanism" (p. 232) for women because it makes their bodily experience secondary to visual knowledge. Such interpretations, however, while shedding critical light on technomedical surveillance over pregnancy and childbirth, may fall into reductionism that renders the visual mode of knowing as essentially detached, voyeuristic and masculine. By framing vision as disembodied and dissociative, these critiques tend to pay scarce attention to how women actually perceive and react to ultrasound imaging during their pregnancy and beyond.

Contrary to the early critiques, recent empirical investigations paint a more nuanced picture regarding how "seeing the foetus" has become an integral part of women's embodied experience with pregnancy (e.g. Harris et al. 2004; Han 2009). A wealth of anecdotal accounts indicates that ultrasound allows expectant mothers to confirm and embody the reality of their pregnancy, evokes pleasure, excitement and emotional bond with the foetus[3] and insofar as foetal normality is assured, alleviates anxieties and fears[4] (e.g. Petchesky 1987; Mitchell 2001; Garcia et al. 2002; Harris et al. 2004; Gammeltift 2007; Han 2009). Georges (1996) in her ethnography with Greek women suggests that ultrasound reconfigures the women's perception of reality by adding a "tactile quality" (p. 164) to the image. Many of her interviewees – especially those at early stages of pregnancy when the foetus is unseen and unfelt – actively interpreted ultrasound images as visual "evidence" of the foetus and reported increased awareness of bearing a child. For these women, "the foetus is *felt* more alive, more present, when it's *seen*" (Georges 1996, p. 164, original emphasis), and the photocopy of the scan they receive becomes tangible proof that they are going to be mothers.

Studies conducted in North America, Europe and Australia commonly report that many women enthusiastically express the pleasure of "meeting" their foetuses on the screen (Garcia et al. 2002). Some women even go through additional scans just to have more opportunities to "see the baby"[5] (Harris et al. 2004; Roberts 2012). The pleasure of seeing the foetus often expands beyond the mothers and encompasses their partners and other family members, for whom visual knowledge is a primary means of participating in the pregnancy. Many expectant fathers interviewed by Draper (2002) described ultrasound scans as "the strongest memory of the pregnancy" (p. 785) that clearly marked their transition to fatherhood and helped them start bonding with their unborn babies. Nowadays a number of commercial companies offer non-diagnostic ultrasound scanning with three-dimensional (3D) and four-dimensional (4D) technologies[6] to satisfy parental demand for a clear, portrait-like image of their foetuses (Roberts 2012). These commercial "keepsake ultrasounds" are designed as a ritual of family and kinship, through which expectant parents and other family members "make specific connections with family identity and history, annotating familiar facial features and behaviours, and weaving the fetus into a network of kinship relations" (Roberts 2012, p, 305).

What seems intriguing here is that while actively engaging in an embodied practice of "seeing the baby," few pregnant women (and their family members) are capable of visually identifying the "baby," especially on the standard 2D scans. Many women interviewed by Mitchell (2001) admitted that they indeed "couldn't recognize anything" (p. 155) until the sonographers pointed to the features of the baby such as the heart, bladder, arms and legs. To the eyes of the expectant fathers in Draper's research (2002) too, the scan appears a "bizarre" "amorphous blob" (p. 785) very different from conventional baby photographs. The fact that lay understanding of the foetus relies heavily on expert interpretations indicates the profound role medical professionals play in the shaping of women's embodied knowledge. In her ethnographic study, Han (2009) observes that sonographers tend to perform two types of scanning: one serves a medical purpose to provide obstetricians with some "good views" on foetal development, while the other aims to "give tours" to parents and take "cute pictures" for them to take home. When "showing the baby" to parents, sonographers actively construct "cuteness" by drawing attention to visual markers of personhood such as fingers, hands and toes that they consider appealing to adults. Referring to the symbolic meaning of baby footprints and handprints in modern American family life, Han (2009) argues that cuteness of the foetal sonography is drawn in part from the conventions of child photography that has long served a significant function of constructing family togetherness and kinship continuity.

The real-time nature of ultrasound scanning also contributes to the manner in which professionals translate the scan into a "baby picture." During her first routine scan at 13 weeks, the first author (Yukari Seko) was shown a 3D sonogram image (Figure 4.1), in which the foetus appeared as if holding its arms up to its face. Pointing out the arms on the screen, the sonographer described "the baby" as "hiding" its face, more specifically, "playing peek-a-boo." Similarly, the other sonographer who conducted Yukari's 22-week routine scan (Figure 4.2) described the image in a manner that ascribed specific personality to the foetus. During this scan the sonographer, having difficulty completing measurements, described the foetus being "too excited" because it was constantly moving away from the transducer. She spoke to the foetus to ask it to "stay still" for the photo, as if the foetus was conscious and

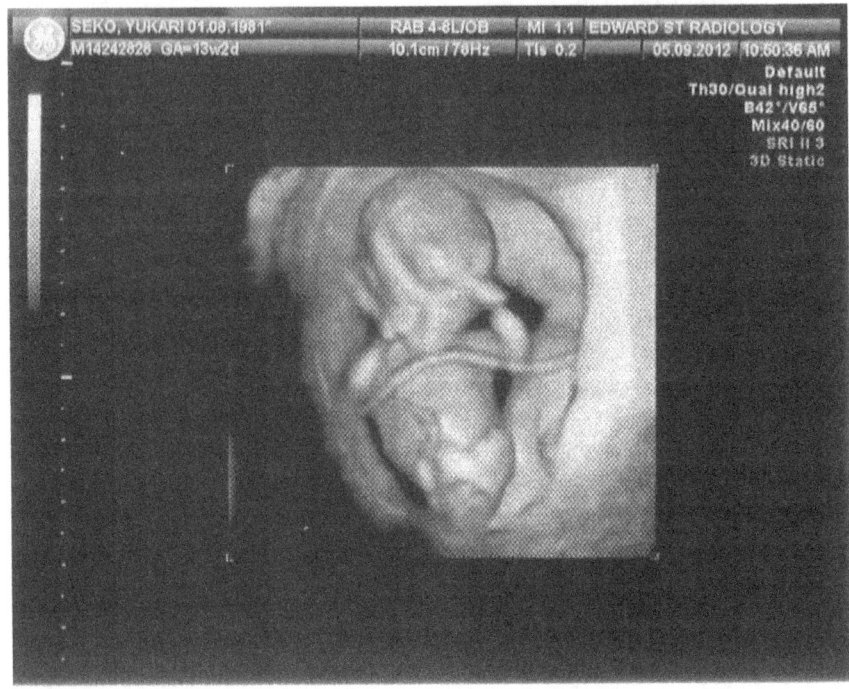

Figure 4.1 This 3D ultrasound image was taken at the first author's 13-week routine scan, in which the foetus was described as "playing peek-a-boo"

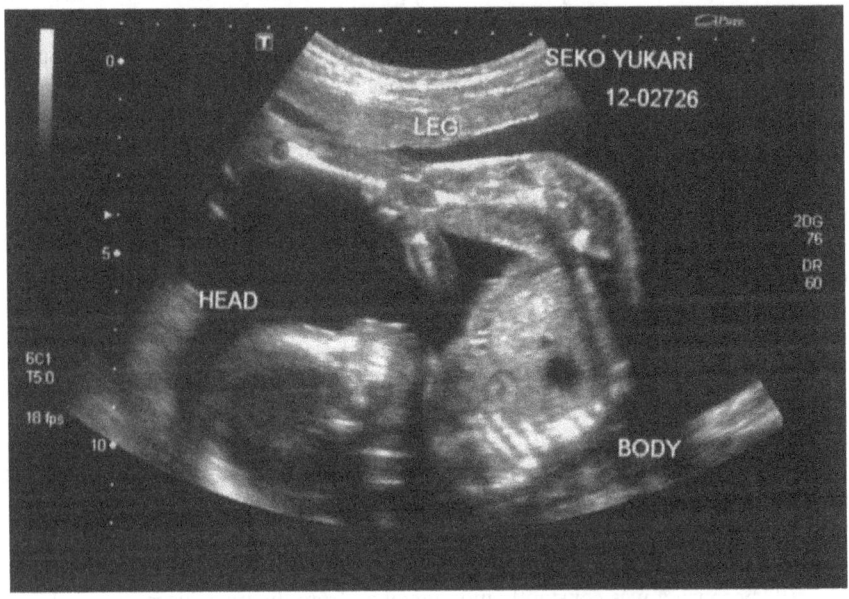

Figure 4.2 The foetal scan taken at the first author's 22-week routine scan. The sonographer described the foetus as "too excited," as it was constantly changing its position

listening to her. These acts of intensive personifications hold remarkable similarity with previous ethnographic observations (e.g. Mitchell 2001; Draper 2002; Han 2009). In her study on commercial 4D scanning in the UK, Roberts (2012) illuminates the way in which sonographers, in collaboration with expectant parents, create an identity for the unborn by ascribing personality to foetal posture and movements. A foetus with hands near the face may be interpreted as "sleepy," "picking its nose" or "blowing a kiss" (p. 306) depending on the personality and family resemblance sonographers and expectant parents wish to impose. Through this "collaborative coding" (Roberts 2012) sonographers and parents work together to construct the foetal image as personal and socially meaningful and "see the baby" accordingly.

Additionally, the way in which sonographers take keepsake snapshots for expectant parents seems shaped by visual conventions of baby photography. During Yukari's second scan the sonographer showed the front view of the foetus on the screen to measure facial features. With black eye sockets and empty nose hole, the foetus on the screen looked like the skull-faced man in *The Scream* by Edvard Munch. "Don't worry," said the sonographer, "I'll give you a better picture to take home." The sonographer's comment dovetails with Mitchell's (2001) observation on the selective gaze of medical professionals, who consider early foetal faces as "weird" or "strange-looking" and may appear "creepy" to expectant mothers (p. 126). Instead of the skull-faced shot, Yukari received a copy of the scan (Figure 4.2) that shows the side view of "the baby" with the contours of the face including the forehead, nose, lips and chin – the features that signify the cuteness of a baby (Mitchell 2001).

Seeing an ultrasound image is therefore not an intuitive, transparent experience but a techno-socially constructed, enculturated practice that translates the diagnostic artefact into a picture of "my baby." Once constructed as such, the animated foetus no longer connotes something unreal. Rather, the image becomes a complex amalgam of medical vision, cultural imagination and parental desire for reality and pleasure that together marks a Deleuzian concept of a virtual, yet-unrealized potential of becoming (Grosz 2005). As Petchesky (1987) aptly points out, it is the dominant cultural codes that determine how expectant parents make sense of the ultrasound scan. Guided by expert interpretations and visual conventions of child photography, parents "see in fetal images what they are told they ought to see" (p. 280).

Cyberbirth of parents

With ultrasonography coming to play a central role in construction of the foetal reality, sharing the "picture of baby-to-be" with family members, friends and the rest of the world has become an integral part of prenatal experience. Photo sharing can occur in person or via postal mail, but digital technologies have added a new dimension to this conventional practice. Once scanned (or photographed/videotaped) and uploaded online, digital sonograms acquire additional attributes compared to their physical counterparts: they become persistent, replicable, scalable, searchable (boyd 2010), as well as widely sharable (Papacharissi & Gibson

2011). As van Dijck (2013) suggests, it is this sociality of digital images and the resultant culture of connectivity that "impose 'sharing' and 'following' as social values" and thus profoundly "alter the nature of our connections, creations, and interactions " (p. 20). Within the social media architectures that prioritize sharing over withholding information (Papacharissi & Gibson 2011), expectant parents are, by default, prompted to share their "baby pictures" with broad and asynchronous audiences.

As exemplified by Piqué tagging Shakira's sonogram as "His first pic! #excited #cute," it is not uncommon for expectant parents to present ultrasound images as their children's first pictures. This not only reconfirms the aforementioned sonographer-initiated social role of the unborn child but also frames the image as the first online milestone, a memento to be followed by many more family photographs to come. By rendering the unborn a social (media) actor, the ultrasound images allow expectant parents to publicly advance their acquisition of a previously nonexistent identity – that of a mother or a father of that particular child. This use of child photographs in negotiating one's transition to parenthood is profoundly gendered, for it is firmly rooted in the tradition of modern family photography which mothers have long been instrumental in producing (Petchesky 1987; Rose 2004, 2014). Rose (2004) in her ethnographic research reports that mothers often felt *compelled* to take photographs of their children especially when they were young. They also felt *obliged* to store, organize, display and circulate these photographs to safeguard the memory of their family. In a more recent publication, Rose (2014) contends that digital technologies have further intensified the practice of family photography by easing mothers' tasks of taking, archiving, organizing and sharing massive numbers of family snapshots. Her assertions seem supported by a recent empirical study on parents' Facebook use at the transition to parenthood (Bartholomew et al. 2012), which found that new mothers were more likely than new fathers to upload a photograph of their child on Facebook, receive more comments on their child's photos and report an increase in their use of Facebook after the birth of their child.

In addition to claiming a new identity, the online announcement of pregnancy provides women with an opportunity to connect with other expectant mothers, exchange advice, share emotional excitement and, in some cases, alleviate anxieties associated with pregnancy. Although research suggests that anecdotal advice from online peers is unlikely to replace traditional sources of medical authority (Song, West, Lundy, & Dahmen 2012), expectant mothers nonetheless turn to the Internet for experiential information and practical support from similar others (Jang & Dworkin 2014; Johnson 2015). Posting information about one's foetus-child on SNSs is reported to help mothers build new social capital beyond their physical social circle (Jang & Dworkin 2014). Within such peer-group environments, sharing sonogram pictures function as the "currency for social interaction" (van Dijck 2008) that circulates among members and helps foster a sense of community and cohesiveness. In this context, the *quality* of "baby's first pic" matters less than the *experience* of sharing and peer bonding, through which expectant mothers gain validation of their new identity.

For expectant mothers, then, the sonograms uploaded online may serve as their own selfies,[7] a visual mode of "self-narration and representation" (Richter & Schadler 2009, p. 171) in a surrogated format. Given the enculturated practice of "seeing my baby" in the ultrasound, the image expresses a narrative of *becoming* that signifies the provisional status of the foetus and the pregnant woman. In this transitional narrative, the boundaries become permeable between the mother and the unborn child, the image maker and the subject, as well as the internal body and the external world. Repurposing ultrasounds into a form of selfie is, in a sense, an act of reclaiming women's embodied subjectivity. By performing their changing identity through the foetal sonograms, pregnant women may visually play out their lives and invite others to their embodied identity construction. In this vein, creating and sharing a surrogate selfie is, as Walker-Rettberg (2014) states, not only a self-expression but also "a form of self-reflection and self-creation" (p. 12).

However, showing off one's sonogram-selfies online is not merely about exploring a new facet of one's identity or finding online peers; it is also a specific way of enacting one's competence as a "good" mother and obtaining public acknowledgement. When entering pregnancy and motherhood, women often negotiate rigid norms and societal expectations placed on them. For mothers in contemporary Western societies, these expectations closely reflect the ideology of "intensive mothering" (Hays 1996) that demands mothers devote themselves entirely to the nurturing of their children. In this form of mothering, socially appropriate childrearing is constructed as "child-centred, expert-guided, emotionally absorbing, labour-intensive and financially expensive" (Hays 1996, p. 8), which requires mothers to commit "not only large quantities of money but also professional level skills and copious amounts of physical, mental and emotional energy" (Hays 1996, p. 4).[8] As Neiterman (2012) reveals in her ethnographic study, pregnant women "do" pregnancy through constant vigilance to food intake, abstinence from potentially harmful actions, compliance with medical advice and – most importantly for our argument – incessant performance of pregnancy to ensure their effort is acknowledged and valued.

In this context, online social platforms provide a promising stage for the performance of pregnancy and mothering. The interactive architecture of social media transforms the digital baby shower into a participatory spectacle that involves friends, families or other expectant parents in the co-construction of prenatal life. The amount and frequency of information uploaded online becomes a marker of "good mothering," while audience reactions are displayed and aggregated in the form of commenting, liking and re-blogging or re-tweeting of images. A plethora of digital self-surveillance and social networking technologies supports expectant mothers to regularly track and update their day-to-day status while constantly checking others' updates. The rise of mobile technologies, especially smartphones and applications (apps), furthers this process by providing mothers with a convenient means to remain connected. In a recent study, Johnson (2014) analyses a series of pregnancy and mothering apps that encourage users to document and share all the facets of their pregnancies by counting foetal kicks, journaling food intake, monitoring weight gain and sharing their sonograms and pictures of their growing bellies. For Johnson, this quantified and highly visualized mode of pre-natal mothering can be called the "puppeteering mother" wherein the pregnant woman transfers her virtual identity onto the foetus and presents the baby as "my measure" that renders her social status calculable and comparable (p. 337).

For women engaging in highly intensive mothering, performing their pregnan-cies online in a measurable and comparable format can be a confidence bolster, as it enables them to publicly demonstrate the "evidence" of good mothering and their strong commitment to their babies-to-be. The digital self-monitoring technologies such as pregnancy apps may also be empowering to these women, who want to exercise control over their bodies and gain calculable, "objective" knowledge of their pregnancy. However, the expectations to engage in incessant monitoring and updating may be overwhelming to expectant mothers who are already laden with an array of responsibilities. Bartholomew et al. (2012) report that mothers who received more comments on their child's photos on Facebook showed greater parental satisfaction, while frequent Facebook use and content management were also associated with higher levels of parenting stress. Although gaining and sharing a particular knowledge of one's own pregnancy may allow a woman to increase self-esteem, this also requires a great deal of physical and emotional labour, and the failure to meet the expectations can cause anxiety and distress.

To the extent that the practice of digital mothering may both empower and disempower expectant mothers, it has a clear resonance with the emergent dis-course of the "digitally engaged patient" (Lupton 2013), an idealized patient who actively employs digital technologies to engage in self-monitoring. According to Lupton (2013), this discourse, while encouraging lay people to generate their own health data and become more conversant with medical knowledge, ultimately induces voluntary self-discipline and compliance with medical authority. Just as ultrasonography requires professional decoding to serve as a "baby picture," user-generated health data often needs to be interpreted and approved by experts and, as such, normalizes medical authority rather than destabilizing it. Given that the compliance with expert advice is one of the crucial components of intensive moth-ering (Hays 1996), we argue that today's motherhood is increasingly implicated with digital health and social media technologies that require one to be highly health conscious and techno-medically savvy. The convergence of the digitally engaged patient model and intensive mothering is extremely powerful, in that it frames quantified data as a part of embodied, subjective knowledge of expectant mothers – just as the practice of "seeing my baby" through ultrasonography. With each "like" and comment received on their sonograms, with each kick recorded on the app, pregnant women accrue confidence and a sense of reality of the baby they grow within. We thus argue that the advancement of social media and digi-tal mothering technologies spurs biomedicine's informal encounter to pregnancy. A pregnant woman who engages in intensive mothering now must take the role of a digitally engaged parent, obliged to incessantly monitor and share their status for the sake of their babies and social validation.

Haunted by digital trace?

While sharing the trials of pregnancy and childrearing online is becoming one of the crucial ingredients of today's motherhood, showing "my baby" over the Internet inseparably involves the creation of the child's digital footprints. A variety of digital data associated with the unborn, not only sonogram scans but also the mother's medical records and her social media trajectories including blog entries, belly photos, comments and likes, altogether constitute extensive digital identity trails of the child by the time he/she is actually born. Given that these online portfolios are obviously made without the child's consent, the phenomenon of digital birth raises concerns with potential risks and harm for the children.

One of the most conspicuous issues is potential breach of children's privacy in both the short and long term. Parents increasingly acknowledge risks associated with Internet use, especially with regard to *which*, *how* and *with whom* information about their children is shared online. In their study on new mothers' privacy considerations, Kumar and Schoenebeck (2015) found that mothers took on responsibilities of "stewarding" their children's privacy when uploading the children's photographs. Many of them reportedly made conscientious decisions when they posted pictures of their children, even though they were tempted to share as many photos as possible to enact good mothering. They were likely to refrain from sharing crying and naked photos of their kids and preferred to post pictures that portray happy and healthy family life. Some mothers also reported the use of privacy features on SNSs, including limiting their profiles to friends only, creating private groups who could see the child's photos or turning off location tracking on their phones (Kumar & Schoenebeck 2015). However, although mothers were aware of the susceptibility of digital information to unexpected use, they might be less cognizant of privacy "loopholes" social media technology retains (Papacharissi & Gibson 2011). "For instance, on Facebook the act of tagging a post or an image can change the visibility of the original post. Once tagged, a copy of the tagged item appears in the profile of the tagged user, regardless of the privacy settings for the original item, and becomes viewable to the 'friends' of the tagged person" (Damen & Zannone 2014). "Parents' ability to control digital content is thus highly dependent on others' perspectives on what constitutes private and public information, which may disrupt their efforts to secure the children's online privacy" (p. 10).

Moreover, persistency of digital data presents a challenge for children who are forced to "inherit their digital profiles as a work in progress from parents" (Holloway, Green, & Livingstone 2013, p. 24). Child and Petronio (2011) introduce an episode of a parent posting a picture of their 18-year-old son as a little boy dressed in a tutu. Once tagged, the picture became accessible to the son's entire group Facebook friends, which compelled him to immediately untag and dissociate the picture from his Facebook profile. This episode suggests that parent-made digital footprints, though not intentionally malicious, may haunt the children later in life. Even if parents post information in accordance to their privacy standards, they may not anticipate how the children perceive such online profiles made without their consent. For young people whose identities increasingly traverse the online and offline contexts, controlling an online profile is quintessential for their identity management. As such, a parent-made digital dossier may conflict with the children's strategies on what to share about themselves online.

Another contested issue is ethical responsibility of parents performing parenthood at the expense of children's autonomy. Mothers' use of their children as "props" or "associates" for their impression management (e.g. Goffman 1963) has been subject to scholarly attention. An empirical study reveals that mothers use well-dressed and -groomed children as a part of their appearance to enhance their own self-esteem and social identities (Collett 2005). These children's appearances and manners are interpreted as the achievements of the mothers who invested financial, social and emotional capital, while the children are deemed vehicles for mothers' ambitions rather than autonomous individuals with full agency. The logic of intensive mothering clearly manifests in this context: mothers exhibit their children as the products of "good" mothering, in which receiving public validation outweighs the risk of exploiting or fetishizing the children.

Parental desire to manage their identities via their children seems to go hand in hand with their urge to monitor and control the children's activities on- and offline. As aforementioned, there are a number of surveillance products available to parents via apps, SNSs and wearable technologies to monitor the activities of their children from newborns on up (Nolan, Raynes-Goldie, & McBride 2011; Johnson 2014; Leaver 2014). Leaver (2014) argues that this parent-oriented "intimate surveillance," even though undertaken with good intensions, may normalize surveillance of young children. Nolan, Raynes-Goldie and McBride (2011) take a step forward to point out an implicit assumption behind parental surveillance that children's voluntary disclosure cannot and should not be trusted. This distrust generates "a moral imperative" that distinguishes "good" parents who actively surveil and control children's (online) activities from "bad" parents who do not (p. 28). The authors further contend that parents engaging in constant surveillance of children "may be negatively impacting how their children learn to trust others or themselves" (p. 29). From this perspective, even though there are benefits to parental control in terms of safety, they may be outweighed by the risk of hindering children's autonomy and psychological well-being in a long run.

These ethical and privacy concerns illuminate the problematic double standards pregnant women and mothers negotiate during their pregnancy and beyond. On the one hand, they face the expectation to incessantly document and share their children's social lives online, and the social cost of non-sharing is quite high for women engaging in intensive mothering. Yet on the other, they are expected to protect their children's privacy by "stewarding" (Kumar & Schoenebeck 2015) or "surveilling" (Nolan, Raynes-Goldie, & McBride 2011) their children in a manner that normalizes a surveillance culture. This dilemma indicates that online media is becoming a complementary identity space[9] to parents and children, wherein both parties have to co-construct social identities and negotiate their right to privacy and autonomy. Given the new affordances of online platforms that prompt sharing (boyd 2010; Papacharissi & Gibson 2011), parents and children together face the challenge of drawing upon mutually agreed privacy boundaries.

In this light, digital literacy education can offer a promising way to circumvent privacy dilemmas parents and children may face. Young people tend to divert from family privacy orientations when they grow into adults (Child & Petronio 2011). Yet family privacy rules have substantial influence on children's perceptions of privacy and the ways in which they engage in identity performance online. Litt and Hargittai (2014) found that young adults growing up in households with clear privacy rules around technology use would make more cautious decisions when uploading personal photographs on social media. They were more likely to post their photos but were more likely to do so with a restricted audience and less likely to share publicly. These findings point to the significance of positive parent involvement in children's digital life and the need for co-developing privacy rules ascribed to by all family members. Future research would benefit from exploring how and to what extent the digital birth and resultant digital footprints influence the child's identity formation and the practice of family building. Interrogating when and in what context children and adolescents interpret parents' posting of their pictures (including sonograms) as a form of privacy invasion would also enrich the understanding of the parent–child relationship in the networked society. Nolan, Raynes-Goldie, and McBride (2011) argue that if parents are able to efficiently "mentor and guide" children to develop and consolidate Internet-related skills, the children will "build their capacity to negotiate their privacy and safety online in a healthy, creative, critically-minded and responsible manner" (p. 31). We therefore advocate research that examines how to nurture the parent–child dialogue on technological and privacy literacy in a way that helps parents, researchers and educators explore how to plant a seed of digital literacy within the family in digital age.

Conclusion

Pregnancy has become highly visible over the past decades – in no small part as a result of routinization of ultrasonography in prenatal care. Through techno-medical vision, the foetus, a mystical creature hitherto hidden deep *in utero*, has entered into public imagination as the unborn child and secured its place in a family album. In a society where mothering is highly intensive (Hays 1996), performing pregnancy with and through digital media becomes a mandatory part of being a "good mother," and a bulk of those performances necessarily takes place online.

In this chapter we have argued that digital birth of a child is inseparably linked to digital birth of the mother (and the father to a lesser degree). In transition to parenthood, expectant mothers seek to verify their emergent identities and constitute their experience as meaningful in the social environments they belong to. As social currency in the culture of connectivity (van Dijck 2013), ultrasound images enable mothers-to-be to establish their authenticity and involve others to their performance of pregnancy. The convergence of intensive mothering and digitally engaged parent/patient model may compel mothers to incessantly document and share their children's growth online, even before their actual birth. Showing "my baby" online, however, can be troublesome due to the ambivalent and transitional nature of ultrasound image that serves both as the mother's selfie and the child's "first pic." Further, the affordances of digital images for being retrieved, modified, and repurposed in unforeseen contexts call into question potential ethical and privacy implications of the digital mothering from the perspective of the children.

While mothers are increasingly aware of the emergent responsibility of safeguarding their children's privacy when curating the children's online identity, how children will actually inherit parent-made online identity remains unknown. We thus emphasized the need for digital literacy education both for parents and children in a way that the family can mutually develop trust, awareness and autonomy, yet that doesn't shame mothers' digital sharing practices which, as we have demonstrated, are pushed on mothers by multiple complimenting discourses. From the digital birth to onward, learning how to autonomously perform online identities is a practice all family members should engage in, in order to help the children develop fully as social actors.

Notes

1 According to Mitchell (2001), the historical changes in Canadian guidelines for foetal ultrasound closely reflect ongoing controversy over the efficacy and cost of routine scanning. In 1981 the SOGC concluded in its guidelines that routine ultrasound "cannot be recommended," whereas its 1994 guidelines recommended at least one mandatory scan during pregnancy. More problematically, Mitchell (2001) also points out that routine scanning is seldom carried out with women's consent. The absence of informed choice around ultrasound technologies is "particularly worrisome" (p. 44) for Mitchell, given the adverse potential of misdiagnosis and emotional distress women may have to go through.

2 The crack baby scandal in the 1980s I the United States is among the most conspicuous examples in which the foetal rights outweighed those of the mothers. Despite the lack of evidence, troubling stories were widespread through the press that children born to mothers using cocaine during pregnancy showed depressed weights and sizes, deformed limbs and considerable developmental delays in brain growth, emotion and learning abilities (Lyons & Rittner 1998). The image of "crack babies" soon became a symbol of bad mothering, and some "crack mothers" were prosecuted for "abusing" their foetuses and had their children taken away from their care. Though most criminal charges against crack-using mothers did not result in guilty verdicts, the mothers and their children have long suffered erroneous stereotyping and stigmatization (Lyons & Rittner 1998).

3 Healthcare professionals frequently suggest that ultrasonography is helpful in promoting parent–child bonding. Nine studies reviewed by Garcia et al. (2002) explicitly addressed the bonding impacts of ultrasound and its potential influence in reducing abortion rates. However, the emphasis on foetal autonomy accompanies the degrading of women's agency. In her analysis of an anti-abortion film *The Silent Scream*, Petchesky (1987) argues that the logic of visual bonding has appeared repeatedly in pro-life propaganda to obstruct and even harass an abortion decision.

4 While some women derive a sense of security from ultrasound, it may generate new fears and concerns among others. Gammerltoft (2007) in her ethnographic research in Vietnam observes that pregnant women in Hanoi often feel compelled to take as many ultrasounds as possible to gain reassurance about foetal normality. Two-thirds of her respondents underwent four or more scans during their pregnancy in order to receive an official guarantee from their obstetricians that the foetuses are "developing normally" (p. 144). For these women living in a society where foetal normality is of paramount

importance, ultrasound is first and foremost a diagnostic tool used to detect foetal abnormalities. Gammerltoft (2007) argues that unlike women in Western countries who view the foetus as an "unborn baby," her interviewees tend to conceive the foetus as a provisional entity, in transition to full personhood. Each scanning is thus seen as contingent and inherently unstable rather than a concrete portrait of an "unborn baby." Although ultrasonography does provide these women with momentary reassurance, "renewed uncertainty soon follows, as does the need for another scan" (p. 145).

5 The entertaining aspect of ultrasonography has given a further impetus to clinical use of this technology. A large-scale population-based study with 1.4 million pregnant women in Canada finds a 55 per cent increase in the use of obstetric ultrasonography from 1996 to 2006. In 2006 nearly one in five women underwent four or more scans, which far exceeded the number recommended by national guideline (You et al. 2010). Given that the tendency to take extra ultrasounds is more pronounced among low-risk women than those with higher risks, You et al. (2010) suggest that the sharp increase in the use (or the overuse) of ultrasound seems driven in part by the "entertainment" value.

6 4D ultrasonography refers to real-time visualization of three-dimensional images, with the fourth dimension being time or motion (Woo 2002).

7 Although what exactly counts as a selfie remains a subject of continuous debate among scholars, selfies are often conceptualized as photographs "taken by oneself using a digital camera especially for posting on social networks" (Merriam-Webster 2015).

8 It is worth noting that the model of intensive mothering is implicitly racialized and classed (Song et al. 2012). Neiterman (2012) argues that this model works predominantly in favor of middle-class, married women with financial stability, while women without such privileges – such as young, unmarried women – are often stigmatized as "unworthy" and positioned "at the bottom of the social ladder of motherhood" (p. 377). Thus the pressure of good mothering women may experience may vary from one person to the other, depending on their social location and their ability to perform "good motherhood."

9 We owe this phrase to Jeremy Hunsinger.

References

AVG Technologies. 2010. *Digital Diaries 2010*. [Online] Available from: http://www.avg.com/digitaldiaries/2010 [Accessed 28 November, 2014].

Bartholomew, M. K., Schoppe-Sullivan, S. J., Glassman, M., Kamp Dush, C. M., & Sullivan, J. M. 2012. New parents' Facebook use at the transition to parenthood. *Family Relations*, *61*(3), pp. 455–469.

boyd, d. 2010. Social network sites as networked publics: Affordances, dynamics, and implications. In Z. Papacharissi (ed.), *Networked Self: Identity, Community, and Culture on Social Network Sites*. New York: Routledge, pp. 39–58.

Butt, K., & Lim, K. 2014. Determination of gestational age by ultrasound. *Journal of Obstetric Gynaecology Canada*, *36*(2), pp. 171–181.

Cargill, Y., & Morin, L. 2009. Content of a complete routine second trimester obstetrical ultrasound examination and report. *Journal of Obstetric Gynaecology Canada*, *31*(3), pp. 272–275.

Casper, M. 1998. *The Making of the Unborn Patient: A Social Anatomy of Fetal Surgery*. New Brunswick: Rutgers University Press.

Child, J. T., & Petronio, S. (2011). Unpacking the paradoxes of privacy in CMC relationships: The challenges of blogging and relational communication on the Internet. In K. B. Wright & L. M. Webb (eds), *Computer-Mediated Communication in Personal Relationships*. New York: Peter Lang, pp. 21–40.

Collett, J. L. 2005. What kind of mother am I? Impression management and the social construction of motherhood. *Symbolic Interaction*, *28*(3), pp. 327–347.

Damen, S., & Zannone, N. (2014). Privacy implications of privacy settings and tagging in Facebook. In W. Jonker & M. Petkovic (eds), *Secure Data Management*. Berlin: Springer International Publishing, pp. 121–138.

Davis-Floyd, R., & Sargent, C. 1997. Introduction. In R. Davis-Floyd & C. Sargent (eds), *Childbirth and Authoritative Knowledge: Cross-Cultural Perspectives*. Berkeley: University of California Press, pp. 1–54.

Draper, J. 2002. 'It was a real good show': The ultrasound scan, fathers and the power of visual knowledge. *Sociology of Health & Illness*, *24*(6), pp. 771–795.

Frith, V. 2013. Jared Padalecki baby: 'Supernatural' actor talks parenthood announces wife Genevieve pregnancy. *Enstars*. [Online] 22 July. Available from http://www.enstarz.com/articles/22015/20130722/jared-padalecki-baby-supernatural-actor-talks-parenthood-announces-wife-genevieve.htm [Accessed 05 January, 2015].

Gammeltoft, T. 2007. Sonography and sociality: Obstetrical ultrasound imaging in urban Vietnam. *Medical Anthropology Quarterly*, *21*(2), pp. 133–153.

Garcia, J., Bricker, L., Henderson, J., Martin, M. A., Mugford, M., Nielson, J., & Roberts, T. 2002. Women's views of pregnancy ultrasound: A systematic review. *Birth*, *29*(4), pp. 225–250.

Georges, E. 1996. Fetal ultrasound imaging and the production of authoritative knowledge in Greece. *Medical Anthropology Quarterly*, *10*(2), pp. 157–175.

Goffman, E. 1963. *Behavior in Public Places: Notes on the Social Organizations of Gatherings*. New York: Free Press.

Grosz, E. 2005. *Time Travels: Feminism, Nature, Power*. Durham, NC and London: Duke University Press.

Han, S. 2009. Seeing like a family: Fetal ultrasound images and imaginings of kin. In V. R. Sasson & J. M. Law (eds), *Imaginings of the Fetus, the Unborn in Myth, Religion and Culture*. Oxford: Oxford University Press, pp. 275–290.

Harris, G., Connor, L., Bisits, A., & Higinbotham, N. 2004. 'Seeing the baby': Pleasure and dilemmas of ultrasound technologies for primiparous Australian Women. *Medical Anthropology Quarterly*, *18*(1), pp. 23–47.

Hays, S. 1996. *The Cultural Contradictions of Motherhood*. New Haven: Yale University Press.

Holloway, D., Green, L., & Livingstone, S. 2013. *Zero to Eight. Young Children and Their Internet Use*. LSE, London: EU Kids Online.

Jang, J., & Dworkin, J. 2014. Does social network site use matter for mothers? Implications for bonding and bridging capital. *Computers in Human Behavior*, *35*, pp. 489–495.

Johnson, S. A. 2014. 'Maternal devices': Social media and the self-management of pregnancy, mothering and child health. *Societies*, *4*(2), pp. 330–350.

Johnson, S. A. 2015. 'Intimate mothering publics': Comparing face-to-face support groups and Internet use for women seeking information and advice in the transition to first-time motherhood. *Culture, Health & Sexuality*, *17*(2), pp. 237–251.

Kumar, P., & Schoenebeck, S. 2015. The modern day baby book: Enacting good mothering and stewarding privacy on Facebook. In *Proceedings of the ACM Conference on Computer Supported Cooperative Work and Social Computing (CSCW '15)*. Vancouver, Canada.

Leaver, T. 2014. Captured at Birth? Presence, Privacy and Intimate Surveillance. Paper presented at the *Annual Conference of the Association of Internet Researchers*, Daegu, South Korea, 21–24 October.

Litt, E., & Hargittai, E. 2014. Smile, snap, and share? A nuanced approach to privacy and online photo-sharing. *Poetics*, *42*, pp. 1–21.

Lupton, D. 2013. The digitally engaged patient: Self-monitoring ad self-care in the digital health era. *Social Theory & Health*, *11*(3), pp. 256–270.

Lyons, P. & Rittner, B. 1998. The construction of the crack babies phenomenon as a social problem. *American Journal of Orthopsychiatry*, *68*(2), pp. 313–320.

Merriam-Webster. Selfie. [Online] Available from http://www.merriam-webster.com/dictionary/selfie [Accessed 06 February 2015].

Mitchell, L. M. 2001. *Baby's First Picture: Ultrasound and the Politics of Fetal Subjects.* Toronto: University of Toronto Press.

Neiterman, E. 2012. Doing pregnancy: Pregnant embodiment as performance. *Women's Studies International Forum*, *35*(5), pp. 372–383.

Nolan, J., Raynes-Goldie, K., & McBride, M. 2011. The stranger danger: Exploring surveillance, autonomy, and privacy in children's use of social media. *Canadian Children Journal*, *36*(2), pp. 24–32.

Oakley, A. 1984. *The Captured Womb: A History of the Medical Care of Pregnant Women.* Oxford: Basil Blackwell.

Papacharissi, Z., & Gibson, P. L. 2011. Fifteen minutes of privacy: Privacy, sociality, and publicity on social network sites. In S. Trepte & L. Reinecke (eds), *Privacy Online.* Berlin Heidelberg: Springer, pp. 75–89.

Pearson, J., 2012. Baby's first picture! Shakira's boyfriend tweets ultrasound scan of their little boy. *Daily Mail.* [Online] 6 December. Available from http://www.dailymail.co.uk/tvshowbiz/article-2244259/Shakiras-boyfriend-tweets-ultrasound-scan-little-footballer-star.html [Accessed 30 November 2014].

Petchesky, R. P. 1987. Fetal images: The power of visual culture in the politics of reproduction. *Feminist Studies*, *13*(2), pp. 263–292.

Ramsdale, S. 2013. Beyoncé talks pregnancy and reveals Blue Ivy ultrasound in new trailer for documentary. *Marie Claire.* [Online] 15 January. Available from http://www.marieclaire.co.uk/news/celebrity/540277/beyonce-reveals-even-more-in-trailer-for-documentary.html [Accessed 15 December 2014].

Richter, R., & Schadler, C. 2009. See my virtual self: Dissemination as a characteristic of digital photography – The example of Flickr.com. *Visual Studies*, *24*(2), pp. 169–177.

Roberts, J. 2012. 'Wakey wakey baby': Narrating four-dimensional (4D) bonding scans. *Sociology of Health & Illness*, *34*(2), pp. 299–314.

Rose, G. 2004. 'Everyone's cuddled up and it just looks really nice': An emotional geography of some mums and their family photos. *Social & Cultural Geography*, *5*(4), pp. 549–564.

Rose, G., 2014. How digital technologies Do family snaps, only better. In J. Larsen and M. Sandbye (eds), *Digital Snaps: The New Face of Technology.* London: I. B. Tauris, pp. 67–86.

Rothman, B. K. 1989. *Recreating Motherhood: Ideology and Technology in a Patriarchical Society.* New York: Norton

Sandeowski, M. 1994. Separate, but less unequal: Fetal ultrasonography and the transformation of expectant mother/fatherhood. *Gender & Society*, 8, pp. 230–245.

Song, F. W., West, J. E., Lundy, U., & Dahmen, N. S. 2012. Women, pregnancy, and health information Online: The making of informed patients and ideal mothers. *Gender & Society*, *26*(5), 773–398.

Terry, J. 1989. The body invaded: Medical surveillance of women as reproducers. *Socialist Review 19*, pp. 13–43.

van Dijck, J. 2008. Digital photography: Communication, identity, memory. *Visual Communication*, *7*(1), pp. 57–76.

van Dijck J. 2013. *The Culture of Connectivity: A Critical History of Social Media.* New York: Oxford University Press

Walker-Rettberg, J. 2014. *Seeing Ourselves Through Technology: How We Use Selfies, Blogs and Wearable Devices to See and Shape Ourselves*. Basingstoke: Palgrave Macmillan.

Woo, J, 2002. A short history of the development of ultrasound in obstetrics and gynecology. [Online] Available from http://www.cfef.org/archives/bricabrac/histoiredesultra sons.pdf [Accessed 3 December 2014].

You, J. J., Alter, D. A., Stukel, T. A., McDonald, S. D., Laupacis, A., Liu, Y., & Ray, J. G. 2010. Proliferation of prenatal ultrasonography. *CMAJ: Canadian Medical Association Journal*, *182*(2), pp. 143–151. doi:10.1503/cmaj.090979

5 Digital by default

Growing into your digital footprint

Vanessa P. Dennen

"Mommy, can I have your phone so I can take a picture?"

This simple query, uttered by my then 3-year-old daughter, made me pause for a moment. If seeking analogous object:action relationships, one would match telephone to making a call and camera to taking a photograph, and yet my daughter wanted a phone, not a camera, in order to take a photograph. As I thought about it, I realized that my daughter's basic concept of a phone was very different from mine. At age 5, for this manuscript, I asked her, "What's the purpose of a phone?" Her reply: "You can text on it, take photos and videos and put them on Facebook, use FaceTime . . ." Nowhere in her reply did she consider making a call.

I was, of course, already aware that my daughter was born into a world full of digital technologies that were not a part of my own childhood. When I was her age, my father took me to his office and showed me a computer so large it had its own room. He asked one of the computer operators to print me a huge Snoopy cartoon figure in ASCII art format. I was amazed by the output and not at all a contributor to the input. Most of my contemporaries had never seen a computer before, nor had many of their parents.

However, my daughter and her peers find it quite normal to have multiple computers in their household and expect that computers can readily be moved around. Technology has gotten smaller, faster, and easier to use, and devices have become increasingly multifunctional – as my daughter readily recognized when asking for a phone rather than a camera in order to satisfy her photography needs.

This chapter tells the story of how the Internet has affected one young child's life, as her Internet presence was born, as she became aware of the Internet, and as she began to interact with and through a variety of information and communication technologies (ICTs). It is the story of digital footprints, virtual relationships, selfies, scrapbooking, privacy concerns, and the ability to understand abstract concepts like the Internet. Her story is annotated with supporting research and enhanced with discussion of child-rearing trends and alternate perspectives.

I approach this story chronologically, dividing it into the major developmental phases of a young child's life. The story starts during gestation and ends as the child begins primary school. The periods between – infancy, toddlerhood, and the preschool years – each bring forward a new set of Internet-related experiences and issues. Each phase represents a developmental transition, but of course these transitions – aside from actual birth – do not occur overnight.

Perspective

Although the main focus of this chapter is young children, the chapter ends up being about parents and other primary caretakers, too.[1] A young child's relationship to the Internet is inextricably intertwined with their parents' beliefs and actions. Parents are the ones who provide their children with initial exposure and access to both devices and bandwidth, and they also are the people most likely to be posting about a particular child online. What parents say and do influences how their children develop initial schema and vocabulary related to ICTs.

The lens used in this chapter is my own. Although it is mine, it is hardly unique. I am a mother of a young child living in a developed country. My family can be described as white collar and upper-middle class. I have high-speed Internet and Wi-Fi in my home and at work. I am rarely more than a few meters from an Internet-connected device. My peer group includes heavy consumers of computers, tablets, smartphones, and cameras. We get our news online first, often through our social networks and newsfeeds. We are on Facebook. We blog, tweet, and pin. We consult online forums for help, and we post our own advice and support to others. We live, or at least share, parts of our lives online. And so, too, do our children – even if only by proxy in the case of the youngest ones.

Privacy is a major concern, and parents have two responsibilities here. First, they must teach children about their privacy rights. Second, they must respect the developing privacy wishes and rights of their children. At one end of the privacy spectrum one might find a parent like Amy Webb, who avoids posting her child's name, photo, and other identifying information online (Webb, 2013). At the other are parents like Mama June, who allowed her family, including a young daughter, to be featured on a reality TV show, resulting in a large digital footprint and a tremendous amount of discussion about her daughter on social media (Goodman, 2012). With regard to my daughter, my husband and I have not always had a planned approach, but we have tried to engage in thoughtful moderation.

Gestation

Obviously there is no way that a gestating foetus, cradled in its mother's womb, can use the Internet. However, it is during gestation that the child's relationship to the Internet begins. During this period of time, three online activities related to the child may occur. The parents may share their joyous news – including periodic updates – as they await birth. And the parents may begin to prepare for the named child's digital presence.

Announcing and waiting

Pregnancy announcements represent not only the moment that friends and family learn that a new life is growing but also the birthplace of digital footprints for those new lives. Online pregnancy announcements have become a creative outlet for many expecting parents, and a quick Internet search yields many sites collecting and sharing ideas for unique ways to share the news with your online world. Nicknames for unborn babies, often private in the past, have become de rigueur in the online world. In fact, they're necessary in order to refer to the baby. Companies have also seen the opportunity to capitalize on this information; they even engage in data mining to figure out who might be pregnant and send targeted advertising information (Oboler, Welsh, & Cruz, 2012).

Not only are pregnancy announcements shared online, but pregnancy milestones and even births are being blogged, posted in status updates, and live-tweeted (Sinclair, 2013). In one well-publicized instance, the live-tweeting of labour and birth culminated in a baby photo, name announcement, and the first post using the newborn's Twitter account (Vingiano, 2014). This example is not unique. In the last 24 hours alone I've seen three newborns on Facebook and another on Twitter, all fresh offspring of people within my network or their close relatives. One had set up a hashtag for the baby, and another tagged the baby in the photo, indicating that he already had a Facebook account set up in his name.

During my pregnancy, I shared information about my developing child and the upcoming birth in a few forums. On Facebook, where my network included about 350 people at the time, I shared that my husband and I were expecting a child along with an image from an ultrasound. We came up with an in-utero name for our child, bambino, which we later occasionally amended to bambina when we learned that we were expecting a girl. Others adopted this name when referring to our child, since we did not share her intended name with anyone.

I did not post heavily on Facebook about the pregnancy, but I did share some belly photos as well as an ultrasound in which my daughter's face was visible about a week before her birth. I was excited and a bit anxious. Part of my online network was in "baby watch" mode, and when I shared that labour finally began people started notifying each other. A college friend posted an announcement to other college friends to send supportive thoughts to the baby and me as we laboured. A family member who was not present but connected via the chain of telephone-based updates unbeknownst to me was providing some online updates.

During pregnancy I also shared a bit of information about my condition on two blogs – one that I had been maintaining independently about other topics and one that we set up to share more information with family and friends who lived far away. My husband and I also shared a wiki to which we posted our baby preparation task lists. This wiki was not shared deliberately with others, but it also was not private. A few years later, when seeking to pull together a memory book for my daughter, I was amazed to find what I had documented. I also felt a bit of tension about it. The Facebook posts did not bother me, but the more detailed blog posts and the wiki were items that, although I was personally delighted to have the information archived, I no longer felt comfortable having posted online. Essentially, I noticed that my sense of privacy had shifted. When my daughter was in my womb, her privacy seemed embedded in mine, and my desired levels of privacy felt sufficient. However, once she was a person moving independently through the world I felt a responsibility to protect her from greater exposure on the Web.

Creating digital presence

Some parents begin thinking about their child's future digital presence and account needs before the child is born. They secure domain names and register email and social media accounts for their offspring as soon as they've settled on a name. Even the aforementioned Amy Webb, who fastidiously seeks to keep her child's name and image offline, admits that she took a two-step approach to this issue before birth (Webb, 2013). First, before selecting a name for her child she searched for that name on the Internet. She wanted to both make sure that she could secure desired usernames for her child and that a Google search for that name did not yield undesirable results. Additionally, she set up various online accounts for her child – not so they could be used but so they would be reserved until the child was old enough to use them.

My own experience was similar, although less thorough and focused. Out of curiosity, I googled the name we had chosen for our daughter and was amused to find that a French singer shares her first and middle names. At the moment, three French women on Facebook have the same name, although I don't recall checking that at the time. It was not until she was an infant that I created two email accounts with her name. I started out of necessity – we needed it for an airline frequent flyer account – but immediately recognized the potential importance of this act in her life. I chose to not reserve a domain name and pay for it each year until she was ready to decide if she wanted to use it, and as I made that decision I realized that the technology landscape when she comes of age and can use these tools and platforms may be totally different.

Infancy

It's difficult to know what infancy is like from a child's perspective, but it is a period of time when many children have a heavy Internet presence despite the inability to use an Internet-connected device. While other people proudly share their photos and seek advice and support about handling them, infants develop a digital footprint. Infancy sets the tone for later expectations.

The omnipresent camera

Perhaps one of the most notable technologies integrated directly in young children's lives is the digital camera. The contrast between current and past generations is notable. When I was a child in the 1970s, a camera required physical film that had to be processed before photos were generated. My parents did not own a camera when I was young but borrowed one on multiple occasions. Photos of my early childhood were taken in occasional spurts, and department-store portraits were done at regular intervals. Photographs were special; you dressed up and posed for them.

My daughter's first digital photo was taken within a few hours of her birth. That photo was texted to family members and posted to Facebook. In the moment when I posted the photo, I did not think about anything beyond sharing my joyous moment and my pride in having such a beautiful newborn. The day after I posted this first photograph, I realized that this baby photo, having been shared online for 24/7 viewing by friends and friends of friends, had taken on a life of its own. A friend downloaded the photo and manipulated it using Photoshop, inserting my daughter's face into several other images, so that she became fictional front-page news, appeared on a billboard, and was featured on a magazine cover. The end result was shared on Facebook, and we enjoyed this creative tribute to our new-born. At the same time, a mere day into motherhood, I realized that I was not in control of my daughter's image. Once I had shared her digital likeness, someone else could grab it and use it for an entirely different purpose.

I felt vulnerable thinking about how easily my daughter's photo could get used for other purposes, but since the actual use had been sweet and funny I pushed the thought quickly to the back of my mind . . . until it resurfaced again. Over the next few months the photographs continued. I was documenting my daughter's life. Since we live far from our family and friends, like many other parents (Baek, 2014) I shared these photographs online so everyone could see how my daughter was growing. Photos are an effective way to tell stories about a young child's everyday life and help distant grandparents feel connected to the new family member (González, Jomhari, & Kurniawan, 2011).

Rather than subject my array of Facebook friends representing segments or parts of my life to endless baby photos, I chose to move photos to flickr, a photo-sharing service that I had already been using. In the past, photos I had shared there had not gotten much notice unless I had tagged and shared them. I told family members how to access the account and then emailed them when I did a big upload. Then, one day while uploading photos I noticed one of my photos had instantly gotten 32 views and been downloaded once. It was a photo of my daughter, lying bare-bottomed on a rug. My photos had been ignored in the past, and suddenly a bare-bottomed baby photo was getting a lot of attention from strangers. Like so many other people, I had been optimistic and underestimated the privacy risk (Baek, 2014). Feeling slightly ill, I toggled the settings so that my baby photos were no longer public. Shortly thereafter I stopped posting photos to flickr altogether. This was a lesson in managing my daughter's online privacy, and like many other parents I began to alter my behaviour and change my privacy settings (Ammari, Kumar, Lampe, & Schoenebeck, 2015).

Photo sharing is a challenging area for a parent to navigate, and the topic of infant photo sharing highlights how little control people (including and especially infants) may have over how their likeness is shared in an online forum (Litt & Hargittai, 2014). This concern extends beyond the current moment. Child and Petronio (2011) recount the story of an adult child who experienced discomfort when his parents shared a photo from his childhood online. Parents need to consider that later in life the child may not agree with them about what is cute and endearing, but once these images are posted online they may not be easily able to retract them.

The array of people who might take and share an infant's photo extends beyond parents. Grandparents and other family members are likely to take and share photographs of young children on a regular basis (Tee, Brush, & Inkpen, 2009). This situation leaves parents to navigate issues such as third-party sharing, even when those third parties are family members (Ammari et al., 2015). Mothers, who are the most likely persons to post and tag a child's photo, typically take on the role of privacy stewards for their children, determining what is and is not acceptable to be shared (Kumar & Schoenebeck, 2015). In this role, they filter out images that are unflattering, of poor quality, or overly private (e.g. naked or depicting personal moments). They also must communicate their photo sharing and privacy preferences to others.

Surveillance

In some ways, today's young children are used to living in a surveillance state. Their induction begins in infancy. In the last 10 years, baby monitor technology has shifted from audio to video. When my daughter was an infant, our state-of-the-art monitor allowed me to hear if she was crying in her bed. When it broke and I sought a replacement 2 years later, I discovered that the new norm was video. Although the traditional use of baby monitors may be to help parents feel secure that their baby is sleeping peacefully and to alert them upon the child's waking, once installed in a child's room the cameras may stay. After relaying my story to several other parents I discovered that it is not unusual for parents to use video monitors to keep an eye on their preschool-aged children. Since I believed that my daughter deserved not only to feel that she had privacy but to genuinely have privacy when physically alone in her bedroom, I was quite surprised. However, research suggests that most parents believe children through preschool age do not require privacy (McKinney, 1998), although preschool-aged children actively seek spatial privacy in spaces like bedrooms (Green, 2011), and sense of privacy may be tied to self-esteem and development of identity (McKinney, 1998).

Baby monitors are just the beginning. Parents may hide webcams or small spy-cams – called nannycams – throughout the household to monitor childcare providers. Once in place, these cameras monitor all interactions in the target location (Mayer, 2003). Outside of the home, webcams have been used by some day-care centres to allow parents to see their child during the day. At one point, I took my then 3-year-old daughter to a dance studio where she was expected to join a class in another room and I was expected to sit in a waiting room with other parents and watch the class via closed-circuit television. Collectively, these examples demonstrate how children are now born into a world where being visually monitored by people in another location is the norm and in which true privacy may be rarely assured, even at home.

Parents seeking support

Infancy is a period when parents are likely to go online seeking online information, support, and community (Madge & O'Connor, 2006). For some parents, online forums are merely a convenience, with the ability to access information and perhaps even have some real-time interaction at any hour of the day – even during a three a.m. feeding. For others, the ability to interact anonymously is attractive. Still others seek online interaction because they have limited opportunities for face-to-face interaction. Contemporary life often means living far from family and friends, but technology can help bridge this distance for adults and, in many cases, children.

The Internet was an important tool for me as a new parent. When my daughter was born, although I lacked a strong local support system, I was able to use technology to connect myself to my family and friends. I was also able to use it to seek advice about caring for a young child and camaraderie among other women who were having similar "new parent" experiences. My experience and the varied people with whom I interacted in some way about parenthood are perfect examples of the phenomenon of networked individualism (Rainie & Wellman, 2012).

The Internet reduced my feelings of isolation as I sat at home alone with my daughter while on maternity leave. I was able to get advice on what baby items to purchase and how to deal with different situations. Much like millions of other mothers, in the Internet I found a source of support, advice, and social interaction as well as a place to document and share my child's development (Morris, 2014). As I returned to work and my days got busier, I did not suffer isolation so much as overload and a change in routine. My days were long, I had little time for myself, and old routines such as going out for drinks with friends were no longer convenient. I continued to use the Internet as a means of connection with the outside world and a space to reflect on and figure out what "life with baby" looks like.

Although the ability to find support and interaction online sounds like a positive, it has a potential downside: contributing to a child's digital footprint. As parents connect with other parents online, they are likely to share information about their child on the Internet. If all that the parent does online is search for information – much as I did to figure out why my 2-week-old baby might be crying and if my 3-month-old baby could really be teething – then the resulting digital footprint may be small and only accessible to others in aggregate, via big data trends. However, in seeking friendship, support, and advice online, often in public forums and among people with whom they do not have prior relationships, some parents disclose a lot of information about their child's health, development, and behaviours (De Choudhury, Counts, & Horvitz, 2013; Morris, 2014). It is at best difficult, and perhaps impossible, for a parent to develop and interact with an online network in this way without an effect on their child.

Toddlerhood

Toddlerhood is a time of great independence. Children learn to walk, amass a large vocabulary, and begin independent play. They also may have their first hands-on experiences manipulating devices. At this stage of development, children are still unable to grasp the abstract concept of the Internet, but they are aware of Internet-connected devices, how people around them use these devices, and how they can use them during play to emulate adults.

Playing with computers and phones

I still remember fondly the day my daughter and I opened a box and found a toy laptop inside. It was made of plastic and more colourful than my laptop, but its form and function were unmistakable to her. She was very excited, and she knew exactly how to place it on her lap, orient it, and begin pressing keys. It's not surprising that she was already proficient at these tasks; she had been watching her parents use laptops for her entire life. Although her laptop keys merely triggered lights and songs, she had a sense that she was engaging in an important behaviour.

Mobile phones are another source of attraction and entertainment for toddlers. Phones are shiny, they have buttons, and the screens light up if you press the right buttons. They can be used to look at pictures and videos. They're obviously important, since almost every adult has one. In one study, more than 70 per cent of adult caregivers were observed with a phone during a meal, and almost 30 per cent were highly absorbed in that device (Radesky et al., 2014). In another, adults reported a high rate of carrying phones at the playground for the purpose of taking photos, and about half of the photo takers indicated that they would also be sharing the photos from the playground (Hiniker et al., 2015). These situations demonstrate one side of what quickly becomes a point of contention between many parents and children. Toddlers may feel that they are competing with devices for their parents' attention and are quick to make their displeasure known. At the same time, parents may alternate between giving devices to children as a distraction when they need an adult moment and restricting device access at other times. Children can easily become confused and upset, wanting more control over both when they may play with a device and when their parents will refrain from using devices. In this way, a complex triadic relationship develops among parent, child, and technology, although the parent is in the position to fully control device ownership and access. However, this situation will continue to grow in its complexity as the child moves through different ages and stages and the parent reaches various points at which some control must be ceded to the child, who starts to own devices, register for online accounts, and interact with others online of his own accord.

The Internet and a child's interpersonal relationships

The Internet supports human connection in a number of ways. It can provide a means of connecting a person with family and established friends between in-person encounters. These "between-meeting" connections may be routine or transactional, such as the messages exchanged by friends to plan a meeting, or they may provide the opportunity to build or extend a relationship despite a geographic distance. At the same time, the Internet can be a platform through which new relationships may be forged, whether or not those relationships are ever realized in a face-to-face environment.

A young child is unlikely to be seeking Internet-based connections on her own, but through parent facilitation a child may nonetheless be developing online relationships with a variety of people. Parents and childcare providers serve as the conduit through which these early virtual relationships develop, such that by age 3 a child might be requesting to initiate virtual communication with someone and shortly thereafter may try to develop new virtual relationships.

While I used the Internet to connect with the world during my daughter's early days, she was introduced to many people via this medium. She has no recollection of being shown off to family members via Skype as an infant, nor does she know about the blog my husband and I tried to keep updated (and gave up on after a year) to share her milestones and cuteness with our family and close friends. However, as a toddler she became quite aware that her grandparents, aunts, uncles, and cousins could all be seen and spoken to in real time on a computer or phone. At times she struggled to grasp the precise ways in which the technology worked. There was a period when I would hand her my phone with the speaker turned on to speak to a grandparent and she would try to wave and interact with the screen. She provided visual rather than verbal responses to the people who spoke with her and was confused that the picture she saw – a profile image associated with the person with whom we spoke – was not moving even though she heard a live voice. However, by the time she was 4 she had developed the ability to differentiate phone conversations from web conferencing. She also began actively requesting to Skype or FaceTime with particular people and initiating those connections on her own if she managed to get access to one of my devices.

Companies have capitalized on the ability to use the Internet to connect adult family members with young children. Several apps have been developed to facilitate storytelling at a distance, marketed toward grandparents as well as parents who travel for business. A commercial for telecommunications company AT&T features a father using the Internet to read his daughter a bedtime story. Although the daughter is at home, the father is sitting at an airport gate, waiting for a flight. In this way, the Internet can maintain family relationships and traditions despite geographic distance.

Although this example focused on connecting a child with known family members between visits, the Internet also facilitates the development of unequal relationships, in which one party learns about the other without any direct interaction or reciprocity. For example, people on Facebook may feel that they know their friends' children even when they've not had any face-to-face encounters. These family friends may have seen photos and videos of special events and everyday life. They may know anecdotes or details shared by parents. At the same time, the child may have no awareness whatsoever of the other person. In some ways this phenomenon predates the Internet. People have long shared photos and stories of their children with far-away family and friends via postal mail and telephone and with colleagues at the office. However, the broadcast abilities of Internet technologies may spread this personal knowledge of children to a wider audience than would be selected for sharing via mail, telephone sharing, or conversations around the office water cooler.

When people "delurk" after observing others in virtual spaces, they may make comments that seem more personal or intimate than are warranted given the one-sidedness of the read-only relationship (Dennen, 2014). It can feel unsettling when a stranger indicates a sense of familiarity. Children who meet people from their parents' online networks may recognize that the person has some genuine underlying connection to their family but likely do not understand the genesis of the false sense of intimacy promoted by the stranger's comments.

In most cases, these unequal relationships are relationships that the parent might actually broker between their child and a friend or relative if geography or other factors were not hurdles. However, in some cases people who might never learn about the child's existence in person may come to feel they know a child quite well by reading about her online. The children of mommy bloggers – women who blog publicly about their lives as mothers – are prime examples. It's not that their mothers are unaware of the public nature of their writing activities. Many mommy bloggers, when posting in fully public spaces, use pseudonyms or initials when discussing their children and may Google their children's names regularly to ensure they have not inadvertently created an unwanted digital footprint (Morrison, 2011). However, to think that they've left no path behind would be naïve. As Powell (2010) notes about her relationship with the mommy bloggers whose writings she regularly reads, "I know the names of their children, the layout of their houses, their favourite drinks and their pet peeves. Like thousands of other readers, I have read of their depressions, their moves, their children's birthdays, and their marital squabbles." Online communication and privacy often are at odds with each other, and it's difficult for parents to share robustly about their own lives and fully maintain the privacy of their children.

Preschool

The preschool years, between ages 3 and 5, are the ones when children seem to develop an awareness of the Internet. They have likely already developed an early digital fluency during toddlerhood, which might be described as a facility with learning how to use new technologies (Palaiologou, 2014). These fearless button pushers and swipers now begin to grasp more fully the potential audience that sits on the receiving end of their actions. Preschool years are pivotal for developing a sense of agency (Sairanen & Kumpulainen, 2014), although actions like digital identity management are still beyond a child's grasp. During these years, parents may notice the first instance of their child exerting their will about whether items should or should not be shared online. Parents themselves must make decisions about what they will document and share online as well as how much time their child can spend online.

Photographs, identity, and control

In the hours, days, and years that have passed since infancy, my husband and I have taken thousands of digital photographs and videos of our daughter. These photos and videos have been taken under many conditions. Sometimes they have occurred with my daughter's knowledge, as she proudly posed. Other times they have not, including photos of her asleep as well as photos covertly capturing her at play. These fill the memory of our phones and several memory cards. They are backed up in the cloud. Many have been shared via text, email, and Facebook. We have printed few, although my parents-in-law have been known to download and print the photos that I share.

However, we're no longer the only photographers in our household. One day I opened the photo app on my phone and discovered several blurry photos of a nose and mouth. My daughter had discovered the joy of taking selfies. When she was 4, she begged for my camera as we were selecting a Christmas tree. I later discovered that she had taken more than 50 photographs of people's backsides on the tree lot, which she thought was very funny. She also received a digital camera as a gift and used it to take both selfies and photos of her dolls. She was proud of the images that she created and wanted to show them to others.

This type of photographic activity is pretty common. As early as age 3, children can be adept at taking, uploading, and managing photographs on a computers (Plowman & McPake, 2013). Children may be emulating the behaviour of the adults around them and also searching for a form of self-expression. They have already observed how their parents share images on social media for the purpose of expression, communication, or promotion (van Dijck, 2013). When they ask to share their photos with others, children are simply following the model they have observed. Although young children typically do not maintain their own social media profiles, profiles may be maintained for them, or images of or created by them may be presented online in support of an adult's need for expression, communication, or promotion.

It's worth noting that control over a child's image becomes increasingly difficult to manage as the child grows. Complete strangers may take your child's photograph and share it online, either inadvertently (e.g. a parent seeking a photograph of his own child on the playground or during the school play who captures additional children in the frame) or intentionally. My family experienced this latter phenomenon, along with feelings of confusion and unease, during a recent trip to China. Wherever we went, we noticed people pointing their cameras toward my daughter and taking her photograph. In some cases, people approached us directly and asked if they might get her to pose with them. In one instance, a queue formed at a tourist site, with people wanting a photograph with her. In another instance, a man with a large, professional-grade camera followed us through a public garden, taking many photos. Although our initial inclination was to be polite and agree to the requests, as a parent I began to feel upset. I realized that while I could say no to the requests, I could not stop the other photographs. Even more troubling, I had no idea whether these photos would be shared online and if so, in what context.

Present and recording

Young children provide a number of photo (and video) opportunities. They say and do a lot of cute things, and parents often want to catch milestones like first steps on camera. By their preschool years, they are putting on performances – whether of their own concoction or via organized recitals and concerts – and participating in sporting events. During my daughter's prekindergarten year, I counted four photo-opportunity events at her preschool and two parent observation days plus a recital for her dance class. By kindergarten, the number of events had grown exponentially. During the last month of the school year alone, I attended two performances of a school play, a classroom showcase, a piano recital, an extracurricular play, and a dance recital.

When attending these events, parents must decide whether to record – and later share – the occasion digitally. Some parents arrive at the auditoriums and theatres early to find a good spot for taking photos or setting up a tripod. In some cases, parents make private recordings even though the event's organizers will later share official ones. During a dress rehearsal for a dance recital, I felt the pressure to make a recording. Parents were explicitly invited to record during the rehearsal, and recordings were strictly prohibited during the actual performance. As I recorded, I noted how the ephemeral experience of watching a live event is pitted directly against the ability to create one's own visual proof of the event. By documenting the moment I had something to share with others, and my family could watch the dance repeatedly, but I had also lost something: the unmediated, immersive enjoyment of the actual event.

These situations raise the question of where the enjoyment lies. Is it in the live performance or moment? Or is it in the attention received when one shares recorded moments with others online? It would be naïve to think that this is strictly a parent issue. Preschool children are acutely aware of when their parents have split attention or are more focused on being reporters than audience members. Depending on the child's intent and preference, they will either request explicitly that a moment be recorded or mandate that a parent put the camera down and give full attention to the live interaction.

Screen time

For parents, preschool is also a time during which concerns about screen time may arise. Screen time refers not only to time spent watching television but also time spent on a computer or mobile device. Screen time for infants and toddlers has been found to be without value (Council on Communications & Media, 2011), and the value of screen time for preschool children is questionable (Ernest et al., 2014). However, most preschoolers enjoy screen time, and for parents it may represent a convenience. Although preschoolers typically exceed the amount of time recommended by professionals (Tandon, Zhou, Lozano, & Christakis, 2011), parents tend to view screen time as a problem that affects other families (Plowman & McPake, 2013). The problem may be more profound with television than computers in this age group (De Decker et al., 2012), although as the popularity of smartphones and tablets continues to grow this may change. Children whose parents who are aware of and communicate limits tend to have less screen time (Carlson et al., 2010), although as one of those limiting parents I'll note that the limits do not come without tensions – especially once children can help themselves to the technology. I will never forget the day that my preschool daughter proudly proclaimed, "I know Daddy's phone code. I watched him. See?" and proceeded to unlock the phone so she could access a game.

Through the child's eyes

The ubiquitous nature of certain types of tools and transactions in contemporary adult lives, such as email, text messages, electronic payments, and social media accounts, means that children become familiar with information and communication technologies but may not really understand how they work or why they are used. As depicted in the opening scenario, a young child may be more likely to identify a phone with photography than with telecommunications. Similarly, a child may be confused by the difference among physically recorded, streaming, and broadcast media since all are displayed on a television. In particular, the temporality of broadcast media can cause great frustration ("Why can't I watch Curious George right now?"), as can the hiccups of an Internet signal. Explaining how a variety of different inputs (DVD, Netflix, cable) may result in the same outcome (entertainment) can be confusing to young children.

Shortly before she entered kindergarten, I had a conversation with my daughter – then age 5 years and 5 months – to learn more about how she perceives various Internet-based and related technologies.[2] Although she's grown up in a technology-heavy world, she's never had anyone explain what the Internet is or how an email and a text message differ. Throughout this conversation transcript, I've added my commentary in square brackets to provide context and explain the potential genesis of her thoughts.

Me: Do you know what the Internet is?

Her: No.

Me: Have you heard that word before?

Her: Yes, but I don't know what it means.

Me: Can you explain what Facebook is?

Her: Facebook. It's where people post things online and send them to other people and other people see them on their phones, iPads, Kindles, and computers.

Me: Ok, so what's a text?

Her: A text is where someone, instead of writing with a pencil, they put some words online. There are speaking texts where it just writes down what you speak and there's just letter texts. And there's a big bunch of punctuation things.

[I use the speech-to-text function frequently when sending messages to my husband because it is faster. She has seen her aunts playing with emoticons.]

Me: How do texts work?

Her: You hit the button that says send on your phone.

Me: And what about email?

Her: Hmmm. Well I know what Snapchat is.

[I have never used Snapchat, but I know she has participated in sending Snapchats from one aunt to another aunt.]

Me: OK. What's Snapchat?

Her: It's something where people take a quick thing and they speak and when the other person gets it, it's like a little video but you don't put it on Facebook.

Me: OK. But back to email. Do you know what email is?

Her: I have no idea. Is it something they put on computers?

[Although her father and I receive and send a high volume of email, it's not an activity with which she's been involved, and we tend to say we're sending a message rather than an email in our home. In contrast, she has participated in composing and sending text messages in the midst of our conversational transactions when we're trying to include a third party who is not physically present.]

Me: How about Google?

Her: That's somewhere where you write down something on your electronics and it gives you the answer in speak or text.

Me: Good. What about FaceTime?

Her: FaceTime is when people take their phones or computer or iPods or iPads and they make another person appear on there with a little picture and they can talk between each other. It's not the same as calling because calling you can't see the person. And the only way for the other person to see you is if your face is in the box on there.

[We use both FaceTime and Skype frequently, and she's had explicit instruction on making sure she's on camera and "in the box." She's also talked to people on speakerphone but tends to not enjoy that experience as much due to the lack of visual.]

Me: And what about Twitter? Do you know what Twitter is? Or what a tweet is?

Her: (shrugs shoulders, looking disinterested) I've heard you say it but I have no idea what it means.

Me: What's a selfie?

Her: A picture people take so they can have a picture of one person and another person to remember. You can print them out and put them in a picture frame or keep them on your phone or other electronic device.

Me: How do you feel about people taking your picture and sharing it online?

Her: Happy because I like being popular.

Me: How do you know if you're popular?

Her: Because I asked you to put [a photo] on Facebook and a lot of people go on Facebook. When I get a lot of likes and comments on it, I really feel really good.

Me: Are there ever photos you don't want people to put online?

Her: Yes, because sometimes my dad takes pictures of my hair sticking up in the bathtub and it really doesn't look good.

This dialogue shows that as she entered her primary school years, my daughter was familiar with a wide range of social media and communication tools. She had a general confidence with any number of Internet tools that have been only indirectly experienced, as well as a clear sense that these tools are for sharing. She was less oriented to Internet-based information-seeking activities, which I anticipate will be introduced more purposefully in a school context or as her reading skills develop. Although her ability to define and differentiate tools and platforms was imprecise, and she didn't even know the word "Internet," my daughter already saw the Internet as a space where she had an audience and where she may have privacy concerns. She didn't question how the technology works but accepted that words, images, and videos transmit to a device.

The foundational knowledge of and experience with the Internet that my daughter and her peer group develop during their first 5 years of life is tightly intertwined with the development of interpersonal relationships, individual identity, and digital footprints. Parents remain the mediators of most online experiences, but by their preschool years children begin to opine about who to communicate with and what to share. As the children born in the early 21st century grow, it will be interesting to see both how these early experiences with the Internet influence later Internet attitudes and use and how they grow into and take control of the early digital footprint that has been created for them.

Notes

1 Throughout the chapter, I refer to the primary caretaker as a parent because that simplifies the discussion. However, many young children's initial relationship with the Internet is influenced by nonparent caretakers, including older siblings, grandparents, aunts and uncles, and nannies.
2 I recorded the conversation with my daughter's permission. I later asked for and received her permission to include it, in the form of typed words, in this chapter.

References

Ammari, T., Kumar, P., Lampe, C., & Schoenebeck, S. (2015). *Managing children's online identities: How parents decide what to disclose about their children online.* Paper presented at the CHI, Seoul, South Korea.

Baek, Y. M. (2014). Solving the privacy paradox: A counter-argument experimental approach. *Computers in Human Behavior, 38*, 33–42. doi: 10.1016/j.chb.2014.05.006.

Carlson, S. A., Fulton, J. E., Lee, S. M., Foley, J. T., Heitzler, C., & Huhman, M. (2010). Influence of limit-setting and participation in physical activity on youth screen time. *Pediatrics, 126*(1), e89–e96. doi: 10.1542/peds.2009-3374.

Child, J. T., & Petronio, S. (2011). Unpacking the paradoxes of privacy in CMC relationships: The challenges of blogging and relational communication on the internet. In K. B. Wright & L. M. Webb (eds), *Computer-Mediated Communication in Personal Relationships* (pp. 21–40). Cambridge, MA: The MIT Press.

Council on Communications and Media. (2011). Media use by children younger than 2 years. *Pediatrics, 128*(5), 1040–1045. doi: 10.1542/peds.2011-1753.

De Choudhury, M., Counts, S., & Horvitz, E. (2013). *Major life changes and behavioral markers in social media: case of childbirth.* Paper presented at the 2013 conference on Computer Supported Cooperative Work.

De Decker, E., De Craemer, M., De Bourdeaudhuij, I., Wijndaele, K., Duvinage, K., Koletzko, B., . . . ToyBox-study, g. (2012). Influencing factors of screen time in preschool children:

An exploration of parents' perceptions through focus groups in six European countries. *Obesity Reviews, 13*(Suppl 1), 75–84. doi: 10.1111/j.1467-789X.2011.00961.x.

Dennen, V. P. (2014). Becoming a blogger: Trajectories, norms, and activities in a community of practice. *Computers in Human Behavior, 36,* 350–358. doi: http://dx.doi.org/10.1016/j.chb.2014.03.028.

Ernest, J. M., Causey, C., Newton, A. B., Sharkins, K., Summerlin, J., & Albaiz, N. (2014). Extending the global dialogue about media, technology, screen time, and young children. *Childhood Education, 90*(3), 182–191. doi: 10.1080/00094056.2014.910046.

González, V. M., Jomhari, N., & Kurniawan, S. H. (2011). Photo-based narratives as communication mediators between grandparents and their children and grandchildren living abroad. *Universal Access in the Information Society, 11*(1), 67–84. doi: 10.1007/s10209-011-0234-z.

Goodman, T. (2012). "Honey Boo Boo": That joke isn't funny anymore. *The Hollywood Reporter.* Retrieved from: http://www.hollywoodreporter.com/bastard-machine/here-comes-honey-boo-boo-alana-mama-364933.

Green, C. (2011). A place of my own: Exploring preschool children's special places in the home environment. *Children, Youth and Environments, 21*(2), 118–144. doi: 10.7721/chilyoutenvi.21.2.0118.

Hiniker, A., Sobel, K., Suh, H., Sung, Y.-C., Lee, C. P., & Kientz, J. A. (2015). Texting while parenting: How adults use mobile phones while caring for children at the playground. In A. Cockburn, J. McGrenere, & J. Rekimoto (eds), *ACM CHI Proceedings of the Conference on Human Factors in Computing Systems.* Seoul, South Korea: ACM.

Kumar, P., & Schoenebeck, S. (2015). *The modern day baby book: Enacting good mothering and stewarding privacy on Facebook.* Paper presented at the 18th ACM conference on Computer-Supported Cooperative Work and Social Computing, Vancouver, Canada.

Litt, E., & Hargittai, E. (2014). Smile, snap, and share? A nuanced approach to privacy and online photo-sharing. *Poetics, 42,* 1–21. doi: 10.1016/j.poetic.2013.10.002.

Madge, C., & O'Connor, H. (2006). Parenting gone wired: Empowerment of new mothers on the Internet? *Social & Cultural Geography, 7*(2), 199–220. doi: 10.1080/14649360 600600528.

Mayer, R. N. (2003). Technology, families, and privacy: Can we know too much about our loved ones. *Journal of Consumer Policy, 26*(4), 419–439. doi: 10.1023/A:1026387109484.

McKinney, K. D. (1998). Space, body, and mind: Parental perceptions of children's privacy needs. *Journal of Family Issues, 19*(1), 75–100. doi: 10.1177/019251398019001006.

Morris, M. R. (2014). *Social networking site use by mothers of young children.* Paper presented at the CSCW '14, Baltimore, MD.

Morrison, A. (2011). "Suffused by feeling and affect": The intimate public of personal mommy blogging. *Biography, 34*(1), 37–55. doi: 10.1353/bio.2011.0002.

Oboler, A., Welsh, K., & Cruz, L. (2012). The danger of big data: Social media as computational social science. *First Monday, 17*(7). Retrieved from: http://journals.uic.edu/ojs/index.php/fm/article/view/3993.

Palaiologou, I. (2014). Children under five and digital technologies: Implications for early years pedagogy. *European Early Childhood Education Research Journal, 24*(1), 1–20. doi: 10.1080/1350293x.2014.929876.

Plowman, L., & McPake, J. (2013). Seven myths about young children and technology. *Childhood Education, 89*(1), 27–33. doi: 10.1080/00094056.2013.757490.

Powell, R. (2010). Good mothers, bad mothers and mommy bloggers: Rhetorical resistance and fluid subjectivities. *MP: An Online Feminist Journal, 2*(6), 37–50.

Radesky, J. S., Kistin, C. J., Zuckerman, B., Nitzberg, K., Gross, J., Kaplan-Sanoff, M., . . . Silverstein, M. (2014). Patterns of mobile device use by caregivers and children during meals in fast food restaurants. *Pediatrics*, *133*(4), e843–849. doi: 10.1542/peds.2013–3703.

Rainie, L., & Wellman, B. (2012). *Networked: The new social operating system*. Cambridge, MA: The MIT Press.

Sairanen, H., & Kumpulainen, K. (2014). A visual narrative inquiry into children's sense of agency in preschool and first grade. *International Journal of Educational Psychology*, *3*(2), 141–172. doi: 10.4471/ijep.2014.09.

Sinclair, M. (2013). The 'Z generation': Digital mothers and their infants. *Evidence Based Midwifery*, *11*(1), 3.

Tandon, P. S., Zhou, C., Lozano, P., & Christakis, D. A. (2011). Preschoolers' total daily screen time at home and by type of child care. *Journal of Pediatrics*, *158*(2), 297–300. doi: 10.1016/j.jpeds.2010.08.005.

Tee, K., Brush, A. J. B., & Inkpen, K. M. (2009). Exploring communication and sharing between extended families. *International Journal of Human-Computer Studies*, *67*(2), 128–138. doi: 10.1016/j.ijhcs.2008.09.007.

van Dijck, J. (2013). 'You have one identity': Performing the self on Facebook and LinkedIn. *Media, Culture & Society*, *35*(2), 199–215. doi: 10.1177/0163443712468605.

Vingiano, A. (2014). A Twitter employee live-tweeted giving birth. *BuzzFeed*. Retrieved from: http://www.buzzfeed.com/alisonvingiano/twitter-employee-live-tweeting-labor.

Webb, A. (2013). We post nothing about our daughter online. *Slate*. Retrieved from: http://www.slate.com/articles/technology/data_mine_1/2013/09/facebook_privacy_and_kids_don_t_post_photos_of_your_kids_online.html.

6 "That's so unfair!"

Navigating the teenage online experience

Abigail Phillips

Introduction

It's a digital world out there. Information flows at an increasing rate via smartphones, laptops, TVs, and other devices. Surprising to few, whether searching, liking, commenting, or lurking, teens are spending significant amounts of time on digital media. In a recent report by Lenhart (2015), 92 per cent of surveyed teens indicated that they go online every day, with 24 per cent going online "almost constantly" (p. 2). Although labelled digital natives, teens have more complex relationships with technology than this label suggests (Agosto, Abbas, & Naughton, 2012). As so-called digital natives, teens are assumed to have an instinctive knowledge about the Internet and digital technologies (Beheshti, 2012). Because teens grew up surrounded by technology, they are believed to "think and process information fundamentally different from their predecessors" (Prensky, 2001, p. 1). Older generations, called digital immigrants, struggle to educate and support this younger, tech-savvy age group (Prensky, 2001). But this isn't a reality. What are teens doing while online? What purposes do digital media have in the daily life of a teenager? To help answer these questions, an examination of the increasingly digital lives of teens including positive and negative realities of these lived experiences is necessary.

In this chapter, the author will first present an overview of the digital lives of teens. Following this, the key roles that digital media and online communication play in the lives of teens will be examined. Then, the darker side of digital media will be assessed. This includes negative online behaviours such as cyberbullying, trolling, cyberstalking, and cyberdating violence. Because cyber violence and abuse are unfortunate realities, it is necessary to study these behaviours from both a researcher and practitioner lens. In the United States, education formally begins at kindergarten and continues until 12th grade. In this article, K–12 refers to the typical education system American students encounter, which begins at age 5 or 6 and ends around age 17 or 18. Upon graduation, most students continue their education in colleges, universities, or technical schools. Finally, this chapter will close with a discussion of implications for K–12 schools, libraries, parents, and community agencies, as well as suggest directions for future research. As role models for teens, these adult figures serve as "media mentors" and create opportunities for teens to develop media skills (Campbell, Haines, Koester, & Stoltz, 2015, p. 1).

The online lives of teens

Teens, defined in this chapter as youth between the ages of 12 and 18, are active consumers and producers of digital media (Ahn et al., 2012). Whether at home, at school, or on the go, youth are connected with digital media. Largely through smartphones, digital teens are staying in touch with friends, creating content, building identities, and seeking information about the world (Itō et al., 2008). But teens are not only using digital media for socializing and entertainment purposes. Two young generations, Millennials and Generation Y, are demonstrating how learning can occur while also engaging in online communities, online gaming, and social media (Partnership for 21st Century Skills, 2009). While participating online, teens are engaging in new literacy practices that occur outside of the traditional K–12 classroom (Davies, 2012). Although some adults may consider the hyper-connected world of teens a cause for concern, teenagers, through their online activities, are establishing the important role of digital media and online communication for 21st-century teaching and learning (Partnership for 21st Century Skills, 2009; Tripp, 2011).

However, not every teen has equal access to reliable and high-speed broadband Internet. Access to broadband both at home and at school provide youth with opportunities for hands-on, informal learning (Mardis, 2013). In rural communities, this access depends largely on socio-economic status and location (Mardis, 2013). For rural teens from poor or working-class families, broadband and data plans for smartphones may financially be out of reach. Additionally, some rural communities in the United States have little or no broadband availability, and if broadband is available, selection among affordable service providers is limited (Alemanne, Mandel, & McClure, 2011). This digital divide leaves rural youth at a disadvantage both in the classroom and in future workplaces.

The roles of digital media

Over the past 10 years, a substantial amount of research from a number of fields has delved into the roles digital media serves in the every day lives of teens (Forte, Dickard, Magee, & Agosto, 2014; Itō et al., 2008; Itō & Antin, 2010; Marwick, Murgia Diaz, & Palfrey, 2010). Two reports, one by Itō et al. (2008) and another by Itō and Antin (2010), stand out in discussions of young adults' use of digital media. In a 2008 article, Itō et al. present three areas of youth media practices: "hanging out, messing around, and geeking out" (p. 1). In a later publication, Itō and Antin (2010) expand on these three "genres of participation" (p. 13). Inspired by these works, this section will highlight four specific roles digital media possess in the lives of teens: identity construction, learning, literacy practice, and creativity.

Identity construction

Through the help of face-to-face and online interactions, teenagers are playing around with identities, exploring who they are, and determining group dynamics. Teens' struggle over identity is nothing new, but digital media has added one more location where a teen's identity construction can occur (Itō et al., 2008). Social networking sites, like Facebook and Instagram, provide teens with arenas in which to publically present, represent, and shape these still-developing identities (Livingstone, 2008). Teens experiment with how they present themselves through the various features of a social networking site or online community. In the passive role of a viewer, teens observe the ways in which their friends present themselves online and often use these observations as guides for constructing their online identities. The social norms that exist in the physical world extend into the online environment (Hargittai & Hinnant, 2008). Influenced by the norms of their peer group, teens build social media profiles, share personal information, and engage in conversations (Livingstone, 2008). Although sharing personal information may trouble parents, this sharing is important for "identity play, expression, and formation" (Marwick, Murgia Diaz, & Palfrey, 2010, p. 23).

Yet the identities teens display online may not be the same as the identity displayed in the physical world (boyd, 2009). As explained by Livingstone (2008), "social networking is about 'me' in the sense that it reveals the self-embedded in the peer group, as known to and represented by others, rather than the private 'I' known best by oneself" (p. 7). The social norms of peer groups dictate what a teen posts, how often, and where. The profiles created on social networking sites allow teens to perform and maintain their social identity (boyd & Heer, 2006). But this identity is both a personal identity and a group identity. Through friending or following, young users communicate shared interests, outlooks, and personalities (boyd & Heer, 2006). Additionally, the features an online community provides young users also restrict self-expression and the ability to represent themselves fully online (boyd, 2010). The absence or inclusion of various capabilities (e.g. uploading pictures, word-count limits, privacy options) unintentionally helps shape the identity teens present online (boyd, 2010).

Learning

While socializing consumes the majority of a teen's online activities, formal and informal learning is also happening (Itō & Antin, 2010). Much of a teen's weekday is spent engaged in formal learning within a classroom. As the Internet has become far more accessible, K–12 teachers have incorporated digital media into lectures, assignments, and activities (Partnership for 21st Century Skills, 2009). Along with this structured learning, digital media offers teens an easy location for informal learning. Much like adults, teens can use social media and online communities to engage in peer-based learning (Itō et al., 2008). This relaxed form of learning allows teens to ask friends, both face to face and online, about shared hobbies and interests instead of relying on the more standard authority figures (e.g. teachers, school administrators) of traditional learning (Itō et al., 2008). In a study of *Final Fantasy XI* teen gamers, Itō and colleagues (2008) investigated how learning and collaborating is encouraged during online gaming. The collaborations within this and similar online games help young users understand how successful and unsuccessful groups operate. They can later apply this understanding of group dynamics to school and/or work group projects (Itō et al., 2008). Through interactions in a virtual world, teens are learning about the physical world and honing 21st-century skills (Partnership for 21st Century Skills, 2009). While improving what is often referred to as transferable skills like organization and successful collaboration, young gamers are also immersed in "learning to be" (Thomas & Brown, 2009, p. 8). As Thomas and Brown described, "these players are learning to give voice to new dispositions within networked worlds and environments which are well suited to effective communication, problem solving, and social interaction" (Thomas & Brown, 2009, p. 19).

Literacy practice

Although hanging out with friends is the main draw of social media, young adults are using these sites to hone digital literacy skills (Braun, Hartman, Hughes-Hassell, Kumasi, & Yoke, 2014). For the purposes of this chapter, digital literacy can be defined as "the myriad social practices and conceptions of engaging in meaning making mediated by text that are produced, received, distributed, exchanged, etc., via digital codification" (Lankshear & Knobel, 2011, p. 5). Young adults are not only accessing information while in online communities, they are also interpreting, evaluating, publishing, and communicating information (Koltay, 2011). Lankshear and Knobel argue that social media is "a member of a family of literacy practices" (p. 256), and outside of the classroom, young adults engage in "self-selected literacy practices", or literacy performances, with social networking sites forming "communities of practices" (Yi, 2008, p. 871). Literacy is a social practice, which takes place through the public environment of digital media (Gee, 2000). With the help of digital media, young adults are creating meaningful content, engaging in thoughtful discussions, and forming informal spaces for learning (Lankshear & Knobel, 2011).

Creativity

Labelled "geeking out" by Itō and Antin (2010), teens are actively creating, uploading, and sharing digital content through sites like YouTube, Instagram, and Vine. The Internet provides teens with a variety of free or inexpensive tools to create new or reimagined content. Ahn et al. (2012) investigated the remix practices among a group of middle school students engaged in digital storytelling. Remixing involves copying, modifying, and recreating print or digital works. Remix culture is one example of how youth use digital media creatively through the creation of memes, fan fiction, video mash-ups, and similar creations (Ahn et al., 2012). On a beginner level, social media sites and apps like Snapchat, Instagram, and Vine allow teens to play around with media production through shared images and videos of themselves, friends, and family. Teens can acquire coding skills as they copy and paste or modify the existing coding of social media profiles and backgrounds (Itō et al., 2008).

To learn more about particular interests, teens join online communities where they can share, collaborate, and learn about digital media projects (Itō et al., 2008). Through the guidance of other community members, teens combine leisure and educational experience. Whether teens are participating in an anime fan group or uploading videos to YouTube, they are seeking and receiving feedback from peers (Itō et al., 2008). For teens, these communities form a support system and source for mentorship (Itō & Antin, 2010). Online communities provide an environment in which teens can hone digital skills and take on new roles as they become more advanced media producers.

What dangers lurk online and offline

Along with meaningful use of social media, these online environments can be locations for violence and harassment for young adults. The deadly consequences of cyberbullying have been reported widely in the popular press (Stanglin & Welch, 2013). However, suicides among cyberbullied teens are rare. Instead, victims suffer life-long negative effects such as low self-esteem, depression, anxiety, and increased aggression (Brown, Demaray, & Secord, 2014). Online harassment does not occur in isolation but is often an extension of offline harassment like traditional bullying (Brown, Demaray, & Secord, 2014). Cyberbullying, cyberdating violence, and trolling are a few of the typical aggressive behaviours that have emerged due to the rise of social media. In many cases of online victimization, the perpetrators and victims are teenagers. Without the face-to-face dimension, anonymous online environments embolden some young users to act and speak in ways they may not have offline. Called the disinhibition effect, this loosening of social norms and restrictions has been cited as one explanation for destructive online behaviours (Mason, 2008). While on social media, users are able to more easily separate real-world identities from online identities and, as a result, separate online actions from real-world accountability (Suler, 2004). In this section, three types of teen online harassment will be discussed: cyberbullying, cyberdating abuse, and trolling.

Cyberbullying

As the popularity of social media has grown since its introduction in 2002, instances of cyberbullying and similar forms of repetitive online violence among young adults have also increased (boyd, 2009). Cyberbullying is "any behaviour performed through electronic or digital media by individuals or groups that repeatedly communicates hostile or aggressive messages intended to inflict harm or discomfort on others" (Tokunaga, 2010, p. 278). While sharing many of the same characteristics as traditional, face-to-face bullying, cyberbullying is distinguished by its online location, perceived anonymity, and flexibility of roles (Bauman, 2010; Bowler, Mattern, & Knobel, 2014). No longer can bullies, victims, and bystanders be easily identified. Instead, cyberbullying is often reciprocal with a role emerging called bully-victim (Dukes, Stein, & Zane, 2009). Cyberbullying is not only a problem for teens; adults also engage in cyberbullying behaviours. But cyberbullying among young adults has received considerably more attention in scholarly research and popular press (Accordino & Accordino, 2011; Dooley, Pyżalski, & Cross, 2009).

Research by boyd and Marwick (2011) illustrated the contrast between the adult-defined practice of cyberbullying and the teen-defined practice of drama. Teens do not perceive themselves as cyberbullies or cyberbullying victims. In its place, they call this behaviour "drama". The term "drama" describes "interpersonal conflict that takes place in front of an audience" (boyd & Marwick, 2011, p. 4). Drama is reciprocal, gendered, social, and interpersonal and involves relational conflict (boyd & Marwick, 2011). Social media provides another public arena in which drama can be performed. For teens, drama takes many forms such as gossip, trash talk, jokes, pranks, and misunderstandings. Not all drama is bullying, but often it can be (boyd & Marwick, 2011). By calling otherwise hurtful and aggressive behaviours drama, teens are able to "save face" and distance themselves from the label of victim.

Cyberdating abuse

Much like cyberbullying, cyberdating abuse is supported by the anonymous and non-stop world of the Internet. Some tech-savvy young adults, still psychologically, emotionally, and physically developing, take romantic frustrations and jealousies online (Zweig, Lachman, Yahner, & Dank, 2014). According to Zweig et al., cyberdating abuse is "the control, harassment, stalking, and abuse of one's dating partner via technology and social media" (p. 1306). By providing perpetrators with easy and unlimited access to victims, social media is a new avenue for extending physical dating violence and abuse online (Zweig et al., 2014). In a recent survey of 5,647 youths by Zweig et al. (2013), more than a quarter reported experiencing "some form of cyber dating abuse victimization" during the last year (p. 1063). One in 10 identified themselves as perpetrators of cyberdating abuse. LGBTQ youth are more likely to be victims of both cyberbullying and cyberdating abuse (Mitchell, Ybarra, & Korchmaros, 2014). Research is limited on cyberdating abuse among young adults. Currently, there is a lack in the literature addressing how teens use digital media to "harass, control, and abuse their dating partners" (Zweig et al., 2013).

Trolling

"Trolling" is a term that has been around since the late 1980s, but it has gained popularity with the ubiquity of the Internet (Schwartz, 2008). An Internet troll can be described as an individual who purposefully and maliciously interrupts online communities (Schwartz, 2008). Instead of focusing on a specific user, trolls typically target entire communities (e.g. discussion board, Facebook group, listserv) and attempt to create argument and discord among members (Buckels, Trapnell, & Paulhus, 2014). A form of cyberbullying formerly called "flaming", trolling is more common among older teens and emerging adults. Although the popular press focuses on cyberbullying as largely a teen activity and trolling as an adult activity, both adults and teens participate in trolling. Within the literature, trolling has been examined as an aggressive online behaviour perpetrated by adults with adult victims (Hardaker, 2010; Herring, Job-Sluder, Scheckler, & Barab, 2002). More research is needed into the trolling activities of teens and the relationship between teen trolling and the teen-defined behaviour of drama.

Implications for K–12 schools and community agencies

Because teens are vibrant and enthusiastic producers and consumers of digital media, it is critical for teachers, librarians, researchers, and other adults to include these online tools in work with teens (Braun et al., 2014). Social media and other digital tools have expanded the ways in which learning can be encouraged and supported. A strictly traditional approach to education is no longer viable for 21st-century learners. As the Internet has become more accessible around the world, many K–12 educators have incorporated gaming, blogging, social media, and other digital media tools into curricula (Pahl & Rowsell, 2006). These progressive teachers recognize the dual nature of digital media – education and entertainment. Through technology-inspired lessons and activities, educators demonstrate the changing nature of the classroom experience and the importance of multimodality in education (Bazalgette & Buckingham, 2013). However, more can be done regarding educating teens about sometimes-overlooked digital skills. To participate fully in the 21st-century workplace, many abilities are required such as correct search engine and database use, online security and privacy, professional social media use, and information analysis (Mills, 2006).

For communities, school and public libraries offer teens a safe space to interact with technology alongside peers and supportive adults (Jones & Delahanty, 2011). One trend among public libraries across the United States is youth Makerspaces such as YOUmedia Chicago, YOUmedia Miami, and the Mix at San Francisco Public Library. These publically available spaces with technology, materials, and dedicated staff "provide engaging learning opportunities for youth" (Sebrine et al., 2013, p. 1). While these are remarkable examples in urban public libraries, Makerspaces are still out of reach for small and rural libraries due to funding and broadband capabilities. To help ease the digital divide, it is imperative for libraries to have appropriate resources to ensure that all children have access to technology. But, as a whole, libraries must improve how they promote digital literacy and digital media skills in youth (Braun, Hartman et al., 2014). As highlighted in a publication by Young Adult Library Services Association (YALSA), "one thing libraries must do more concertedly and aggressively is support teens' acquisition of media-literacy skills" (2014, p. 7). In a study of young adults' use of the Internet, Livingstone (2003) found that teens lack persistence for online searching and are limited in research skills. This age group also does not possess the skills needed to evaluate online resources (Livingstone, 2003). Additionally, a digital divide exists among middle-class, urban, and more resource-rich teens and poorer, rural, and minority teens (Hargittai & Hinnant, 2008). While schools and libraries can assist in resolving some of these inequalities that teens experience at home, limited funding, staff training, and staff availability can make this task difficult.

While the majority of teens' digital media use is positive, cyberbullying, cyber harassment, and cyber violence do occur. To prevent these behaviours, teens must be educated about ethical and responsible use of the Internet, and to do so requires a community approach (Childnet International, 2007). A white paper by Jenkins and colleagues (2006) examines the challenges and possibilities for media education by K–12 schools, after-school programs, and parents. One challenge Jenkins et al. highlight is the need for youth to be "socialized into the emerging ethical standards that will shape their practices as media makers and as participants within online communities" (2006, p. 56). Schools, public libraries, school libraries, and youth-focused organizations can play a key part in teaching teens about digital citizenship. Digital citizenship is composed of nine elements: digital etiquette, digital communication, digital literacy, digital access, digital commerce, digital law, digital rights and responsibilities, digital health and wellness, and digital security (Oxley, 2011). Along with each of the elements, an understanding of empathy and compassion is necessary for teens to become digital citizens. A whole-community approach is needed to not only instruct teens about ethical online use but also model these responsible behaviours.

Conclusion

For teens to have well-rounded and healthy online experiences, assistance from parents, teachers, school administrators, librarians, and other concerned adults is critical. Because of the evolving nature of digital media, the online habits of teens offer numerous directions for future research. Research of digital media requires constant awareness of new and emerging trends. This is particularly true for researchers concentrating on teens, an age group always on the hunt for what's trending and popular. As discussed throughout this chapter, digital media has become an important component of a teen's daily life. Additional research is needed into how schools and libraries can further encourage teens' use of digital media for creative and educational purposes. Another area currently lacking research is how educators can incorporate media literacy skills fully into curricula. Instead of simply adding digital literacy to existing lesson plans, digital literacy must be a part of day-to-day classroom activities. Connected learning, defined as "socially embedded, interest-driven, and oriented towards educational, economic, or political opportunity", empowers teens to take ownership over how they learn (Braun et al., 2014, p. 8). This peer-driven style of learning can be found in the activities youth take part in while online.

Although the moniker "digital natives" may be unfounded, teens are inventive, enthusiastic, and active users of digital media. Teens view the Internet as "a central and indispensable element" in their lives (Lenhart, Purcell, Smith, & Zickuhr, 2010, p. 11). During everyday online use, this age group engages in play, socialization, creativity, communication, and learning. Yet the same technology that enables teens to take part in these rich experiences also allows them to engage in destructive and sometimes deadly behaviours. Cyberbullying, cyberdating violence, and trolling are realities for many online teens. However, with guidance from adults about ethical and responsible use of digital media, these behaviours may be prevented and kindness may be spread online.

References

Accordino, D. B., & Accordino, M. P. (2011). An exploratory study of face-to-face and cyberbullying in sixth grade students. *American Secondary Education, 40*(1), 14–30.

Agosto, D. E., Abbas, J., & Naughton, R. (2012). Relationships and social rules: Teens' social network and other ICT selection practices. *Journal of the American Society for Information Science and Technology, 63*(6), 1108–1124. http://doi.org/10.1002/asi.22612.

Ahn, J., Subramaniam, M., Fleischmann, K. R., Waugh, A., Walsh, G., & Druin, A. (2012). Youth identities as remixers in an online community of storytellers: Attitudes, strategies, and values. *Proceedings of the American Society for Information Science and Technology, 49*(1), 1–10.

Alemanne, N. D., Mandel, L. H., & McClure, C. R. (2011). The rural public library as leader in community broadband services. *Library Technology Reports, 47*(6), 19–28.

Bauman, S. (2010). Cyberbullying in a rural intermediate school: An exploratory study. *The Journal of Early Adolescence, 30*(6), 803–833. http://doi.org/10.1177/0272431609350927.

Bazalgette, C., & Buckingham, D. (2013). Literacy, media and multimodality: A critical response. *Literacy, 47*(2), 95–102.

Beheshti, J. (2012). Teens, virtual environments and information literacy. *Bulletin of the American Society for Information Science and Technology, 38*(3), 54–57.

Bowler, L., Mattern, E., & Knobel, C. (2014). Developing design interventions for cyberbullying: A narrative-based participatory approach. In *iConference 2014 proceedings* (pp. 153–162). Berlin, Germany. http://doi.org/10.9776/14059.

boyd, d. (2009). Why youth (heart) social network sites: The role of networked publics in teenage social life. Retrieved from http://papers.ssrn.com/sol3/papers.cfm?abstract_id=1518924.

boyd, d. (2010). Social network sites as networked publics: Affordances, dynamics, and implications. In Z. Papacharissi (ed.), *Networked self: Identity, community, and culture on social network sites* (pp. 39–58). Retrieved from http://www.danah.org/papers/2010/SNSasNetworkedPublics.

boyd, d., & Heer, J. (2006). Profiles as conversation: Networked identity performance on Friendster. In *System Sciences, 2006. HICSS'06. Proceedings of the Hawaii International Conference on System Sciences* (Vol. 3, p. 59c–59c). IEEE. Retrieved from http://ieeexplore.ieee.org/xpls/abs_all.jsp?arnumber=1579411.

boyd, d., & Marwick, A. (2011). *Social steganography: Privacy in networked publics.* Boston, MA: International Communication Association.

Braun, L. W., Hartman, M. L., Hughes-Hassell, S., Kumasi, K., & Yoke, B. (2014). *The future of library services for and with teens: A call to action* (pp. 1–59). Chicago, IL: Young Adult Library Services Association.

Brown, C. F., Demaray, M. K., & Secord, S. M. (2014). Cyber victimization in middle school and relations to social emotional outcomes. *Computers in Human Behavior, 35,* 12–21. http://doi.org/10.1016/j.chb.2014.02.014.

Buckels, E. E., Trapnell, P. D., & Paulhus, D. L. (2014). Trolls just want to have fun. *Personality and Individual Differences, 67,* 97–102. http://doi.org/10.1016/j.paid.2014.01.016.

Campbell, C., Haines, C., Koester, A., & Stoltz, D. (2015). *Serving Youth* (pp. 1–12). Association for Library Service to Children. Retrieved from http://www.ala.org/alsc/sites/ala. org.alsc/files/content/2015%20ALSC%20White%20Paper_FINAL.pdf.

Chicago Public Library. (2015). *YOUmedia Chicago.* Retrieved from http://www.chipub lib.org/youmedia/.

Childnet International. (2007). *Cyberbullying: A whole-school community issue* (pp. 1–8). Sydney, Australia: Australian Communications and Media Authority.

Davies, J. (2012). Facework on Facebook as a new literacy practice. *Computers & Education, 59*(1), 19–29. http://doi.org/10.1016/j.compedu.2011.11.007.

Dooley, J. J., Pyżalski, J., & Cross, D. (2009). Cyberbullying versus face-to-face bullying: A theoretical and conceptual review. *Journal of Psychology, 217*(4), 182–188. http://doi. org/10.1027/0044–3409.217.4.182.

Dukes, R. L., Stein, J. A., & Zane, J. I. (2009). Effect of relational bullying on attitudes, behavior and injury among adolescent bullies, victims and bully-victims. *The Social Science Journal, 46*(4), 671–688. http://doi.org/10.1016/j.soscij.2009.05.006.

Forte, A., Dickard, M., Magee, R., & Agosto, D. E. (2014, February). What do teens ask their online social networks? Social search practices among high school students. In *Proceedings of the 17th ACM Conference on Computer Supported Cooperative Work & Social Computing* (pp. 28–37). ACM.

Gee, J. P. (2000). Teenagers in new times: A new literacy studies perspective. *Journal of Adolescent & Adult Literacy, 43*(5), 412–420.

Hardaker, C. (2010). Trolling in asynchronous computer-mediated communication: From user discussions to academic definitions. *Journal of Politeness Research. Language, Behaviour, Culture, 6*(2). http://doi.org/10.1515/jplr.2010.011.

Hargittai, E., & Hinnant, A. (2008). Digital inequality: Differences in young adults' use of the Internet. *Communication Research, 35*(5), 602–621. http://doi.org/10.1177/0093650 208321782.

Herring, S., Job-Sluder, K., Scheckler, R., & Barab, S. (2002). Searching for safety online: Managing "trolling" in a feminist forum. *The Information Society, 18*(5), 371–384. http://doi.org/10.1080/01972240290108186.

Itō, M., & Antin, J. (2010). *Hanging out, messing around, and geeking out kids living and learning with new media.* Cambridge, MA: MIT Press. Retrieved from http://site.ebrary. com/id/10347251.

Itō, M., Horst, H., Bittanti, M., boyd, d., Herr-Stephenson, B., Lange, P. G., Pascoe, C. J., & Robinson, L. (2008). Living and learning with new media: Summary of findings from the Digital Youth Project. John D. and Catherine T. MacArthur Foundation. Retrieved from http://eric.ed.gov/?id=ED536072.

Jenkins, H., Purushotma, R., Weigel, M., Clinton, K., & Robison, A. J. (2009). *Confronting the challenges of participatory culture: Media education for the 21st century.* Boston: MIT Press.

Jones, K. R., & Delahanty, T. J. (2011). A viable venue: The public library as a haven for youth development. *Children and Libraries: The Journal of the Association for Library Service to Children, 9*(1), 41–44.

Koltay, T. (2011). The media and the literacies: Media literacy, information literacy, digital literacy. *Media, Culture & Society*, *33*(2), 211–221. http://doi.org/10.1177/0163443710393382.

Lankshear, C., & Knobel, M. (2011). *Digital literacies*. New York: Peter Lang Publishing, Inc.

Lenhart, A. (2015). *Teens, social media & technology overview 2015*. Washington, DC: Pew Internet & American Life Project. Retrieved from http://www.pewinternet.org/2015/04/09/teens-social-media-technology-2015/.

Lenhart, A., Purcell, K., Smith, A., & Zickuhr, K. (2010). *Social media & mobile Internet use among teens and young adults* (pp. 1–51). Washington, DC: Pew Internet & American Life Project. Retrieved from http://eric.ed.gov/?id=ED525056.

Livingstone, S. (2003). Children's use of the Internet: Reflections on the emerging research agenda. *New Media & Society*, *5*(2), 147–166.

Livingstone, S. (2008). Taking risky opportunities in youthful content creation: Teenagers' use of social networking sites for intimacy, privacy and self-expression. *New Media & Society*, *10*(3), 393–411. http://doi.org/10.1177/1461444808089415.

Mardis, M. A. (2013). What it has or what it does not have? Signposts from US data for rural children's digital access to informal learning. *Learning, Media and Technology*, *38*(4), 387–406. http://doi.org/10.1080/17439884.2013.783595.

Marwick, A. E., Murgia Diaz, D., & Palfrey, J. (2010). *Youth, privacy and reputation* (pp. 1–66). Cambridge, MA: The Berkman Center for Internet & Society at Harvard University. Retrieved from http://147.237.72.56/NR/rdonlyres/4CA36194-FEFE-4DE8-965A-3A1464118554/26314/Perceptions_SSRNid15881632.pdf.

Mason, K. L. (2008). Cyberbullying: A preliminary assessment for school personnel. *Psychology in the Schools*, *45*(4), 323–348. http://doi.org/10.1002/pits.20301

Mills, K. A. (2006). Critical framing in a pedagogy of multiliteracies. In *Proceedings Australian Literacy Educator's Association/Australian Association of the Teaching of English National Conference 2006: Voices, Vibes, Visions: Hearing the Voices, Feeling the Vibes, Capturing the Visions*. Retrieved from http://eprints.qut.edu.au/00004844.

Mitchell, K. J., Ybarra, M. L., & Korchmaros, J. D. (2014). Sexual harassment among adolescents of different sexual orientations and gender identities. *Child Abuse & Neglect*, *38*(2), 280–295.

Oxley, C. (2011). Digital citizenship: Developing an ethical and responsible online culture. *Access*, 5–9.

Pahl, K., & Rowsell, J. (2006). The new literacy studies and teaching literacy: Where we were and where we are going. In *Literacy and Education: Understanding the New Literacy Studies in the classroom* (pp. 1–24). Thousand Oaks, CA: Sage Publications Inc.

Partnership for 21st Century Skills. (2009). *P21 framework definitions* (pp. 1–9). Washington, DC: Partnership for 21st Century Skills. Retrieved from http://ipkt.org:8080/modul/DPLI/index_htm_files/21ST%20CENTURY%20SKILLS.p.

Prensky, M. (2001). Digital natives, digital immigrants part 1. *On the Horizon*, *9*(5), 1–6.

Schwartz, M. (2008, August 3). The trolls among us. *The New York Times*. Retrieved from http://www.nytimes.com/2008/08/03/magazine/03trolls-t.html.

Sebrine, P. B., Brown, E. R., Julian, K. M., Ehrlich, S. B., Sporte, S. E., Bradley, E., & Meyer, L. (2013). *Teens, digital media, and the Chicago Public Library* (pp. 1–67). Chicago, IL: The University of Chicago Consortium on Chicago School Research. Retrieved from http://ccsr.uchicago.edu/sites/default/files/publications/YOUmedia%20Report%20-%20Final.pdf.

Stanglin, D., & Welch, W. M. (2013, October 16). Two girls arrested on bullying charges after suicide. *USA Today*. Retrieved from http://www.usatoday.com/story/news/nation/2013/10/15/florida-bullying-arrest-lakeland-suicide/2986079/.

Suler, J. (2004). The online disinhibition effect. *Cyberpsychology & Behavior*, *7*(3), 321–326.

Thomas, D., & Brown, J. S. (2009). Why virtual worlds can matter. *International Journal of Media and Learning*, *1*(1), 37–49. Retrieved from http://www.mitpressjournals.org/doi/full/10.1162/ijlm.2009.0008.

Tokunaga, R. S. (2010). Following you home from school: A critical review and synthesis of research on cyberbullying victimization. *Computers in Human Behavior*, *26*(3), 277–287. http://doi.org/10.1016/j.chb.2009.11.014.

Tripp, L. (2011). Digital youth, libraries, and new media literacy. *The Reference Librarian*, *52*(4), 329–341. http://doi.org/10.1080/02763877.2011.584842.

Yi, Y. (2008). Relay writing in an adolescent online community. *Journal of Adolescent & Adult Literacy*, *51*(8), 670–680.

Zweig, J. M., Dank, M., Yahner, J., & Lachman, P. (2013). The rate of cyber dating abuse among teens and how it relates to other forms of teen dating violence. *Journal of Youth and Adolescence*, *42*(7), 1063–1077. http://doi.org/10.1007/s10964-013-9922-8.

Zweig, J. M., Lachman, P., Yahner, J., & Dank, M. (2014). Correlates of cyber dating abuse among teens. *Journal of Youth and Adolescence*, *43*(8), 1306–1321. http://doi.org/10.1007/s10964-013-0047-x.

7 Living social

Comparing social media use in your 20s and 30s

Natalie Pennington

There are many different reasons to use information communication technologies (ICTs), with the most common being to foster connections and relationships between users (Haythornthwaite, 2005). Those relationships vary from strong to weak tie connections, but one element unique to ICTs is the ability to maintain more weak ties than ever before, and with growing ease (Haythornthwaite, 2005). Additionally, we know that through the use of ICTs weak ties can be turned into strong ties over time (Baym, 2000). This ability to use technology to allow for the development of interpersonal relationships and communication, while once thought to be impossible, is now one of the most common ways to engage online (Baym, 2010; Jones et al., 2009). One of the most commonly used forms of ICTs today for interpersonal communication, particularly by younger adults, is a social networking site.

While social media existed prior to 2004 (MySpace, Friendster, anyone?), many mark the introduction of Facebook that year and its meteoric rise to be the pre-eminent social networking site as proof of the prevalence of social networking sites in the lives of many today. Now just over 10 years old, what started as a college-access-only site has become one of the most-trafficked websites on the Internet, ranking number two in the world and holding steady for the past few years (Fitzgerald, 2012). Indeed, Facebook now boasts more than 1.35 billion monthly active users (*Facebook Newsroom*, 2015). These numbers make it not all that surprising that users of the site have expanded beyond those who first adopted it (college and high school students).

According to the latest study from the PEW Research Center's Internet and American Life Project, 71 per cent of the adults that are online are using Facebook (Duggan et al., 2015). While comparative results of their data from 2013 to 2014 showed a continued small climb in use by 18- to 29-year-olds (87 per cent from 84 per cent), they also found a decrease in use of the site for users 30 to 49 (down to 73 per cent from 79 per cent). This was the only age group to see a decline in use in the last year, with those in the 65+ age group category seeing the biggest gain, jumping from a 45 per cent to 56 per cent penetration rate (Duggan et al., 2015). PEW also reports a continued increase in the use of various other social networking sites such as Twitter, Instagram, Pinterest, and LinkedIn since 2013, with the most noticeable leaps forward in Instagram for almost every demographic and LinkedIn for college students

(Duggan et al., 2015). Knowing who is using these site(s) is only the start of the battle for researchers, however, as the next important question becomes: *how* are these sites being used?

The aim of this chapter is to discuss the various ways in which users in their 20s and 30s engage with and through social media by summarizing current research on the question while also discussing the results of research conducted by the author of this chapter within the last year. To try to summarize all possible uses of social media (e.g. interpersonal, political) and all the various sites (e.g. Facebook, Twitter, Instagram) is difficult within such a limited frame as a single chapter in a book. The goal of this chapter, therefore, is to consider the relational (interpersonal) uses of social media by users in their 20s in 30s as particular life stages. Given the heavy focus of research on college-aged samples and Facebook, the chapter will begin by surveying the existing literature addressing how college students engage with Facebook. The discussion will then turn to comparative work that exists both in terms of other age groups but also other social networking sites. Last, the chapter will conclude with recommendations for future research on social media for users in these particular life stages while highlighting the need to consider the importance of affordances and functions of sites rather any one site for future work.

Identifying the early adopter: Facebook and college students

Most research on Facebook use is focused on college students in some capacity. College students were the early adopters and are an easily accessible population for many researchers, making them an obvious choice for analysis. That does not make that research any less relevant to the discussion but rather provides ample evidence with which to compare the results for those who either never attended college or are not currently in a collegiate setting. Unfortunately, few studies provide a comparative lens.

The most often-cited use of Facebook for college students is built into the nature of the site: it is for social networking and connecting with friends and family. Ellison, Steinfield, and Lampe's (2007) study of Facebook is one of the earliest to study Facebook use by college students and offers several promising findings on benefits to networking through the site: participants used the site to meet new people, maintain long-distance high school friendships (weak ties), as well as other close local (strong) ties, which in turn increased social capital. As a follow-up, Ellison, Steinfield, and Lampe (2011) looked more closely at the communication patterns of Facebook users and the benefits of Facebook, suggesting that users typically engage in one of three communicative strategies: initiating (meeting new people, which was the least-used strategy), maintaining (close ties), and the third they labelled "social information-seeking", wherein users would turn to Facebook to learn more about someone they had met offline. The researchers explain how this is a unique benefit of Facebook (and social network sites in general): meeting someone in passing, a person can turn to social media, find that person (likely tied to someone else they know), and learn more about them

(Ellison, Steinfield, and Lampe, 2011). After they connect (friend that person) they're turning a latent tie into a weak tie and potentially into a strong-tie relationship over time, acting as what the researchers call a "*social lubricant*" (Ellison, Steinfield, and Lampe, 2011, p. 887).

Given that Facebook is used to maintain a variety of both strong and weak ties, it is not surprising that studies on the site's use have shown that the more one uses Facebook, the more bridging and bonding capital they have (Ellison, Steinfield, and Lampe, 2007; Ellison et al., 2014). Similarly, research on social support (Rozzell et al., 2014) has found that users are able to gain information and emotional support through Facebook – by having access to a larger network of weak ties, users feel the responses will be less judgmental and more objective and offer a greater diversity of opinions than might be gained in a small circle of close friends (strong ties).

Additional research since that initial study by Ellison and colleagues supports these claims: Urista, Day, and Dong (2009) suggest that building and maintaining interpersonal relationships in a convenient and efficient manner is one of the biggest benefits to Facebook. Valenzuela, Park, and Kee (2009) found a positive relationship between Facebook use by college students and social capital. In addition, this study found that increased Facebook use was positively related to increased life satisfaction, social trust, and civic and political participation (Valenzuela, Park, and Kee, 2009). While in this case "*use*" was measured in terms of building relationships and time spent simply being *on* the site, coupled with the results from Ellison, Steinfield, and Lampe (2007, 2011), it is clear that an integral part of gaining any sort of benefits from Facebook is communicating through the site.

Wright et al.'s (2013) study found that Facebook support network satisfaction was associated with lower levels of self-reported depression, but that it was not as high as face-to-face (FtF) network satisfaction. Yet, as the researchers rightfully point out, their sample (college students) could skew these results: users of social media who are more socially isolated (which social isolation can increase with age) may benefit even more from Facebook use in terms of mental health (Wright et al., 2013). This would point to the importance of research on looking beyond college students for study of the benefits and drawbacks of the use of Facebook. That said, there are elements in studies of college students that point to the need for social support through the Internet. Pennington (2013) cites research on the experience of death by college students as a reason to focus on this sample for grief communication. Pennington found that Facebook became an ideal outlet for many to grieve when they were not geographically close enough to participate in more traditional outlets. Likewise, Manago, Taylor, and Greenfield (2012) note that in a "geographically mobile" world, the growth of social networks for college students is important to help improve life satisfaction in college students. While various studies suggests that college students in particular have large social networks (Litt et al., 2014; Sosik and Bazarova, 2014), this particular study is interesting in that it suggests that having a larger network for college students (just perceiving the audience as there and watching) can improve well-being and perceptions of social support (Manago, Taylor, and Greenfield, 2012). My own research on this question of network size and college students (Pennington, 2015) suggests that college students in particular seek to "bulk up" their network and connections, fearing the potential loss of relationships and as a result going out of their way to avoid confrontation through social media that could cause them to sever a tie. This is true not only of Facebook but also of Twitter and Instagram (Pennington, 2015).

In addition to Facebook use, 18- to 29-year-olds are also the heaviest users of Instagram, Twitter, and Pinterest (Duggan et al., 2015). While not all of those within this demographic category are college students, research by Jones et al. (2009) suggests that it is college students in particular that are the early adopters of new tools on the Internet, with the authors noting,

> Many online tools have been adopted first by college students. Facebook, MySpace, BitTorrent, online games, and numerous other phenomena seem to have had a head start on college campuses, or, in cases like Facebook, were primarily conceived for college students.

As Jones et al. also point out, it is also likely that being introduced to and having technology heavily integrated into everyday life in college increases the likelihood that after the fact, Internet use will remain high among those with a college education. While this may be the case in terms of general Internet use, can the same be said for interpersonal engagement through social media?

We all grow up (post-college engagement)

One of the more fascinating studies done comparatively in the past few years regarding changes in the use of social media by users since leaving college was an analysis of language use that analysed more than 15.4 million Facebook status updates by 75,000 participants (Schwartz et al., 2013). While a large focus was on considering possible personality differences that existed (e.g. extroversion, emotional stability), a part of the study also considered the effect of age on language use. The researchers found, through the use of differential language analysis, that the language frequently used online correlates heavily with life stages. Nineteen- to 22-year-olds are more likely to post about, for example, what they refer to as "drunk topics" using words such as "drunk", "hungover", or "wasted", whereas someone that is 23 to 29, they note, is more likely to engage in the "beer topic" including words like "beer", "drinking", and "ale" (Schwartz et al., 2013). Other common life stage differences emerge between those in college and now in the workforce, with 19- to 22-year-olds more likely to use words such as "semester", "class", "exam", "roommates", and "assignments", while 23- to 29-year-olds are more likely to use words like "work", "wedding", "babies", and "vacation". The researchers found no major differences once users reached 30, grouping together the 30 to 65+ year old group, noting that common words included "children", "family", "prayer", and "blessed".

In addition to differences in topic, Schwartz et al. also noticed a stark difference in tone for language use. Nineteen- to 22-year-olds were far more likely to engage in negative emotions and content through social media, with common words like "fuck", "damn", and "bullshit" highlighted in the word cloud provided. Conversely, 23- to 29-year-olds had a much more positive tone, with common words including "excited", "thankful", and "celebrate". The 30 to 65+ age group continues this trend with words such as "wonderful", "blessed", and "grateful". These shifts in language use on social media are important to consider, as they highlight changes in perspective as users move through life stages. The stressors of college and instability in relationships that can be more prevalent in younger age groups increase the potential for negative affect and emotional outpourings, while as one ages, the probability of "settling down" leads to reflection and more positive affect within language use. While there are additional variables to consider (e.g. gender, personality), it follows that life stage would have a large impact on how one communicates (and what about) on social media.

Besides research on language use, McAndrew and Jeong (2012) conducted a series of correlations between possible uses of Facebook and age and found that as users get older they use Facebook less, but when they do use the site it is for one-on-one interaction and engaging with family, versus younger users who are more likely to have a higher number of friends on the site, spend more time, and do things like post pictures and engage in social comparison. This is fairly consistent with what we know of other research – this desire to talk about and engage with family as one ages and have a larger social support network of friends when one is in college (Ellison, Steinfield, and Lampe, 2007, 2011; Schwartz et al., 2013).

When it comes to comparative claims about social media use across sites (e.g. Twitter, Facebook, Instagram), less exists to understand what is used and why. Hughes et al. (2012) suggest that younger adults prefer Facebook because they view it as a social site, whereas older users prefer Twitter because it can be used to gain information. Twitter has been touted as a social networking site on one hand and a political and news source on the other (van Dijck, 2011). These varied uses of the site allow for a wider audience to pull in, which has allowed it to grow and find its own unique place among the most popular social media today.

My own research (Pennington, 2015) on the question of Facebook, Twitter, and Instagram suggests that younger adult users (18–29) prefer Twitter and Instagram (though also use Facebook) and that as users enter their 30s, there is almost always a sole preference for Facebook. This study used both a college sample and Amazon's Mechanical Turk to access participants, which gave diversity to the sample in terms of experience attending college (which has been shown to increase the use of social media; see Jones et al., 2009). By asking participants questions about what different sites they used (and preferred) and relational decisions, the study was able to assess possible differences that exist as a result of age (Pennington, 2015).

Similar to McAndrews and Jeong's (2012) findings, the results suggested that frequency of use of a social networking site (be it Facebook, Twitter, or Instagram) differed across age groups but not in quite the same pattern as they found. Those in their younger 20s (20–23) used social media the most, followed by those in their 30s and then those in their older 20s (24–29). While the younger 20s and 30s were significantly different in terms of use from those in their older 20s, they were not significantly different from each other (Pennington, 2015). This pattern would suggest that users take a "break" post-college from social media, decreasing use of the Internet to focus on face-to-face communication. In addition to the survey data reported in the above mentioned study (Pennington, 2015) focus groups were conducted with users in their 20s and 30s to validate these results. Users in their late 20s indicated that privacy concerns kept them from using social media much, whereas those in their early 20s suggested little concern for sharing and connecting online with others (Pennington, 2015).

Similar to past research, network sizes were also the largest for those in their younger 20s, showing a significant decrease down into the late 20s and again into the 30s, moving from an average of 579.96 friends/followers down to 384.54 friends/followers (Pennington, 2015). A correlation was also found to exist between age and past experience with "un-friending/following" through social media that would account for this decrease in network size as users of social media got older (Pennington, 2015).

One feature of Facebook that is considered a benefit across age groups is the ability to "reconnect" with old friends (e.g. old high school friends) through the site (Lewis and West, 2009; Ramirez and Bryant, 2014). This can be seen as particularly true for older age groups when they first join social media – the chance to reconnect with old ties is more likely to lure in older users versus a college student who would find other reasons to join but may also benefit from this feature.

Valentine's (2011) analysis of uses of Facebook in users 35 years old and older found that communication was a primary use for participants; 60 per cent of participants indicated that they read and responded to their newsfeed at least weekly, with 45.1 per cent indicating this was a daily habit. It is worth noting that of the sample, 72.8 per cent were 35 to 54 years old, with the remainder of participants primarily in the 55 to 64 age group (22.3 per cent) and a small subset over 65 years old (3.7 per cent; Valentine, 2011, p. 26). Valentine's survey asked participants if they "interacted with applications, quizzes, or games", and 59.1 per cent of the respondents indicated that they never did so, while 11.7 per cent said they did so daily. Unfortunately, Valentine (2011) does not indicate the primary age group of that 11.7 per cent, and one can only speculate that it is the older users in the sample, similar to Ancu (2012) noting that the use of social media for entertainment purposes is common in users over 50 years old.

Altogether this research shows a consistent picture of behaviours of users in their 20s and 30s and their use of social media (whether it be Facebook, Twitter, or Instagram). While fewer studies exist on the latter sites, comparative work that does exist suggests that users engage for similar reasons across sites and that age does play a role in the number of connections and how users relate to those strong and weak ties through each site. Before concluding, it is important to consider the potential that exists for differential use as a result of age and education, as much of the research that exists focuses on college-educated individuals and their engagement with social media.

A (possible) digital divide

With an increased presence online and a growing number of users each year, it is important to address the role that social media plays not only in the lives of early adopters of the sites but of all social media users. While some research exists that focuses solely on older adult users of social media as already summarized (Ancu, 2012; Baker et al., 2013; Valentine, 2011), the majority of studies we know primarily are concerned with how young adults are using social networking sites (Ellison, Steinfield, and Lampe, 2007, 2011; Valenzuela, Park and Kee, 2009). But does this unequal representation in research correlate to use and knowledge?

Hargittai and Walejko (2008) note that unequal participation in the use of digital media can create a divide wherein those who participate more set the norms and expectations for use of a given medium or site. While early research on the digital divide focused almost entirely on questions of access, research in the last decade and a half has addressed what has been known as the "second-level digital divide" – questions of knowledge and use (Friemel and Signer, 2010; Katz and Rice, 2002; Loges and Jung, 2001). Facebook can be seen as an example of a digital divide that began as a question of access but now may be more about use: in its earliest years it was only available to college students, then high school students, and finally opening up to the public in late 2006 – giving some young adults more than 2 years of access to learn how to use the site ahead of older adults around the world. While the gap in use has closed, younger adults having used it for a longer period of time may give them an advantage in understanding all that the site has to offer in terms of potential benefits.

Friemel and Signer (2010) suggest that experience with the Internet (earlier access) can account for a larger second-level digital divide: younger adults have spent more time using Web 2.0 technology, like Facebook, and as a result are more comfortable using it to their benefit, while older adults who make the leap to join social media stick with what they are comfortable with – games that they can play without having to actively communicate and engage in the capabilities afforded to them by this form of new media (e.g. building social capital, receiving social support, and networking). Livingstone and Helsper (2007) in discussing the results of their study on the digital divide write,

> The findings support the implicit yet widespread policy assumption that basic use makes for a narrow, unadventurous, even frustrating use of the internet, while more sophisticated use permits a broad-ranging and confident use of the internet that embraces new opportunities and meets individual and social goals.
>
> (p. 692)

It is not enough to know how to *sign up* for social media but to be able to benefit from all the nuances of the site(s) available.

Hargittai (2007) suggests a variety of reasons that older adults may hesitate engaging in ICTs – for example, not knowing how to properly "copy" recipients on an email and concerns for privacy can prevent use of email. Similarly, on Facebook, lacking knowledge of privacy mechanisms for status updates and sharing images, a user may opt to not post at all for fear of someone seeing it they do not want to communicate with. While this may seem easy to those comfortable in that particular online space, it can be overwhelming to a new user, and as a result they can miss out on the potential benefits of a given medium, with research suggesting that a lack of skill or know-how contributed heavily to not engaging in the Internet, due in some part to a fear of technology and concern for privacy (Livingstone and Helsper, 2007; Loges and Jung, 2001).

While this is certainly more likely for the 50- to 65-year-olds and 65+ age categories highlighted in Ancu's (2012) study of Facebook users and Duggan et al.'s (2015) report on social media use in general, the numbers do not lie in showing that the earliest adoption of most social media comes in the 18 to 29 age group. For example, 53 per cent of 18- to 29-year-olds that are online use Instagram, the popular photo-sharing site, while only 25 per cent of 30- to 49-year-olds use it (Duggan et al., 2015). These gaps in use are likely to close over time – Instagram will be just 5 years old when this chapter reaches publication, half the age of Facebook, in terms of its public face, with roughly half the penetration rate in 18- to 29-year-olds. With time one can imagine that Instagram, much like Twitter in a few more years, may continue to gain across all age groups. What this means in terms of knowledge is a separate question, as younger adults will still have that edge on recognizing the potential interpersonal (and in some cases professional) benefits that are gained from social networking sites. This can be seen in the results of the studies previously discussed: older users hesitate in sharing personal information online and have smaller networks. Both self-disclosure and the presence of increased strong and weak ties have been shown to be helpful to users in the various studies discussed, making it important to continue to consider ways to encourage all individuals (regardless of age) to see the benefits of social media use.

Conclusions, suggestions for future work

Summary work of the last decade on research on social media has found an overwhelming focus on Facebook and college students (Rains and Brunner, 2015; Wilson, Gosling, and Graham, 2012). While this creates a clear picture regarding the use of at least one social network site (Facebook) by college-aged individuals, much more work must be done regarding social media as a whole and the various users across age groups and backgrounds. As the PEW Research Center's Internet and American Life Project demonstrates, the use of multiple social networking sites is on the rise, particularly with older adults (Duggan et al., 2015). Their study results show that 52 per cent of adults use two or more social networking sites (Duggan et al., 2015), which is promising to future researchers in this area. It is crucial that future work on who is using social media and *how* continues to expand the focus to address not just one site and what it can do but the affordances that can be attributed to all sites in terms of communication theory and practice.

Bryant, Marmo, and Ramirez (2011) note that social networking sites are "playing an increasingly important role in the communication of young adults and are even beginning to gain reputation as a viable tool for adults" (p. 14). Their chapter that highlights the functions of social networking sites is an important contribution to the overall literature as we consider the placement of social media in society today. With a growing number of sites that are used for different (and sometimes overlapping) reasons, it is important to address in research what can, in a broader sense, be gained (or lost) by a user. At the same time, keeping in mind those differences is important – differences in users and life stages is just one such way to categorize the use of ICTs and, more specifically, social media, but it is an important one to keep in mind as we attempt to navigate what is sure to be a long-lasting web of information sharing online for years to come.

References

Ancu, M. (2012). Older adults on Facebook: A survey examination of motives and use of social networking by people 50 and over. *Florida Communication Journal*, 40(1), 1–12.

Baker, P. M. A., Bricout, J. C., Moon, N. W., Coughlan, B., and Pater, J. (2013). Communities of participation: A comparison of disability and aging identified groups on Facebook and LinkedIn. *Telematics & Informatics*, 30(1), 22–34.

Baym, N. K. (2000). *Tune in, log on: Soaps, fandom, and online community.* Thousand Oaks, CA: Sage.

Baym, N. K. (2010). *Personal connections in the digital age.* Cambridge, UK: Polity Press.

Bryant, E. M., Marmo, J., and Ramirez, Jr., A. (2011). A functional approach to social networking sites. In *Computer-mediated communication in personal relationships*, edited by K. B. Wright and L. M. Webb, New York: Peter Lang Publishing, 3–20.

Duggan, M., Ellison, N. B., Lampe, C., Lenhart, A., and Madden, M. (2015). Social media update 2014. *Pew Research Internet Project.* Retrieved on January 9, 2015 from: http://www.pewinternet.org/2015/01/09/social-media-update-2014/.

Ellison, N. B., Steinfield, C., and Lampe, C. (2007). The benefits of Facebook 'friends': Exploring the relationship between college students' use of online social networks and social capital. *Journal of Computer-Mediated Communication*, 12(4), 1143–1168.

Ellison, N. B., Steinfield, C., and Lampe, C. (2011). Connection strategies: Social capital implications of Facebook-enabled communication practices. *New Media & Society*, 13(6), 873–892.

Ellison, N. B., Vitak, J., Gray, R., and Lampe, C. (2014). Cultivating social resources on social network sites: Facebook relationship maintenance behaviors and their role in social capital processes. *Journal of Computer-Mediated Communication*, 19(4), 855–870.

Facebook Newsroom. (2014). Key facts. Retrieved on December 15, 2014 from: http://newsroom.fb.com/Key-Facts.

Fitzgerald, B. (2012, August 10). Most popular sites 2012: Alexa ranks the 500 most-visited websites, *The Huffington Post.* Retrieved on August 20, 2014 from: http://www.huffingtonpost.com/2012/08/09/most-popular-sites-2012-alexa_n_1761365.html.

Friemel, T. N., and Signer, S. (2010). Web 2.0 Literacy: Four aspects of the second level digital divide. *Studies in Communication Sciences*, 10(2), 143–166.

Hargittai, E. (2007). A framework for studying differences in people's digital media uses. In *Cyberworld unlimited?*, edited by N.K. a. H.-U. Otto, Wiesbaden: VS Verlag für Sozialwissenschaften/GWV Fachverlage GmbH, 121–137.

Hargittai, E. and Walejko, G. (2008). The participation divide: Content creation and sharing in the digital age. *Information, Communication and Society*, 11(2), 239–256.

Haythornthwaite, C. (2005). Social networks and Internet connectivity effects. *Information, Communication, & Society*, 8(2), 125–147.

Hughes, D. J., Rowe, M., Batey, M., and Lee, A. (2012). A tale of two sites: Twitter vs. Facebook and the personality predictors of social media usage. *Computers in Human Behavior*, 28(2), 561–569.

Jones, S., Johnson-Yale, C., Millermaier, S., and Pérez, F. S. (2009). Everyday life, online: U.S. college students' use of the Internet. *First Monday*, 14(10), http://firstmonday.org/article/view/2649/2301.

Katz, J. E., and Rice, R. E. (2002). *Social consequences of Internet use: Access, involvement, and interaction.* Cambridge, MA: MIT Press.

Lewis, J., and West, A. (2009). 'Friending': London-based undergraduates experience on Facebook. *New Media & Society*, 11(7), 1209–1229.

Litt, E., Spottswood, E., Birnholtz, J., Hancock, J., Smith, M. E., and Reynolds, L. (2014). *Awkward encounters of an "other" kind: Collective self-presentation and face threat on Facebook.* Paper presented at the 2014 Annual CSCW Conference, Baltimore, MD.

Livingstone, S., and Helsper, E. (2007). Gradations in digital inclusion: Children, young people and the digital divide. *New Media & Society*, 9(4), 671–696.

Loges, W. E., and Jung, J. Y. (2001). Exploring the digital divide: Internet connectedness and age. *Communication Research*, 28(4), 536–562.

Manago, A. M., Taylor, T., and Greenfield, P. M. (2012). Me and my 400 friends: The anatomy of college students' Facebook networks, their communication patterns, and well-being. *Developmental Psychology*, 48(2), 369–380.

McAndrew, F. T., and Jeong, H. S. (2012). Who does what on Facebook? Age, sex, and relationship status as predictors of Facebook use. *Computers in Human Behavior*, 28, 2359–2365.

Pennington, N. (2013). You don't de-friend the death: An analysis of grief communication by college students through Facebook. *Death Studies*, 37(7), 617–635.

Pennington, N. (2015). *Building and maintaining relationships in the digital age: Using social penetration theory to explore communication through social media*, PhD thesis. University of Kansas.

Rains, S. A., and Brunner, S. R. (2015). What can we learn about social networking sites by studying Facebook? A call and recommendations for research on social network sites. *New Media & Society*, 17(1), 114–131.

Ramirez, Jr., A., and Bryant, E. M. (2014). Relational reconnection on social network sites: An examination of relationship persistence and modality switching. *Communication Reports*, 27(1), 1–12.

Rozzell, B., Piercy, C. W., Carr, C. T., King, S., Lane, B. L., Tornes, M., Johnson, A. J., and Wright, K. B. (2014). Notification pending: Online social support from close and nonclose relational ties via Facebook. *Computers in Human Behavior*, 38, 272–280.

Schwartz, H. A., Eichstaedt, J. C., Kern, M. L., Dziurzynski, L., Ramones, S. M., Agrawal, M., Shah, A., Kosinski, M., Stillwell, D., Seligman, M.E.P., and Ungar, L. H. (2013). Personality, gender, and age in the language of social media: The open-ended vocabulary approach. *PLOS One*, 8(9), 1–16.

Sosik, V. S., and Bazarova, N. N. (2014). Relational maintenance on social network sites: How Facebook communication predicts relational escalation. *Computers in Human Behavior*, 35, 124–131.

Urista, M. A., Dong, Q., and Day, K. D. (2009). Explaining why young adults use MySpace and Facebook through uses and gratifications theory. *Human Communication*, 12(2), 215–229.

Van Dijck, J. (2011). Tracing Twitter: The rise of a microblogging platform. *International Journal of Media and Cultural Politics*, 7(3), 333–348.

Valentine, A. (2011). *Uses and gratifications of Facebook members 35 years and older*, M.A. thesis. University of North Texas. Available at: http://digital.library.unt.edu/ark:/67531/metadc84293/m2/1/high_res_d/thesis.pdf.

Valenzuela, S., Park, N., and Kee, K. F. (2009). Is there social capital in a social network site?: Facebook use and college students' life satisfaction, trust, and participation. *Journal of Computer-Mediated Communication*, 14(4), 875–901.

Wilson, R. E., Gosling, S. D., and Graham, L. T. (2012). A review of Facebook research in the social sciences. *Perspectives on Psychological Science*, 7(3), 203–220.

Wright, K. B., Rosenberg, J., Egbert, N., Ploeger, N. A., Bernard, D. R., and King, S. (2013). Communication competence, social support, and depression among college students: A model of Facebook and face-to-face support network influence. *Journal of Health Communication*, 18(1), 41–57.

8   Blurring boundaries

Social media and boundary maintenance at midlife

Kelly Quinn

Digital media use, as viewed from the perspective of the life course, yields interesting twists on commonly held beliefs about digital life, and midlife is perhaps one of the most interesting yet understudied periods to reveal the everyday impacts. Internet and social media use is frequently examined from the vantage point of younger users, possibly due to their high adoption rates and rapid embrace of new media forms, but this view can be incomplete, as it neglects the effects of accumulated life experience on perceptions, attitudes, and behaviours. Though lagging behind youth and young adults, digital media use by adults at older ages has grown rapidly in recent years (Ofcom, 2014; Smith, 2014b) and, not surprisingly, usage patterns of older persons appear to be different from those of younger persons both in terms of adoption of specific technologies and in how they are employed (Zickuhr, 2010). This signals that embedded relational practices and values may be reflected in everyday digital media use, a condition which potentially offers opportunities to contemplate not only a wider array of uses but also how these technologies might be considered and interpreted differently in various life phases.

This chapter highlights the attitudes and practices of midlife adults surrounding the act of connection on social media platforms. Employing data gathered from in-depth interviews of social media users between the ages of 45 and 65 years, it explores the social strategies that are used, often in combination, as processes of social boundary regulation. These practices and dispositions often result from accumulated life experiences and distinguish social media use at midlife as unique from that of younger persons. Examination of social media use at midlife, therefore, underscores some influential ways in which these technologies have shaped everyday life.

Midlife

Midlife is a life stage that is qualitatively different from other life stages (Neugarten, 1968), and yet it defies definition from a calendar point of view (Wahl and Kruse, 2005), though many estimates peg it as the period between 40 and 60 years of age (Lachman, Teshale and Agrigoroaei, 2014). It is often viewed as a period "in the middle," both because it connects the life phases between "younger" and "older" adulthood (Hunt, 2005; Neugarten, 1971) and also because it defines the midpoint of most individuals' lives. Recognition that one is aging (Atchley, 1988) and an enhanced awareness of the finite nature of life (Carney and Cohler, 1993) characterize midlife, and it has been descriptively termed as the "turning point between the rise and decline of the flow of life" (Wahl and Kruse, 2005, p. 7).

Midlife is an age of both developmental growth and loss: professional expertise and competence in family matters, such as dealing with adolescents, are often accomplished by this life stage, but high-level physical functioning, such as with athletics or fertility, begins to decline (Heckhausen, 2001). At younger ages, cognitive development is strongly influenced by education and training; at older ages, physiological declines play a major role. In contrast, cognitive performance at midlife is seen as being at peak levels for high-order and complex functions such as vocabulary, verbal memory, inductive reasoning, and spatial orientation (Willis and Schaie, 1999).

Though there are exceptions, in general midlife adults tend to be more secure about themselves than their young adult counterparts and have a high level of self-esteem (Robins et al., 2002). They are effective at regulating emotion (Magai and Halpern, 2001), and most have achieved balance among societal expectations, personal goals, and environmental demands (Dörner, Mickler and Staudinger, 2005). Complex relational contexts and the simultaneous fulfillment of contrasting roles are common in midlife (Lachman, 2004). Family obligations are often at a peak during midlife, due to the simultaneous caring for aging relatives and children still living in the home (Martin and Zimprich, 2005), and midlife adults occupy a high number of social roles (Antonucci, Akiyama and Merline, 2001), both as a result of the melding of present and past identities and as a result of a succession of occupational positions. Overall, midlife is a stable life stage from a developmental perspective and, coupled with the numerous and varied social roles that adults at midlife hold, possesses significant value for social research.

Social media, sharing, and connection

All relationships begin somewhere – a chance meeting at a social gathering, being seated next to someone at a meeting. In the world of social media, a relationship begins with the act of connection, sometimes called "friending." Platforms such as Facebook, LinkedIn and Twitter have varying forms of connection: some are uni-directional, or acknowledged by only one party ("following" in the parlance of Twitter); others are bi-directional ("Friends" in the jargon of Facebook). The aggregation of these connections is the equivalence of a social network and, in social media, these networks are publicly visible and personally curated (Ellison and boyd, 2013). Offline friendship networks grow smaller throughout the life course (Kalmijn, 2003), and correspondingly older persons tend to have smaller social networks on social media sites than younger persons (Smith, 2014a). In addition, because the use of social media declines with increasing age (Smith, 2014b), the "network effect" (Easley and Kleinberg, 2010) may also play a role in network size: an individual's social media network will reflect their offline network of relationships that also use the particular social media platform; with fewer social media participants at older ages, a smaller proportion of one's network may be available for connection through a given platform.

A defining characteristic of social media technologies is the sharing of user-generated content. Platforms such as Facebook, LinkedIn, and Twitter are designed to spread the details of daily living with other users with whom an individual shares connection. This information is also provided to platform sponsors, as the platforms often trade on user-generated content to secure and maintain their economic viability. To protect these economic interests, the ways in which information is used and shared are often opaque to the individual (Sar and Al-Saggaf, 2013). In addition, platform privacy tools can be difficult or challenging to effectively employ, and it is not uncommon for information to accidently leak to unintended recipients despite an individual's deployment of the available privacy controls (Strater and Lipford, 2008).

Social media platforms are also designed to address multiple audiences as one, and this quality of broadcast alters the control an individual has over the intended audience for disclosure (Tufekci, 2008). This results in the communication of decontextualized content, when disclosure is communicated beyond the imagined audience (Litt, 2012), and "context collapse" (boyd, 2008), which occurs when disparate social contexts converge into a single space. These qualities challenge the processes associated with social boundary maintenance, a process especially important to relational development (Altman and Taylor, 1983) and to the regulation of privacy (Petronio, 2002).

Finally, activities within digital media possess characteristics related to their digital nature, including, among others: (1) easy replicability, or an ability to be copied and pasted elsewhere; (2) scalability, or the ability to be readily transmitted and forwarded effortlessly to large(r) audiences; and (3) compactness, which allows information that is generated within these platforms to persist over time and be preserved (boyd and Marwick, 2011a; Samuelson, 1990). These characteristics give tangibility to our social actions, leaving digital traces of contact, communication, and connection and permitting examination of social interactions in new ways.

Social boundaries and boundary work

"Boundary" is a metaphor used to delineate the "physical, temporal, emotional, cognitive, and/or relational limits that define entities as separate from one another" (Ashforth, Kreiner and Fugate, 2000, p. 474). Though often unseen, boundaries are integral to the way individuals order their environment and reveal how individuals' identities are structured (Zerubavel, 1991). They arise in environmental contexts, as with making a distinction between home and work; in role identity, such as distinguishing between being a parent and worker; and in privacy negotiation, such as with limiting disclosures. At midlife, adults are required to play many varied and complex roles (Lachman, 2004) and operate in multiple social spheres at once. This provides significant opportunity for establishing boundaries and for boundary crossings and transition, that is, the psychological movement between roles and contexts (Ashforth, Kreiner and

Fugate, 2000). Thus, the challenges of navigating these social boundaries come into sharp focus at midlife, when the variety, number, and complexity of social roles and contexts are great.

Studies of boundary transitions and boundary work, or the strategies, principles, and practices by which we create and maintain cultural categories and role identity (Nippert-Eng, 1996a), are illuminating because they provide insight into the ways in which individuals create and understand their environment and self and how they give meaning to everyday life. Significant attention has been paid to the examination of work–family boundaries in offline contexts (e.g. Ashforth, Kreiner and Fugate, 2000; Nippert-Eng, 1996a, 1996b; Rothbard, Phillips and Dumas, 2005), but few studies have examined how this activity is carried out in online spaces. Activities in the social media milieu reflect a microcosm of this boundary-crossing activity, so the perceptions midlife adults bring to these behaviours and the strategies used to carry out this boundary work online illustrate some of the influences of social media on everyday life.

Midlife adults can provide perspective on the change potential of these newer communication technologies. The Internet's arrival into everyday use occurred approximately in the mid to late 1990s (Haythornthwaite and Wellman, 2002), and by 1998 it was reported to be available in approximately 50 per cent of US high school classrooms (Wells and Lewis, 2006). As this timing places midlife adults as being exposed to the Internet and acquiring the necessary skills for Internet communication technology use well into the life phase of continuous work, they have been able to observe the adaptation processes in their entirety and are therefore able to articulate differences between traditional communication forms and newer platforms such as social media. Because of their later position in the life course and accumulated lived experience, midlife adults' views on boundary management within the social media environment also offer an alternative perspective to the well-studied, younger adult user groups as well.

The use of social media at midlife

Twenty-three social media–using adults, aged 45 to 65 years, participated in in-depth, face-to-face interviews regarding their attitudes toward the Internet, privacy, and social media sites and social strategies related to privacy protection and identity management. The sample was composed of 15 females and eight males; ten participants fell into the younger, 45- to 54-year-old, half of the age range and 13 participants fell into the older, 55- to 64-year-old range. Seventeen of the participants used both Facebook and LinkedIn, while six individuals used one or the other exclusively. While the interviews were conducted as part of a larger study which explored Internet use by midlife adults, this chapter specifically highlights the findings related to privacy negotiation, boundary control strategies, and perceptions related to Internet and social media use.

The interview data was thematically analyzed and clustered into an explanatory framework consistent with the interview texts. Through this process, the connections that are undertaken on social media platforms emerged as an important site for the construction and maintenance of social boundaries at midlife and illustrate ways in which these digital platforms subtly impact the understanding of self and the social environment.

Establishing social boundaries in social media

Individuals differ in the degree of flexibility and permeability of the boundaries between social spheres. Flexible boundaries allow individuals to change the physical time and location in which a role is enacted; permeability refers to the degree to which an individual physically located in one domain must be psychologically concerned with another (Hall and Richter, 1988). The more inflexible a boundary is, the greater the constraints on role performance in alternative environments (Ashforth, Kreiner and Fugate, 2000) and the less opportunity for role identity failure. Social media platforms and their propensity for context collapse have some impact on boundary flexibility; however, by their very nature, they increase the level of boundary permeability between social spheres significantly.

Participants in this study suggested that they sometimes have a preference for keeping certain social spheres distinct and delineated more rigid social boundaries based on the environment of the relationship. A common site of such boundary establishment for many individuals is the work/personal life boundary, and participants in this study described how they navigated between these social spheres. Tim, a participant in the study, described his awareness that connections on social media platforms make his work/personal life boundary more permeable, which, based on previous offline life experiences, was perhaps not a desirable outcome:

> *I'm starting to see this come up more in the forefront of, you know, do you really want your coworker to know, be your friend on Facebook? Do you want them to know things going on in your personal life and things of that nature? I've seen what happens in the old way, when sometimes the wrong person, or someone or something happens, and then all of a sudden there's a "hmm . . ."*

> Tim, Male, Age 54

One mechanism that participants used to make social boundaries less permeable was in the selection of the specific social medium through which they connected with certain individuals. It was not unusual for participants to establish boundaries by connecting with certain individuals on one site, for example, Facebook, but not another, such as LinkedIn. Participants described distinct differences in their perceptions of various social network sites, especially between what they viewed as the "business" or "professional" context of LinkedIn and the "social" or "friends and family" context of Facebook. They described each forum as having certain etiquette, or rules which guide norms and behaviour. Wanda, another participant, described her perception of these differences and highlights some of the underlying reasons for her connection preferences:

> *Okay, I think of LinkedIn by and large as a social network of working people. And as such, since I am old, there's a certain level of decorum and etiquette*

associated with the work place. So, I guess I take comfort that there are certain boundaries that won't be crossed in LinkedIn, whereas you know, Facebook seems like no rules.

Wanda, Female, Age 57

Beyond the question of which social media platform to connect on, participants noted that the decision of not to connect with specific others is also a mechanism to enforce boundary impermeability. For example, the familiarity promoted by the sharing of personal information on social media platforms can be detrimental to role boundary maintenance, so denying a connection is another way in which social boundaries can be enforced. An example given by Sue demonstrated this decision-making process: by *not* connecting with her teenage son's friends, she was able to maintain an appropriate social distance in her role as a parent.

I didn't accept [my] younger kid's friends. I just thought it was kind of inappropriate. . . . I wasn't interested in reading what they had to say on my Facebook feed, and I didn't think they'd be interested in me either. . . . When I tell them that they can't drink in my [home] – you know, these are 18-year olds – I don't want our relationship to be so casual that I comment on their silly things. . . . I think there needs to be that separation between being a parent and you know, being someone's mom.

Sue, Female, Age 54

Segmentation, or the act of boundary creation, also extends beyond the delineation of roles and whether they can be performed in the social media environment. Personal boundaries, or those which an individual may draw to preserve privacy and provide identity, are also enforced in the social media environment. Laura described how her decision not to connect with some individuals reflects the reality of her relationships and reinforces these already-established personal boundaries:

There are actually some people on there (Facebook) that I will not friend, (such as) disagreeable work people that I've worked with. And I'm just like, I know you . . . but at the same time I'm like, no, because I don't want to deal with you in any way, in any format (she laughs).

Laura, Female, Age 46

Finally, a third strategy used by participants to create and maintain social boundaries was the creation of multiple profiles within a given social media platform. Candace described how she created three separate profiles to help reinforce the social roles she enacted in her daily life. By selectively connecting with others using a specific profile, she was able to maintain the various boundaries that segmented her social spheres.

I am a rep for [XYZ Cosmetics Company]. So, in order to reach more people, I have an account [profile] for that. Then I have another account for my

*family and friends. And then, at the church, we are in charge of the youth. So
I also opened another account where I did a small group there, so that we can
communicate with the young people.*

Candace, Female, Age 50

In summary, the strategies used by the participants in this study to define social
boundaries included selection of a particular social media through which connection occurred; careful consideration of the decision to connect with an individual; and creation of multiple profiles to interact in distinct social spheres. These
online practices serve to segment roles and environments, effectively making the
respective social boundaries more rigid, and help guide participants to appropriate behavioural frameworks. In particular, these mechanisms are responsive to the
characteristics of digital media that foster boundary permeability and especially
context collapse but also lend insight to how these digital spaces are interpreted
in the everyday.

Boundary work in social media

The process of managing social boundaries, boundary work, involves the integration, or blurring, of role boundaries as well as the segmentation, or separation,
of roles and environments. In a sense, these two processes are the extremes of a
continuum: for example, the fully integrated work/personal life position would
see "work" and "personal life" as one and the same; in a fully segmented view,
the realms are distinct and have no conceptual overlap. In everyday life, either
extreme is unusual, and the boundary management strategies for most individuals
fall somewhere on this continuum of integration to segmentation (Nippert-Eng,
1996b), depending on individual preferences and identities (Rothbard, Phillips
and Dumas, 2005).

Social media, fundamentally designed to promote the sharing of social information, fosters integration of social boundaries in many ways. The scalability of
social media means that information can move easily among platforms, sometimes in automated ways, spreading easily to larger and wider audiences as it is
repeated and shared. Context collapse requires identity performance in multiple
social spheres at once, as individuals connect with family, friends, co-workers,
and classmates. The compact nature of digital media, which allows for low-cost
data storage, also requires identity integration over time, as personal information
and memories are collected and preserved. The social media strategies and practices that serve to integrate information and identity are therefore also boundary
work in this environment.

A fundamental way in which the participants controlled information flow in
their social media was manifested in their practices of connection. Most of the
participants in this study characterized their connections not just as acquaintances
but as relationships with substance that were grounded in personal history. Often
describing themselves as "picky" and "discriminating" about their connection
decisions, they described "knowing" their connections, with definitions of "knowing" ranging from having knowledge of one's important relationships (typically,

children and/or spouses) and social preferences to having a shared personal history. As Wanda put it, *"We've either been friends or been in a professional relationship at some point"* (Wanda, Female, Age 57). Connection activity which preferences a shared relationship history enables a degree of trust between connections; this permits greater context transparency and minimizes potential harm in the event of a context failure but also evidences an integration activity between an individual's social spheres.

Ignoring connection requests fits into this process too. When a request is received from someone that is not "known," it is sometimes ignored by these participants. As Laura described, *"It's easy enough, I've had a couple of requests that I've ignored. I've not friended them, and then unfriended them. It's just been like, uh, no, ignore"* (Laura, Female, Age 46). These types of requests are placed in a "wait and see" category, to be re-evaluated in the event that the relationship progresses to a more substantial level where integration between social spheres is less threatening.

Some connections form bridges between the environmental boundaries that an individual establishes. A primary example can be found in personal relationships which develop over time between co-workers; these relationships often serve to make established boundaries more permeable. Pat described an example of how certain professional connections had become friends through long-term association; these individuals have become personal friends, and they now naturally shared information about interests and activities outside the workplace. But their presence in her work sphere was not to be confused with other professional connections:

> *And so, it's [social media] a way for us to stay connected and to know that Colleen in Hong Kong is doing Funky Dance and I'm doing Zumba. And I'm okay for her to know I'm doing Zumba, but it's not okay for, you know, the Head of HR [or the] office hacks to know I'm doing Zumba. I don't want to be associated with that. . . . So there's a small group of people that I, it is okay that we know our personal lives.*
>
> Pat, Female, Age 55

Aware that these connections cross the work/personal life boundary, Pat highlights that it is the self-disclosure that occurs in her social media use that makes connection inappropriate with professional contacts. Social media promote self-disclosure in overt ways, such as inviting users to update their status, and in more opaque ways through features such as "like" and "share" buttons. Conscious that information might unintentionally be spread, the midlife adults in this study also carefully consider the information that they post via social media platforms. Discursive strategies, then, are a second form of boundary work in social media environments.

Multiple audiences of varying contexts have the potential to misconstrue the intention or reading of posted content, so participants in this study took active steps to avoid misinterpretation. This is a deliberate process that is accomplished by careful wording and making explicit those circumstances in which humor or sarcasm is a part; it also considers the possibility for varying interpretations of the content. Jayla described the approach she took to posting content and indicated her interest in not presenting conflict with her role as a business owner:

> *Yes, I have to be very careful because I run a business. . . . I had to be very careful about how I phrased my thoughts and what I said so we don't insult anyone's delicate sensibility. . . . And, you know, reputation is everything.*
>
> Jayla, Female, Age 63

Perhaps due to prior experiences with context failure, participants were mistrustful of the privacy controls built into social media platforms. Participants agreed that while privacy controls are a feature of the social media environment that aid in managing social boundaries, continual changes by social network site sponsors and difficulties in deployment led them to lack confidence in their effectiveness. While they used such features to regulate boundaries, participants suggested that they also self-censored their disclosures via social media platforms. Clarice described this process:

> *I make sure that it's not able to be seen by the entire world. And, you know, you never put anything out there that, even if it's a private email from one person to another or even a private post on Facebook, that you wouldn't want your – I mean, my mother has passed [away] – but you wouldn't want your mother to read, you know what I mean? . . . I'm mindful that anybody can read this.*
>
> Clarice, Female, Age 60

Another discursive strategy used to manage boundaries is to post "artificial" content, or content which may be considered false or misleading. Often, the fabricated nature of such content is known to close connections and might include the use of "junk email account" addresses or the use of generalized information, such as claiming a major metropolitan location instead of a smaller hometown. As Fiona described, this strategy helps her navigate personal boundaries:

> *I, when I started out on Facebook. And I mentioned that I do like to protect my privacy. There were a couple things I lied about (she laughs) just from a privacy perspective. And one was my birth date. Not the year, I didn't post the year at all (she laughs), but I lied about the date. . . . Everybody who knows me, knows my age. I'm not shy about that. But I did lie about the birth date, and part of that is because I do use my birth date in a lot of ways they tell you not to use them.*
>
> Fiona, Female, Age 59

Such self-censoring activity is limiting, however, and indicates a lower level of engagement for midlife adults in the social media environment. Rosie described these limitations to expressing her identity, implying that not only is the resulting picture incomplete but also that it is readily decontextualized. Importantly, she acknowledges agency in this boundary navigation:

> *I see the entity of Facebook there. And what I put on there, people are going to respond to that. They're going to see it in a very, very, in a small vacuum. I mean, even though Facebook has gotten a lot better, they're only going to see that one portion of it. And you select what you put on there.*
>
> Rosie, Female, Age 55

Finally, when boundaries become too difficult to maintain, disconnection may also be undertaken as a strategy for boundary curation. Unfriending, or the process of disconnection, was seen as unusual and unnatural by these midlife participants, especially given the careful consideration given to the decision for connection. Unfriending activity decreases as age increases (Madden, 2012), and this may be due in part to the social consequence that it imparts (Bevan, Pfyl and Barclay, 2012). Participants in this study noted that, in their view, it would be better to ignore a request and take time to evaluate the situation rather than undo it. The public nature of the connection activity may be what prompts these midlife participants to respond in this way, but there is also sensitivity to the potential for further damage to the underlying relationship, however weak it may be. As Fiona described:

> *I don't ever want to hurt someone. I mean, I just am cautious friending some-one . . . Have I had friends in my life that I've kind of drifted from on purpose? Yeah. Do I want to do that on a social media where everyone can see it? No, I don't. So I hope I'm never in that situation. You know, because I wouldn't want to do it.*
>
> Fiona, Female, Age 59

Loss of trust in the connection, however, is a fundamental prompt for disconnection, as this effectively makes boundaries permeable and therefore less manageable. Candace described her disconnection for this reason:

> *Yeah, I remember I canceled [the connection], and it's because of the friends that they had and I didn't want my postings to be open to them. When I have friends, I kind of know, either I know or I don't know how their settings are. So if I know that this person has a tendency for narcissism [which for Candace meant openly connecting with unknown others], I don't want her or him as my friend, because I'm afraid whatever I post is open.*
>
> Candace, Female, Age 50

In summary, the integrating boundary work done by midlife adults in their social media use takes several forms. The initial act of connection is carefully considered, as connection with known others is a primary mechanism for boundaries to be coordinated and curated and evidences an acknowledgement that the boundaries between environments and roles are permeable and flexible. Discursive strategies and especially the careful curation of content are a second mechanism for boundary management; by carefully managing the content that is created or placing limits on the accuracy or quality of the information that is produced about oneself, midlife adults are able to integrate multiple environments into a single forum and multiple roles into a unified identity. Finally, disconnection, an alternative taken reluctantly, is a boundary management strategy that is employed when boundary transitions become too difficult to navigate or too uncertain to manage; it is a practice that signals an integration failure and heralds renewed segmentation.

Conclusion

As individuals age, they accumulate a myriad of contexts through which they develop relationships with others. To successfully order their social worlds online and offline, they establish and navigate boundaries to order their environments, accomplish role identities, and manage privacy. Context collapse, inherent in the social media milieu, complicates these processes, especially because they are designed to collapse contexts into a single audience or forum. This challenges the established processes of boundary management and prompts adaptation to navigate the emerging environment.

Midlife adults often accomplish boundary management through implicit social norms and social strategies and carry these processes to their online experiences. These mirror the online practices of teens and young adults, who use strategies such as social steganography and networked privacy to navigate social boundaries in their digital media use (boyd and Marwick, 2011a, 2011b). But teens and young adults often have fewer relationship contexts than midlife adults through which to navigate. It is not that younger people do not have multiple relationship contexts; rather at midlife, there is an accumulated life experience of professional careers, multiple career paths, and role responsibilities that younger persons have not yet experienced. Therefore the ways in which midlife adults segment their environment and role performance in their social media use provide opportunities to understand social boundary navigation in a digital environment in new ways.

Examination of midlife social media practices highlights strategies that are used to segment social spheres and enhance social boundaries, such as the use of multiple social media platforms and the denial of connection, perhaps due to an increased need to perform social roles. It also highlights additional processes of social sphere integration, such as the careful curation of content or adopting a "wait and see" approach toward connection, as these strategies aid in navigating across and transitioning between social worlds and roles. These strategies and practices are not (yet) widely deployed by younger users or even considered acceptable in young adult user groups (McLaughlin and Vitak, 2012), perhaps because of an earlier positioning in the life course; however, they illuminate the subtle ways in which digital media enter and shape our everyday life and interaction with others.

References

Altman, I. and Taylor, D. A., (1983). *Social penetration: The development of interpersonal relationships.* New York: Irvington.

Antonucci, T. C., Akiyama, H. and Merline, A., (2001). Dynamics of social relationships in midlife. In: M. E. Lachman (ed.), *Handbook of midlife development.* New York: John Wiley & Sons. pp. 571–598.

Ashforth, B. E., Kreiner, G. E. and Fugate, M., (2000). All in a day's work: Boundaries and micro role transitions. *Academy of Management Review,* 25(3), pp. 472–491.

Atchley, R. C., (1988). *Social forces and aging: An introduction to social gerontology.* Belmont, CA: Wadsworth Publishing.

Bevan, J. L., Pfyl, J. and Barclay, B., (2012). Negative emotional and cognitive responses to being unfriended on Facebook: An exploratory study. *Computers in Human Behaviour,* 28(4), pp. 1458–1464.

boyd, d., (2008). Facebook's privacy trainwreck: Exposure, invasion, and social convergence. *Convergence: The International Journal of Research into New Media Technologies,* 14(1), pp. 13–20.

boyd, d. and Marwick, A. E., (2011a). Social steganography: Privacy in networked publics. *International Communication Association Annual Conference,* Boston, MA, 28 May.

boyd, d. and Marwick, A. E., (2011b). Social privacy in networked publics: Teens' attitudes, practices, and strategies. *Privacy Law Scholars Conference,* Berkeley, CA, 2 June.

Carney, J. K. and Cohler, B. J., (1993). Developmental continuities and adjustment in adulthood: Social relations, morale, and the transformation from middle to late life. In: G. H. Pollack and S. I. Greenspan (eds), *The course of life: Volume VI. Late adulthood.* Madison, WI: International Universities Press, pp. 199–226.

Dörner, J., Mickler, C. and Staudinger, U. M., (2005). Self-development at midlife. In: S. L. Willis and M. Martin (eds), *Middle adulthood: A lifespan perspective.* Thousand Oaks, CA: Sage. pp. 277–317.

Easley, D. and Kleinberg, J., (2010). Network effects. In: D. Easley and J. Kleinberg (eds), *Networks, crowds, and markets: Reasoning about a highly connected world.* New York: Cambridge University Press. pp. 509–542.

Ellison, N. B. and boyd, d., (2013). Sociality through social network sites. In: W. H. Dutton (ed.), *The Oxford handbook of Internet studies.* Oxford, UK: Oxford University Press. pp. 151–172.

Hall, D. T. and Richter, J., (1988). Balancing work life and home life: What can organizations do to help? *Academy of Management Executive,* 2(3), pp. 213–223.

Heckhausen, J., (2001). Adaptation and resilience at midlife. In: M. E. Lachman (ed.), *Handbook of midlife development.* New York: John Wiley & Sons. pp. 345–394.

Haythornthwaite, C. and Wellman, B., (2002). The Internet in everyday life: An introduction. In: C. Haythornthwaite and B. Wellman (eds), *The Internet in everyday life.* Malden, MA: Blackwell. pp. 3–41.

Hunt, S., (2005). The challenge of mid-life. In: S. Hunt. *The life course: A sociological introduction.* New York: Palgrave MacMillan. pp. 169–183.

Kalmijn, M., (2003). Shared friendship networks and the life course: An analysis of survey data on married and cohabiting couples. *Social Networks,* 25(3), pp. 231–249.

Lachman, M. E., (2004). Development in midlife. *Annual Review of Psychology,* 55, pp. 305–331.

Lachman, M. E., Teshale, S. and Agrigoroaei, S., (2014). Midlife as a pivotal period in the life course: Balancing growth and decline at the crossroads of youth and old age. *International Journal of Behavioral Development,* 39(1), pp. 20–31.

Litt, E., (2012). Knock, knock. Who's there? The imagined audience. *Journal of Broadcasting & Electronic Media*, 56(3), pp. 330–345.

Madden, M., (2012), 24 Feb. *Privacy management on social media sites*. Washington, DC: Pew Research Center. Available at: http://www.pewinternet.org/2012/02/24/privacy-management-on-social-media-sites/ [Accessed July 12, 2013].

Magai, C. and Halpern, B., (2001). Emotional development during the middle years. In: M. E. Lachman (ed.), *Handbook of midlife development*. New York: John Wiley & Sons. pp. 310–344.

Martin, M. and Zimprich, D., (2005). Cognitive development in midlife. In: S. L. Willis and M. Martin (eds), *Middle adulthood: A lifespan perspective*. Thousand Oaks, CA: Sage. pp. 179–206.

McLaughlin, C. and Vitak, J., (2012). Norm evolution and violation on Facebook. *New Media & Society*, 14(2), pp. 299–315.

Neugarten, B. L., (1968). The awareness of middle age. In: B. L. Neugarten (ed.), *Middle age and aging: A reader in social psychology*. Chicago: University of Chicago Press. pp. 93–98.

Neugarten, B. L., (1971). Grow older with me: The best is yet to be. *Psychology Today*, 5(2), pp. 45–48.

Nippert-Eng, C. E., (1996a). Calendars and keys: The classification of "home" and "work." *Sociological Forum*, 11(3), pp. 563–582.

Nippert-Eng, C. E., (1996b). *Home and work: Negotiating boundaries through everyday life*. Chicago: University of Chicago Press.

Ofcom, (2014). *Adults' Media Use and Attitudes Report*. London: Ofcom. Available at: http://stakeholders.ofcom.org.uk/market-data-research/other/research-publications/adults/adults-media-lit-14/.

Petronio, S., (2002). *Boundaries of privacy: Dialectics of disclosure*. Albany: State University of New York Press.

Robins, R. W., Trzesniewski, K. H., Tracy, J. L., Gosling, S. D. and Potter, J., (2002). Global self-esteem across the life span. *Psychology and Aging*, 17(3), pp. 423–434.

Rothbard, N. P., Phillips, K. W. and Dumas, T. L., (2005). Managing multiple roles: Work-family policies and individuals' desires for segmentation. *Organization Science*, 16(3), pp. 243–258.

Samuelson, P., (1990). Digital media and the changing face of intellectual property law. *Rutgers Computer and Technology Law Journal*, 16(2), pp. 323–340.

Sar, R. K. and Al-Saggaf, Y., (2013). Propagation of unintentionally shared information and online tracking. *First Monday*, 18(6). Available at: http://firstmonday.org/ojs/index.php/fm/article/view/4349/3681 [Accessed January 17, 2015].

Smith, A., (2014a), 3 Feb. *6 new facts about Facebook*. FactTank: News in the Numbers. Available at: http://www.pewresearch.org/fact-tank/2014/02/03/6-new-facts-about-facebook/ [Accessed January 17, 2015].

Smith, A., (2014b), 4 Apr. *Older adults and technology use*. Washington, DC: Pew Internet & American Life Project. Available at: http://www.pewinternet.org/2014/04/03/older-adults-and-technology-use/.

Strater, K. and Lipford, H. R., (2008). Strategies and struggles with privacy in an online social networking community. In: D. England (ed.), *BCS-HCI '08 proceedings of the 22nd British HCI group annual conference on people and computers: Culture, creativity, interaction – volume 1*. British Computer Society, pp. 111–119.

Tufekci, Z., (2008). Can you see me now? Audience and disclosure regulation in online social network sites. *Bulletin of Science, Technology & Society*, 28(1), pp. 20–36.

Wahl, H.-W. and Kruse, A., 2005. Historical perspective of middle age within the life span. In: S. L. Willis and M. Martin (eds), *Middle adulthood: A lifespan perspective*. Thousand Oaks, CA: Sage. pp. 3–34.

Wells, J. and Lewis, L., (2006). *Internet access in U.S. public schools and classrooms: 1994–2005* (NCES 2007–020). Washington, DC: U.S. Department of Education, National Center for Education Statistics. Available at: http://nces.ed.gov/pubsearch/pub sinfo.asp?pubid=2007020.

Willis, S. L. and Schaie, K., (1999). Intellectual functioning in midlife. In: S. L. Willis and J. D. Reid (eds), *Life in the middle: Psychological and social development in middle age*. San Diego, CA: Academic Press. pp. 234–247.

Zerubavel, E., (1991). *The fine line: Making distinctions in everyday life*. New York: The Free Press.

Zickuhr, K., (2010). *Generations 2010*. Washington, DC: Pew Research Center. Available at: http://pewinternet.org/~/media//Files/Reports/2010/PIP_Generations_and_Tech10. pdf.

9 Retrospective narratives about life with anxiety

Considering the role of the Internet for sufferers across the life course

Catherine Brooks

Introduction

Today, millions of people in the United States suffer from anxiety and anxiety-related disorders. From general anxiety disorder (GAD) to post-traumatic stress disorder (PTSD) and obsessive-compulsive disorder (OCD), this growing mental health crisis has been only marginally examined by social scientists studying eHealth or the Internet. This particular chapter examines how those suffering from mental illness and anxiety engage the Internet across the life course. The life course approach for understanding the role of the Internet relative to mental health suffering is particularly valuable because many people experience heightened illness effects during certain periods or around events tied to particular life stages. Sometimes events can happen at any life stage (e.g. abuse), and other events are directly tied to a particular life period (e.g. military involvement) – though these events happen differentially across time periods, they have an acute impact on mental health. Child labour is an example of an experience that is particularly tied to certain life stage and has been clearly linked to some illnesses related to anxiety (Lochner et al., 2002, Vasconcelos et al., 2007). Thus, a focus on the life course and the role of the Internet for support across periods is particularly germane to understanding mental health and the role of the Internet in anxiety's evolution over time.

The rise of the Internet shepherded in a variety of shifts in health care. With foci on how people find health information, how they find support as patients or caregivers, how they engage as members of online health communities, or how people navigate new data management tools and plans, researchers from across the academic spectrum have taken interest in studies of eHealth. Kivits (2014) describes the importance of Internet-related health studies overall, describing eHealth research in this way:

> A vast literature on the Internet and health care has emerged over the last decade. Studies in this area have the peculiarity of drawing on a range of disciplines, including medicine, sociology, psychology, geography, IT, and

information studies. The result has been the emergence of a new field of study, often referred to as eHealth studies, a generic term for research examining health and the Internet.

(p. 992)

Interest in the Internet relative to health management and wellness is thus a broad and continually burgeoning area for practitioners, scholars, and other readers from across sectors and fields of work or study.

The Internet can provide a means of support for sufferers and their families, and certainly a number of practitioners and researchers are paying attention to the various roles it plays in health management. Some scholars situate the Internet as a source of knowledge and information (e.g. Dolce, 2011) or as a place for sharing personal health scores and progress, as in the example of sharing blood sugar readings for diabetes management (Hunt and Koteyko, 2015). Other studies situate the Internet as a place for finding social and community support for struggles tied to depression (e.g. Houston et al., 2014), cancer (e.g. Bender et al., 2011), sexual violence (e.g. Yeager, 2011), psychiatric disabilities (e.g. Kaplan et al., 2011), or other medical concerns. Scholars like Shillair, Rikard, Cotton, and Tsai (2015) examine online social support for aging adults, and others, like Whittaker et al. (2008), focus on youth interventions and the Internet. This particular chapter examines anxiety sufferers as a particular group of people struggling with mental health issues and complements a body of literature that examines Internet use for social connection across life periods. The Internet provides a safe and potentially anonymized site for finding information and sharing experiences with others, so stigmatized health issues like anxiety and related mental concerns or distinctly private disorders like OCD (Brooks, 2011) provide a particularly rich basis for eHealth discussions among Internet researchers.

For this study, the Internet is situated as an influential site through which mental health sufferers seek assistance, knowledge, advice, guidance, support, and social connections with others. Though most involved in this current project were not familiar with the Internet in their youth (i.e. it did not exist for most when they were young), this work interrogates how people of differing ages utilized or intersected with the Internet as they aged and how their talk about online support is informed by previous life periods. To that end, the following research questions guided this particular project:

R1: How does the Internet function across the life course for anxiety sufferers?
R2: How does the Internet get integrated into the stories of anxiety sufferers, and how are those stories of Internet use informed by previous life periods?

This research

This study relied on an interpretive methodological design involving life history interviews with nine participants (audio recorded and 1–2 hours in length) that were transcribed and functioned as empirical data. The interviews talk about living with anxiety was analyzed iteratively, beginning with a broad reading, then the assignment of initial codes, then a narrowing to a smaller set of broad themes (Miles and Huberman, 1994). The interpretive coding procedures for this study follow those that typify qualitative work, analytic processes that are prescribed in a number of relevant reference materials (Creswell, 2007, Humphreys, 2005, Silverman, 2000). Given the focus on human stories, and because anxiety issues typically happen in coordination with a set of other mental health concerns (see for review Friborg et al., 2013, Goes et al., 2012, Marcks et al., 2011), an interpretive research approach was warranted to examine, from the data themselves, how the Internet emerges in and works across people's life stories.

Participants were recruited from a network of people involved with a large online support group, and all recruitment and interview procedures to include an informed consent process were carried out with approval from an institutional review board. After the first few interviews with participants recruited from the online support community, this research relied on a snowball sampling technique, a kind of referral process in order to reach others willing to tell their stories of living with anxiety. The conversations with interviewees were unstructured, always began with a broad opener such as "tell me about your life with anxiety," and while the researcher guided the life-story narration to a degree, the interviewer interfered little with each participant's pattern of storytelling. To protect participants' identities, a set of pseudonyms is used in the next sections that present the findings that emerged from this project.

Findings

Across the life course, for these participants, the role of the Internet was distinct for each participant and shifted over time. Most interviewees had lived long enough to recall not having the Internet when they were young but talked about using the Internet now to find information, to learn about their symptoms, and to meet other people in similar life scenarios. Many were like Gwen, a participant who viewed the Internet as an ongoing source of "news and companionship" over time. The findings of this work speak to variegated periods along the life course, pointing to the role of the Internet for youth, teens, and mid- to late-life adults – regretfully, aged or elderly adults were not involved in this study, a population deserving additional research. The primary themes working across life stages were tied to learning about one's illness or disability by hearing the stories of others (i.e. the comfort afforded by learning about the experiences of others, the fear that ensues when hearing about difficulties), as well as the mixed experiences in and perspectives on online communities for health support. These primary themes are the focus of the next sections.

Using the Internet to learn about illness

The Internet functioned for many as a tool for finding out about particular mental health issues, and for most, that information seeking happened early in life. As mentioned, most interviewees did not have access to the Internet as children, but Seth was a younger participant – he explained that his mother had turned to online venues in order to find out more about his particular mental health issues. Others were like Seth and his mother, seeking out information online in the early stages of their illnesses. Some spoke of not having any idea that they were suffering from their particular mental health issue without having read listed symptoms on the Internet – if not making these connections as youth, most engaged in this kind of information-seeking behavior as young adults.

Ann, the youngest interviewee, was a teen participant, and was unique in her level of involvement with others online. She reported being very involved in a teen-based and youth-directed online support community. Instead of learning about her issues from websites or organized online resource materials, she learned the most from hearing the stories of others. She explained:

> Well, I learn more and more when I hear about people's stories. I learn about symptoms that I haven't even been through. It makes me realize how much people are really – how much people suffer . . . it almost makes me feel better knowing officially that there's tons of people out there that are going through the same thing. Now that I know how to deal with it, I feel really good being able to read the stories and help people get through them . . . . I like being able to learn more about people and help them.

As the youngest participant in this research, she talked about the online community discussing youthful topics like how to get by "at school." Her voice was a particular window into the stories told by teens, a view into how members of her population wrangle with, learn about, and share in their mental health concerns.

Hearing the experiences of others online was of particular benefit for most participants – Ann was one of several who recognized the power of stories online. She explained that "every story is interesting and is completely unique" and especially helpful to hear and absorb. Kathy actually had little sense of what she was experiencing in her life until hearing the stories of others online – she figured out her issue by accident while listening to someone talk about their day-to-day challenges tied to their mental health issues. Kathy was concerned about her own "getting really angry when things would just, [when] people would do things that were just not right," and she noticed she reacted more extremely than others around her. Once she had a sense of what was happening for her based on people telling their stories online, she went after particular kinds of information (e.g. looking up specific symptoms) on the Internet. She said "the Internet was just there, and I started reading up on things. I didn't have the typical, I had more of the atypical stuff." Kathy implied that the atypical nature of her struggle rendered her diagnosis difficult – the Internet gave her the space to explore some of her symptoms, to hear the stories of others, and to work to understand what was happening for her.

In addition to learning from the stories themselves, participants reported that connecting socially with online community members was also helpful. Gwen explained how she just felt generally better after talking online with others. She explained that up until her connecting with those in an online group with a similar mental health issue, she'd "never spoken to another person" with a comparable set of problems. She said:

> Suddenly I was in a [chat] room with 15, 16 people who all had it, I listened to all their stories. We were all so similar with the same kind of thoughts and feelings and the worries about, "Am I ever gonna feel good again?" It was just incredible to know that there were other people that had the same thing I did. Yeah, very, very – just extremely comforting . . .

For Gwen and others like her, beyond being helped by stories shared by other people online, the social connections enhanced their overall sense of comfort. However, there were also some negative aspects of hearing the stories of others online, as discussed next.

The dark side of Internet-based stories

Certainly stories can function to shape the meaning of events, and stories are carved tales of personal experiences. But they can bring about a variety of outcomes for the audience members for whom the story is told. For these participants, the impact of stories was not always viewed positively.

Some feared sharing stories online because they might hurt other members of their community. Gwen, for example, reported a similar kind of fear, talking about a friend who took great care and responsibility with regard to sharing stories, experiences, and advice online. She talked about this friend of hers as someone who "has an obsessive fear that she will say something that will cause someone harm."

Others reported having been hurt by hearing the stories of others online. Certainly Mike was one of these participants, voicing a downside to engaging people on the Internet for sharing stories. In expressing how he felt when he was first diagnosed, he had this to say:

> Well, initially, I went online, which was probably the worst thing that I could do. In a lot of the comment forums . . . and online support groups, you have a lot of people who will say stuff like, "It's getting worse." "I've been dealing with this in its worst form for decades." When I was at my bottom, I just thought, "There's no way, I would probably kill myself if I had to be like this for the rest of my life," and I meant it. It was horrible.

Mike explained that he was severely and negatively impacted by hearing some of the stories of others. He evolved and, over time and upon reaching his midlife, he learned to survive with and manage his particular challenges – but his memories of those early stories heard online vastly differ from the positive story-sharing experiences of Ann and others.

Uniquely for Ben, events across the life course impacted the way that he heard, received, and considered his own online story sharing. Ben was kind of an extreme case, explaining that he "would not want to bother others or trust people" with his stories, emotions, and experiences on the Internet. When asked more about his concerns with sharing in the online support group, he asserted, "I don't want my personal information in anybody else's house." Ben reflected on his military background in his youth and how that shaped his thinking about himself, the assumptions made about sharing experiences and emotions online. In some ways, Ben seemed to take on a compassionless stance, calling members of online support communities "whiners" and explaining that he did not want to engage in that way. He explained that he had been taught as a child to "be a man" and not share his difficulties with others – he trusted his medical doctor only. Ben's perspective and potential to engage in an online community as a middle-aged suffering man was influenced by his military training and early-year development. The Internet, indeed, functions in particular ways for differing online participants, but one's previous and youthful experiences inform how they see themselves in relation to the Internet to begin with. The next section moves into analyzing talk about online communities and related participation more directly.

The online support community

A few participants had experience with online support groups that went beyond participation – they acted as facilitators and in some cases they'd originated their own groups of various types. Gwen offers a particularly poignant tale of the beginnings of one of several online support communities for those suffering mental health issues. She was just about 30 years old when she began doing this kind of work and now is facilitating a large online support group for those suffering from particular kinds of mental health issues. She explained the development of her group:

> [I]n 1993 – we had just gotten our first computer in 1990 – and I had joined little groups online for cat lovers and for, I had guinea pigs at the time, so I joined a guinea pig owners group. One day I said, "Whoa, hey, I wonder if there's a support group somewhere on here." I was on the Prodigy network back then, which is long gone, but I went onto their health bulletin board. . . . so I posted a message, and . . . I started to get responses from people, and so I had a – we have a little group of about maybe five or six people that were talking about it, and that was the beginning of what I do today. I started out with five people, and now I have 4,200 *[laughter]*.

Like Gwen and as mentioned previously, Ann was very involved in an online community, but Ann's work was designed for teens in particular and a group that had formed only recently. Her group was smaller than Gwen's, and she explained, "I think there's about a hundred members now." She also described the composition of the online community: "It is international. I don't know how people find out about it. There's somebody from Indonesia. There's somebody from England. I'm like, 'Whoa, that's pretty cool.'" Across the life course, Gwen had more than 20 years of memories encompassing the onset of the Internet in her life of mental illness, while Ann used the Internet currently – she was a teen talking about teen talk online. These two cases, in particular, exhibit some of the distinct perspectives offered by participants of differing ages and how their experiences are indeed influenced by their existence within distinct life stages. For both Gwen and Ann, online communities were viewed as beneficial for participants and facilitators, but as was the case with online stories, there were also difficulties expressed among participants with regard to sharing in online communities.

The dark side of sharing online

As described previously, Ben faced difficulty sharing with others online and lacked trust in the process – feelings he explained were spurred by his particular kind of upbringing and also by his military involvement. Like Ben, Seth also lacked some degree of trust in the online support process and talked about the social indifference found online. He was not hesitant to share his stories and experiences online with strangers, but he knew his input might not be received well. He explained this idea this way:

> I think what's hard sometimes . . . but I feel like it's not just that list. I feel like it's just online in general . . . there's no compassion. They're looking at words on a screen. I know if I have a conversation with someone online or through text it can be much more cold [compared to face-to-face talk].

Seth pointed to the coldness in the medium itself – that sometimes the Internet lends itself to unsympathetic, unkind, emotionless, and impersonal interactions when heartfelt responses and earnest recognition are needed, especially in the context of mental health suffering, experiences, and related stories. When humans need empathy, they may be met with distance and impersonal contact, from Seth's perspective.

Seth also explained a kind of "double edge" to the online community. While a site for support, sharing similar stories, and talking with like-minded or similarly struggling people, it also holds potential as a place for misaligned notions of appropriateness.

> I know one thing that I always tell people is, when I was sick I would imagine myself on a podium in front of an audience of like 2000. I would say what I do. I would imagine would everybody in the audience go, "Yeah. Yeah. Absolutely, I do that all the time." or would everybody look at me like what the hell? For me it was like I would stand up there and say I cannot buy anything at a grocery store that is in the same aisle as the pest control stuff . . .

Seth went on to explain that this kind of thinking worked to help him know when his behaviours were out of synch with what non-sufferers were doing in their day-to-day lives. Though he was just trying to convey the kind of audience needed when trying to discern how problematic his behaviours were, one can imagine that this kind of scenario would not work with an online audience built around like-minded thinking and shared experiences. The very nature of human–human comparisons and the way people socially negotiate a shared sense of normalcy are mediated by the Internet in the online support group. Most in the online community were likely ready to help Seth know what behaviours were appropriate and which were inappropriate, but Seth began to articulate that there may be differences in the degree to which or how online and face-to-face supporters measure and "call out" inappropriate behaviour. Given the international and distributed nature of the online support group, its members may have less of a firm grip on what is considered "normal" behaviour given the lack of physically, geographically, and locally contextualized cultural knowledge. Future research – especially given what Goffman (1959) says about contextualized performance and norms of behaviour – ought to push these ideas forward and interrogate them specifically in the context of online mental health support.

Overall, the findings uncovered by this study suggest that computing histories over the life course were different for each interviewee. Ann as a teen is online now, and Gwen began her computing life in 1990 – she remembers the Prodigy network. Seth's age lies somewhere between that of Ann and Gwen, and his memories of Internet use in his youth are non-existent with the exception of his mother's reach online for information about her son's mental health. Ben is middle-aged (late 40s), does not trust the Internet as a safe space for sharing, and was always taught to keep emotions in "like a man." While all participants gave voice to these varying perspectives, those quoted here in this chapter are simply those whose words most clearly exemplify salient themes in the data. The next and final section offers some final discussion points on how this line of research on Internet use for sufferers of mental health issues can be understood and advanced.

Concluding remarks

By considering the role of the Internet for mental health sufferers, we can uncover new understandings of anxiety as a lived social experience in a mediated age. By engaging a set of interviews analytically from a life course perspective, this chapter points to some of the ways Internet use may shift over time and also how it may morph relative to life events and age periods. Across age groups, hearing the stories of others online was asserted to be important but also in some cases problematic. Across participants, too, making social connections in communities beyond just the stories themselves was a helpful endeavour for one's sense of knowing, hope, and health management even though online venues may seem "cold" from time to time. This chapter also addresses how youth development may inform how the Internet is utilized later in life – a point Ben exemplified.

With an increasing reliance on the Internet for health information seeking, for sharing in the doctor-patient-health management processes, and for participating in online health communities, a focus on how these processes happen across life periods is an important site for continued research. While the Internet functioned to connect these participants in this study with others in varying ways, some of these social connections (e.g. connecting sufferers with one another, connecting sufferers with doctors who were paying attention) may well have literally saved lives. Therefore, the importance of the Internet across the life stage, though it is experienced differentially across ages and contexts, cannot be missed.

Findings presented here may offer insight and implication for mental health interventions and treatment. Not to say that treatment or caregiving were salient goals of this project, but readers from across the patient, caregiver, medical practitioner, and scholar spectrum will find meaning in the data presented in this chapter. These findings point to additional areas for study, such as (1) how the Internet exists as a tool and also as an integrated system of social networks needed when people face anxiety-producing life events in their day to day lives, (2) how people might engage in identity work related to their anxiety management (e.g. avoiding social stigma, enacting roles deemed appropriate within and across public and private contexts), and (3) how some of the more traditional modes of treatment and support (e.g. face-to-face clinic sessions, conferences) are working alongside some of the continually emerging avenues for Internet-based support (e.g. online sites, eHealth) in the daily lives of contemporary sufferers. Additional research in these areas is certainly warranted along with additional focus on aged populations, who were not readily available for participation in this project.

This work contributes to an ongoing conversation about the interplay between human life and the Internet, not that the Internet is simply a thing humans take up and use when needed but rather that lives are connected and health management, recovery, and wellness are domains shot through with mediated connectivity. Speaking specifically about social networking and health, Koteyko, Hunt, and Gunter (2015) put it this way:

> Aside from the binary rhetoric of hope and fear, visions of SNSs based on tool metaphors separate the technology from its users as well as from the contexts of its use. This representation of SNSs in isolation, as a tool adding certain features to online health-related activities (or impacting on them) is reductive, implying that the concepts of online participation, health and illness management and social media are both already known and unchanging. Taking into account the diverse and multiple factors that shape health-related behavior we should instead be focusing on why, when and how these new technologies contribute to the everyday management of illness.
>
> (p. 480)

This chapter gets beyond an analysis of Internet activity as tool use and into this ongoing conversation about the fluidity with which lives unfold and happen with emerging technologies.

The Internet and its related technologies are taken up by humans differentially over time, but how people perceive the Internet, its history, its role in their life, and appropriate online activity shift, change, and are impacted by stages in the life course. The Internet is a site through which more than just human connections and information-seeking processes happen, although many will and should continue to examine factors that impact online information retrieval (e.g. Hogan et al., 2015, Scaioli et al., 2015). A large number of scholars continue to point to the Internet as an information "resource" and call for future work considering how its resources are organized (e.g. Kernisan et al., 2010). This chapter, however, argues that there is a sociality overall to the ways in which the Internet gets taken up and situated in memory and in differing stages of the life course – this is not a new argument but one to be emphasized. Health care professionals, Internet or eHealth scholars, and others will be helped by continually thinking about the ways the Internet phases in and through people's lives over time and by continuing to consider the important social processes at work beyond the level of information seeking or online searching techniques.

References

Allen, J. L., Rapee, R. M., & Sandberg, S. (2008). Severe life events and chronic adversities as antecedents to anxiety in children: A matched control study. *Journal of Abnormal Child Psychology*, 36, 1047–1056.

Bender, J. L., Jimenez-Marroquinn, M.-C., & Jadad, A. R. (2011). Seeking support on facebook: A content analysis of breast cancer groups. *Journal of Medical Internet Research*, 13. Retrieved from: http://www.jmir.org/2011/1/e16/.

Brooks, C. F. (2011). Social performance and secret ritual: Battling against obsessive-compulsive disorder. *Qualitative Health Research*, 21, 249–261.

Creswell, J. W. (2007). *Qualitative inquiry and research design: Choosing among five approaches*. Thousand Oaks, CA: Sage Publications, Inc.

Dolce, M. C. (2011). The Internet as a source of health information: Experiences of cancer survivors and caregivers with healthcare providers. *Oncology Nursing Forum*, 38, 353–359.

Friborg, O., Martinussen, M., Kaiser, S., Overgard, K. T., & Rosenvinge, J. H. (2013). Comorbidity of personality disorders in anxiety disorders: A meta-analysis of 30 years of research. *Journal of Affective Disorders*, 145, 143–155.

Goes, F. S., McCusker, M. G., Bienvenu, O. J., Mackinnon, D. F., Mondimore, F. M., Schweizer, B., Depaulo, J. R., & Potash, J. B. (2012). Comorbid anxiety disorders in bipolar disorder and major depression: Familial aggregation and clinical characteristics of comorbid panic disorder, social phobia, specific phobia and obsessive compulsive disorder. *Psychological Medicine*, 42, 1449–1459.

Goffman, E. (1959). *The presentation of self in everyday life*. New York: Doubleday.

Gothelf, D., Aharonovsky, O., Horesh, N., Carty, T., & Apter, A. (2004). Life events and personality factors in children and adolescents with obsessive-compulsive disorder and other anxiety disorders. *Comprehensive Psychiatry*, 45, 192–198.

Hogan, T. P., Hill, J. N., Locatelli, S., Weaver, F. M., Thomas, F. P., Nazi, K. M., Goldstein, B., & Smith, B. M. (2015). Health information seeking and technology use among veterans with spinal cord injuries and disorders. *PM&R*. Retrieved from: http://www.sciencedirect.com/science/article/pii/S1934148215007522.

Houston, T. K., Cooper, L. A., & Ford, D. E. (2014). Internet support groups for depression: a 1-year prospective cohort study. *American Journal of Psychiatry*, 159(12), 2062–2028.

Humphreys, M. (2005). Getting personal: Reflexivity and autoethnographic vignettes. *Qualitative Inquiry*, 11, 840–860.

Hunt, D. & Koteyko, N. 2015. "What was your blood sugar reading this morning?" Representing diabetes self-management on Facebook. *Discourse and Society*, 26, 445–463.

Kaplan, K., Salzer, M. S., Solomon, P., Brusilovskiy, E., & Cousounis, P. (2011). Internet peer support for individuals with psychiatric disabilities: A randomized controlled trial. *Social Science & Medicine*, 72, 54–62.

Kernisam, L. P., Sudore, R. L., & Knight, S. J. (2010). Information-seeking at a caregiving website: A qualitative analysis. *Journal of Medical Internet Research*, 12. Retrieved from: http://www.jmir.org/2010/3/e31/?utm.

Kivits, J. (2014). Health, the Internet, and media. In: Cockerham, W. C., Dingwall, R., & Quah, S. R. (eds), *The Wiley Blackwell encyclopedia of health, illness, behavior, and society*. New York: John Wiley & Sons.

Koteyko, N., Hunt, D., & Gunter, B. (2015). Expectations in the field of the Internet and health: An analysis of claims about social networking sites in clinical literature. *Sociology of Health & Illness*, 37, 468–484.

Lochner, C., Du Toit, P. L., Zungu-Dirwayi, N., Marais, A., Van Kradenburg, J., Seedat, S., Niehaus, D. J. H., & Stein, D. J. (2002). Childhood trauma in obsessive-compulsive disorder, trichotillomania, and controls. *Depression and Anxiety*, 15, 66–68.

Marcks, B. A., Weisberg, R. B., Dyck, I., & Keller, M. B. (2011). Longitudinal course of obsessive-compulsive disorder in patients with anxiety disorders: A 15-year prospective follow-up study. *Comprehensive Psychiatry*, 52, 670–677.

Miles, M. B. & Huberman, A. M. (1994). *An expanded resource: Qualitative data analysis*. Thousand Oaks, CA: Sage.

Scaioli, G., Bert, F., Galis, V., Brussaferro, S., De Vito, E., La Torre, G., Manzoli, L., Messina, G., Torregrossa, M., & Ricciardi, W. (2015). Pregnancy and Internet: Sociodemographic and geographic differences in e-health practice. Results from an Italian multicenter study. *Public Health*, 129(9), 1258–1266.

Shillair, R., Rikard, R., Cotten, S., & Tsai, H. (2015). Not So Lonely Surfers: Loneliness, Social Support, Internet Use and Life Satisfaction in Older Adults. *iConference 2015 Proceedings*. Retrieved from: https://www.ideals.illinois.edu/bitstream/handle/2142/73666/218_ready.pdf?sequence=2.

Silverman, D. 2000. Analyzing talk and text. In: Denzin, N. K., & Lincoln, Y. S. (eds), *Handbook of qualitative research* (pp. 821–834). Thousand Oaks, CA: Sage Publications, Inc.

Vasconcelos, M. S., Sampaio, A. S., Hounie, A. G., Akkerman, F., Curi, M., Lopes, A. C., & Miguel, E. C. (2007). Prenatal, perinatal, and postnatal risk factors in obsessive–compulsive disorder. *Biological Psychiatry*, 61, 301–307.

Whittaker, R., Maddison, R., McRobbie, H., Bullen, C., Denny, S., Dorey, E., Ellis-Pegler, M., Van Rooyen, J., & Rodgers, A. (2008). A multimedia mobile phone–based youth smoking cessation intervention: Findings from content development and piloting studies. *Journal of Medical Internet Research*, 10(5), e49.

Yeager, J. 2012. A content analysis of an online support group for survivors of sexual violence. In: Smedberg, A. (ed.), *E-health communities and online self-help groups: Applications and usage* (pp. 85–106). Hershey, PA: IGI Global.

10 Older adults and social media

Foreshadowing challenges of the digital future?

Kelly Quinn

Scholarship on the use of media at older ages, while not an emerging field, is an area that has received increasing attention in recent years due to the ubiquity of digital media in today's society. Primarily arising in the disciplines of computer science, information science and gerontology, this research offers sharp contrasts to digital media use studies that are undertaken from the perspectives of the young. Studies of youth and young adults often provide views of user attitudes and emerging practices and acknowledgement of the widespread engagement in digital media at these ages. Research on these populations frequently highlights opportunities for future platform development and underexplored dimensions of values and norms or the individual user social and psychological characteristics that are invoked or exploited during use.

Studies of older adults, in contrast, are frequently focused on aspects of digital media non-use or the barriers to increased digital media usage, as well as the potential benefits that increased digital media participation may hold for those at older ages. This overt presumption that increased digital engagement at older ages is highly desirable holds strong undertones of digital utopianism; however, it also reflects national policy efforts toward digital inclusion, as societies and governments increase reliance on the Internet as a primary communication medium for shopping, banking and access to government services. Because studies of older adult digital media use focus on dimensions of non-use, however, they portend some of the practical ways in which routines have *not* been impacted by the presence of digital media and, at the same time, emphasize areas in which digital media might become more relevant or useful to daily living.

As a specific form of digital media, social media have rapidly moved to the forefront in terms of everyday use for many adults today and asserted their prominence for social connection in a digital world. A review of the literature on older adults and social media engagement, then, becomes an important mechanism for understanding of not only how these media might be better integrated and ingrained in everyday life but also the future challenges that these media forms may hold for younger persons.

To provide opportunities for such insight, this chapter will review literature on older adults and social media. It will begin with an overview of how aging processes overlap with technology use and then highlight prevailing research themes. Finally, it will highlight the predominant theoretical frameworks that have guided this research and suggest new directions for study. Such a review will not only aid in understanding of social media's impact on those at older ages but also provide a broader understanding on how digital media shapes everyday living at all ages.

At the intersection of aging and technology

Despite today's older adults being healthier and better educated than previous generations, physical, perceptual and cognitive changes coincident with aging present some unique challenges to the use of the Internet and especially social media. As one ages, physical changes result in declines in response times, coordination and the ability to maintain continuous movements; these changes often make the use of input devices, such as a keyboard or mouse, more difficult than at younger ages (Rogers et al., 2005). Functions such as clicking, dragging and fine positioning on a screen become more difficult (Czaja and Lee, 2008), and these debilities becomes especially inhibiting as devices become smaller and more tactile via the use of touch screens.

Vision function decreases at older ages too, specifically in the areas of visual acuity, colour perception and contrast discrimination (Rubin et al., 1997). This decreased functioning is especially pertinent to aspects of screen-based materials such as the size of text, colour gradation, and the centrality/periphery of navigational features, and impacts how efficiently an individual reads and comprehends websites and other visual information via a screen (Czaja, 2005; Leonard, Jacko and Pizzimenti, 2005); it also may inhibit finding important navigational tools such as menus and help links (Romano Bergstrom, Olmsted-Hawala and Jans, 2013). Hearing deficiencies also increase at older ages (Chien and Lin, 2012), and functions such as synthetic speech recognition and sensitivity to pure tones may be reduced (Czaja and Lee, 2008); while traditionally a lower concern in the visually oriented web environment, these declines in functionality are heightened with the increasing prevalence of multimedia content.

Declines in cognitive function at older ages impact digital media use as well. Fluid intelligence, which involves processes such as working memory and perceptual speed, declines with age (Czaja et al. 2006; Czaja and Lee, 2006). As such functioning is important to the acquisition of new skills (Czaja and Lee, 2006), retrieving information and working in interactive, web-based environments (Sharit et al., 2008), these declines may negatively impact the ability to accurately input information into web spaces and to find information sought through web searches. Finally, it is important to note that while age-related changes to motor skills and perception can be addressed through the use of technological measures, such as expanding the use of trackballs and providing an ability to enlarge text sizes in web browsers, age-related cognitive decline is much more difficult to accommodate in digital media use.

Older adults and social media

The use of social media has grown rapidly in recent years, and these technologies have become a near-universal means of connecting and interacting with others.

While often thought of as popular with younger persons, the use of social media has grown rapidly with adults at older ages (Ofcom, 2014; Smith, 2014). In 2014, for example, more than 56 per cent of US adults over the age of 65 and more than 30 per cent of UK adults over the age of 65 reported using social media sites (Duggan et al., 2014; Ofcom, 2014). Perhaps not surprisingly, though, adoption of specific platforms and how they are employed have emerged in different ways (Ofcom, 2014; Smith, 2014; Zickuhr and Madden, 2012). Of note is the presence of a "grey divide" (Millward, 2003), or a particularly steep decline in use between those in the 'younger-old' group (i.e. those younger than 70 years), and those that are 'older-old,' often characterized as age 70 years and above. The presence of this grey divide has been previously noted for Internet use (Duggan and Brenner, 2013; European Commission, 2012; Friemel, 2014; Ofcom, 2014); it is quite pronounced in social media use too, with social media usage rates dropping precipitously beyond the age of about 80 years (Smith, 2014). Nonetheless, while reports demonstrate very large increases in social media use by older adults over the past several years, they also point out that participation in most social media platforms by older adults lags behind that of youth and young adults by a considerable degree.

Social media platforms, such as Facebook, Twitter and LinkedIn, are characterized by the ease with which users can share information. They are 'networked communication platforms' in which participants have a unique profile, visible lists of connections to other users and streams of content that takes the form of news, information and comments from other users and system-generated data such as birthday reminders and sponsored advertising (Ellison and boyd, 2013). One-to-many broadcast capabilities are designed into these platforms and facilitate the dissemination of content between users. Specifically encompassing social network sites, more broadly defined social media platforms also may include online communities, such as SeniorNet and GreyPath, content-sharing sites such as You-Tube and discussion boards such as those found on AARP.org.

The networks of connections that are represented through these media forms are often conflated for an individual's social network, or the system of relationships to which one is connected. However, while a social medium may map a large proportion of one's social network, it can only embody the portion of connections that are represented within such platform. Given the high adoption rates of platforms such as Facebook for younger persons, the network mapped by a particular medium often represents a large proportion of their social networks. For older adults, however, the overlap between these two network forms may be significantly less due to lower usage rates of these technologies at older ages. Herein therefore, references to a social network are deemed to be the totality of an individual's social connections and not just those represented in a given social media platform.

Researchers have pursued an understanding of social media forms not only as mechanisms for communication but also as cultural icons and sites of identity performance. Studies of social media use at older ages, however, tend to highlight social media's utilitarian role in everyday life. The focus of much of this research is concentrated in three primary streams of knowledge. The first targets reduced levels of social media engagement at older ages and examines potential barriers to social media use; the obvious focus of many of these studies is to increase engagement levels. A second and related nexus of research has emerged around older adults who do participate in social media. These studies examine the ways in which social media are employed differently among user groups of different ages, to again understand the gap in age-related engagement. Finally, as social media are often seen as a low-cost/low-barrier mechanism for social connection (Donath, 2007; Donath and boyd, 2004), the third line of scholarship examines the social benefits of social media use. Studies of young adult populations suggest that social media users are more socially connected and less lonely than non-users (Lee, Lee and Kwon, 2011; Lee, Noh and Koo, 2013) and, given the evidence between social ties and life quality (e.g. Cherry et al., 2013; Smith and Christakis, 2008), these studies explore whether similar benefits extend to older adults. The following sections will provide an overview of these three research themes and discuss the ways in which these research trends reveal the influences these technologies impart on everyday life.

Barriers to social media use

Given the overall popularity of social media platforms today, social scientists have aggressively pursued an understanding of the slower adoption rates by older adults. The incidence of chronic illness and disability at older ages is frequently cited as functionally interfering with the use of digital technologies (e.g. Lee, Chen and Hewitt, 2011; Smith, 2014), but studies of social media non-use and barriers to its use at older ages do not address these functional aspects. Instead, extant literature revolves around attitudinal, perceptual and skills-related obstacles; a deficiency in digital media skills; a lack of perceived benefit; and attitudes related toward privacy and security. These foci offer some evidence that values, interaction styles and, especially, entrenched patterns of communication with existing relationships are determining factors in social media adoption and suggest that social media technologies may be influencing the ways in which interpersonal interaction takes place.

Access and skill deficiencies are often attributed as barriers to social media use, with older adults lacking both access to broadband connection and the necessary literacy skills to navigate the emerging social media environment (van Deursen and van Dijk, 2009). Broadband Internet connections are often critical to optimized social media use, and older adults lag their younger counterparts in access to broadband connection (Ofcom 2014; Smith, 2014). In addition, older users often cite a lack of skills or lack of confidence in their own skills as reason to not engage in social media platforms (Lee, Chen and Hewitt, 2011; Lehtinen, Näsänen and Sarvas, 2009; Lüders and Brandtzæg, 2014; Smith, 2014). Finding pathways to acquire skills at older ages is therefore an important avenue of research, and studies have demonstrated that the provision of instructional support engenders social media participation (Gibson et al., 2010; Lüders and Brandtzæg, 2014; Xie et al., 2012). This is a barrier that should diminish over time, as those acquiring digital skills through education and training (a primary means for acquiring digital skills for those currently at younger ages) eventually reach older age.

Studies of Internet and social media non-use have also highlighted that lower levels of engagement sometimes result from preference, due to a lack of relevance to everyday living. Specifically, several studies point to a lack in perceived benefit in using social media platforms (Braun, 2013; Lampe, Vitak and Ellison, 2013; Lehtinen, Näsänen and Sarvas, 2009; Luders and Brandtzæg, 2014; Sundar et al., 2011). Perception of benefit has been found to be a strong motivator for technology use by older adults (Czaja et al., 2006; Sayago, Forbes and Blat, 2013), and this concept appears to extend to social media use as well. Social media platforms are often perceived as a lesser form of interaction than more traditional forms (Lehtinen, Näsänen and Sarvas, 2009; Luders and Brandtzæg, 2014) or as a forum that is oriented exclusively toward youth (Hope, Schwaba and Piper, 2014). Older adults who perceive higher benefits for social media participation are more likely to use it (Braun 2013), and connection with family members is an important reason to consider using social media (Bell et al., 2013; Luders and Brandtzæg, 2014; Sundar et al., 2011). However, social media adoption is dependent on a 'critical mass' of one's friends and acquaintances also using the specific platform (Hargittai, 2008; Hendler and Golbeck, 2008), so if one's social network is not reflected in the users of a particular platform, the relevance of that platform and/or medium is significantly reduced, and non-use may result.

Concerns about privacy and security are a third stream of research related to the non-use of social media at older ages. Often fueled by media reports, older adults have been characterized as cautious about providing personal information online (Dumbrell and Steele, 2015; Gibson et al., 2010). Concern about identity theft and suspicion of platform provider motive have been reported by older adults as reasons not to use specific social media services (Dumbrell and Steele, 2015; Hope, Schwaba and Piper, 2014; Luders and Brandtzæg, 2014). Perceptions that social media providers do not take sufficient action to protect individual privacy also may lead to non-use or pre-empt certain online interactions between users (Dumbrell and Steele, 2015; Lampe, Vitak and Ellison, 2013; Lehtinen, Näsänen and Sarvas, 2009; Xie et al., 2012). Further, older adults often find privacy controls on social network sites difficult to navigate and implement (Brandtzæg, Lüders and Skjetne, 2010), fueling their concerns about being able to protect their privacy when using these platforms. While there are few significant differences in the privacy attitudes of older and younger adults or in the engagement of privacy controls (Hoofnagle et al., 2010; Madden, 2012), younger adult users appear more confident in their use of strategies to protect their privacy (Brandtzæg, Lüders, and Skjetne, 2010; Madden, 2012).

Examining these barriers to social media use at older ages is enlightening to the understanding of the impact of digital technologies in everyday life. First, these studies demonstrate the importance of digital skills for the use of these technologies and lend significance to a continued focus on efforts toward skill development and digital inclusion at all ages. As these studies evidence, the lack of digital skills generates substantial difficulty in social media participation and, given its importance in today's society, are a potential barrier to sociality if not effectively addressed.

Second, perception of benefit is a central element for social media engagement. These studies suggest that appreciation of the benefits of social media use may shift throughout life and that current platforms may be optimized for use at younger ages when the acquisition of social relationships is at its peak. Older adults' inattention to the social media benefit for maintaining weak relationships is a stark counterpoint to its emphasis on relationship accumulation. This lack of perceived benefit may point to a subtle but notable shift in the way individuals maintain interpersonal connection over time and highlight an additional shift in the social influence of these technologies.

Finally, privacy and security concerns related to social media use are relevant to all individuals, but, significantly, the ways in which older adults accommodate these concerns hold relevance to how social media are impacting everyday life. Withholding information, such as photos or other personally identifying information, or not engaging in certain online interactions, such as discussion of specific topics, are ways in which privacy concerns are mitigated by older adults (Lehtinen, Näsänen and Sarvas, 2009). These mechanisms, which reflect attitudes related to the privacy and security of social media use, point to an important shift in everyday interpersonal communication. The use of these media has prompted shifts in the amount and ways that information is shared between individuals and especially with individuals with whom ties are weaker.

Generational differences

A second stream of research focuses on older adults who do use social media and highlights the differences that surface when such use is compared to other user groups, especially youth and young adults. While pointing out the existence of such dissimilarities, it is interesting to note that few scholarly attempts have sought to place these in the context of life experiences. Instead, the focus appears centered on functional dimensions of social media use, with three varieties of comparison taking prominence: activities of social media engagement the characteristics of networks represented within social media platforms and the motivation for social media use. Examination of this line of research points to ways in which the demands of daily living evolve throughout the life course and, correspondingly, how the users of social media technologies may adjust to these patterns.

Comparative studies of older and younger adult social media users establish that older users spend less time using social media platforms than younger persons (Van Volkom, Stapley and Amaturo, 2014; Van Volkom, Stapley and Malter, 2013) and that, as age increases, social media activities such as seeking personal information about other individuals and impression management decreases (McAndrew and Jeong, 2012). Older adults are less likely to share created content, such as photos, videos and status updates, often due to lower levels of technology proficiency and the previously mentioned concerns about privacy (Brandtzæg,

Lüders and Skjetne, 2010; Karahasanović et al., 2009; McAndrew and Jeong, 2012). But when older adults are using social media platforms, they are more likely than younger persons to be interacting with individuals directly, looking at family photographs and spending time on their own pages (McAndrew and Jeong, 2012). Distinctions are made between 'young-older adults' (under 65 years) and 'old-older adults' (over 65 years) in their social media use as well, with those in young-older groups reporting higher levels of social media engagement (Bell et al., 2013; Sundar et al., 2011).

Research on the characteristics of social networks represented in social media platforms illustrates differences between younger and older adult users as well. Older adults have fewer connections with others on these platforms (McAndrew and Jeong, 2012; Van Volkom, Stapley and Malter, 2013), and the age dispersion among those connections is wider (Arjan, Pfeil and Zaphiris, 2008); that is, youth have more connections with other users of a similar age than do older adult users. This difference perhaps may be attributable to the lower levels of social media adoption among the older adult population: with fewer social media users at older ages, the available number of similarly aged social media connections is less. Simply put, if an individual's social network is not represented within a social media platform, he or she cannot connect with it.

Motivations for using social networks sites differ between older and younger users, with older adults indicating they use these platforms to stay in touch with family while younger users look to stay in touch with friends (Bell et al., 2013; Zickuhr and Madden, 2012). Unlike youth and younger adults, however, older adults use social media to maintain connection with extended family and friends who are not in everyday circles, that is, their weaker connections (Brandtzæg et al., 2010). An emerging use of social media at older ages is reconnection with friends and colleagues from one's past (Quinn, 2013), a practice that may also be more limited with younger social media users due to briefer life experiences and an introduction to these connection-preserving technologies at younger ages. These results also are consistent with socio-emotional selectivity theory, which suggests that as individuals grow older, they look to spend more time with familiar and rewarding relationships (Carstensen and Mikel, 2005).

The existence of these age-related differences in social media use underscores the importance of examining social media use at different points in life to assess their impacts. These studies provide evidence that social media use changes in tandem with the social, psychological and cognitive development of an individual throughout the life course, changes which may be relevant to how its impact on everyday life is perceived and understood.

Social media use and social well-being

Research on sociality and well-being strongly indicates that individuals at older ages with larger and stronger social networks are healthier and experience greater social support and reduced levels of cognitive decline (Cherry et al., 2013; Smith and Christakis, 2008); however, studies on the role of the Internet and social media in expanding social networks and enhancing life quality has been mixed. The use of social media has been positively linked to social capital creation and maintenance for adults at all ages (Burke, Marlow and Lento, 2010; Cotton, Anderson and McCullough, 2013; Ellison, Steinfield and Lampe, 2007), but research on the relationship between social capital creation and life quality is thin and only recently garnering attention (Nyqvist et al., 2013). Moreover, some studies have found that Internet and social network site use are not linked to quality of life at older ages (Lee et al., 2010; Leung, 2010; Slegers, Van Boxtel and Jolles, 2008; Sundar et al., 2011).

A key factor in producing these conflicting results may lie in the lower participation rates in social media at older ages. With fewer available connections on a platform, social capital benefits may be less easily realized. In addition, lower usage rates also limit the types of individuals that can be studied, favouring the inclusion of novice social media participants (Leist, 2013), who may need social media platform use longevity to derive social value. Increasing social media participation at older ages may mitigate these limitations and provide additional opportunity for clarification.

Social media use generally has been connected with reduced feelings of loneliness for both younger and older adults (Ballantyne et al., 2010; Burke, Marlow and Lento, 2010; Sheldon, 2012) and, in particular, those with greater numbers of connections report lower levels of loneliness (Burke, Marlow and Lento, 2010). Research on increased feelings of social connectedness and social media use at older ages (Ballantyne et al., 2010; Bell et al., 2013) is consistent with findings on Internet use generally, which shows that Internet-using older adults incur higher contact frequency with friends and family than non–Internet users (Hogeboom et al., 2010). Social media use by older adults also encourages self-disclosure, which in turn may lead to higher levels of social support (Lee, Noh and Koo, 2013).

Importantly, this avenue of research points to some positive effects that social media have fostered. The use of social media enhances connection with others, which reduces loneliness and ultimately enhances well-being (Lee, Noh and Koo, 2013). While not unique to older adults, these benefits are highly relevant at older ages because factors such as retirement and mobility limitations diminish social connection, which in turn is associated with poorer health outcomes (Cornwell and Waite, 2009). The prominence of this research line is significant and provides support of the constructive influence these technologies may hold for everyday living.

Future directions

Taken together, these studies collectively not only reveal the strong role that interpersonal connection plays in the use of social media technologies but also emphasizes the role of offline connection to their use. Studies of older adult use of social media underscore the requirement for a certain level of digital proficiency to enable social media use and, thus, to recognize its potential benefits. While reduced digital skill levels at older ages may diminish over time, as those acquiring digital skills through education and training eventually reach old age, the significance of perception of benefit as an important motivator to digital media use should not be lost.

Perception of benefits and the studies of older adult social media adoption that align with this concept often refer to the technology acceptance model (TAM). TAM is based on the theory of reasoned action (Ajzen and Fishbein, 1980) and attempts to identify a predictive relationship between perceptions of technology and its actual use, and specifically identifies perceptions of the benefit and ease of use as important factors (Davis, Bagozzi and Warshaw, 1992). Despite that factors associated with aging such as declines in vision, cognitive processing speed and psychomotor function make technology use more difficult at older ages, ease of use appears to matter less than perceived utility with social media (Braun, 2013).

Benefits of social media use to older adults include 'keeping up' with the everyday lives of younger family members, sharing photos and videos with individuals seen less frequently and being able to contact multiple people simultaneously (Gibson et al., 2010). As adults age, however, their social networks reduce in size as they become more selective of the relationships that are maintained (Carstensen, 1992). This reduction in network size at older ages is considered to be a deliberate process, and it potentially relegates the importance of one of the primary benefits of social media platforms, facility in creating and maintaining weak social ties. Studies of older adult social media use, therefore, highlight the significance of understanding how the utility of these media forms may shift for different life phases and provide evidence of change in how these media support aging processes throughout life.

Social media provide low-cost mechanisms to support weaker relationships and, like all communication media, reduce the significance of physical distance for social interaction. Maintaining social connections often becomes more difficult at older ages due to factors such as retirement, bereavement, mobility limitations and chronic disease. Social disconnectedness and loneliness are, in turn, associated with poorer mental and physical health outcomes (Cornwell and Waite, 2009; Lee, Noh and Koo, 2013). As such, researchers have reasoned that social media technologies should benefit aging users by reducing the impact of mobility restrictions to maintaining relational ties and also by helping maintain a broader base for social and emotional support.

Social capital theory (Lin, 1999) has been used as a theoretical foundation to connect social media use to the health and psychological benefits of sociability and underscores much of the research that involves motivation for social media use. Social capital theory posits that investment in one's network of relationships provides a mechanism through which resources are developed and accessed (Lin, 2008), resources such as information, social credentialing and social and emotional support (Lin, 1999). Two forms of social capital are typically facilitated in social media use: bonding social capital, which is typically found in strong relationships and provides access to social and emotional support, and bridging social capital, which is typically found in more diverse and weaker relationships and provides access to broader world views or more varied information resources (Burke, Marlow and Lento, 2010; Ellison, Steinfield and Lampe, 2007).

These studies suggest that additional research on the relationship between social media use and adaptive mechanisms to sustain social connection may be an important future direction of study, especially as the relationship between social capital and well-being is not well mapped (Nyqvist et al., 2013). Indeed, the social capital needs of adults at later life stages may well differ from those at earlier points in the life course, so additional work on older adult social media use will be important to the identification of how social media support social well-being generally, as well as the relevance of this support for varying life stages.

Conclusion

The rapid proliferation of social media mundane and pervasive use in today's society bears examination, especially for its effects on everyday social interaction. Older adults, while rapidly adopting these media forms, have not embraced their use to the same degree as younger users. For this reason, examination of the scholarly work on social media use and non-use at older ages, particularly, becomes an important means for understanding how these media are integrated and ingrained into everyday life. Studies of attitudes and practices are revealing of the ways in which social media may be shaping routine communications but also to what future challenges these media forms may hold for younger persons. As such, these studies provide important linkage to broader awareness of how digital media are shaping everyday living more generally at all ages.

References

Ajzen I. and Fishbein, M., 1980. *Understanding attitudes and predicting social behavior.* Englewood Cliffs, NJ: Prentice-Hall.

Arjan, R., Pfeil, U. and Zaphiris, P., 2008. Age differences in online social networking. *Proceeding of the 26th Annual Conference on Human Factors in Computing Systems-CHI'08.* New York: ACM Press, pp. 2739–2744.

Ballantyne, A., Trenwith, L., Zubrinich, S. and Corlis, M., 2010. "I feel less lonely": What older people say about participating in a social networking website. *Quality in Ageing and Older Adults*, 11(3), pp. 25–35.

Bell, C., Fausset, C., Farmer, S., Nguyen, J., Harley, L. and Fain, W. B., 2013. Examining social media use among older adults. *Proceedings of the 24th ACM Conference on Hypertext and Social Media-HT'13*, pp. 158–163.

Brandtzæg, P. B., Lüders, M. and Skjetne, J. H., 2010. Too many Facebook "friends"? Content sharing and sociability versus the need for privacy in social network sites. *International Journal of Human-Computer Interaction*, 26(11–12), pp. 1006–1030.

Braun, M. T., 2013. Obstacles to social networking website use among older adults. *Computers in Human Behavior*, 29(3), pp. 673–680.

Burke, M., Marlow, C. and Lento, T., 2010. Social network activity and social well-being. *Proceedings of the 28th International Conference on Human Factors in Computing Systems-CHI'10*, pp. 1909–1912.

Carstensen, L. L., 1992. Motivation for social contact across the life span: A theory of socioemotional selectivity. In: J. E. Jacobs (ed.), *Developmental perspectives on motivation.* Lincoln: University of Nebraska, pp. 209–254.

Carstensen, L. L. and Mikels, J. A., 2005. At the intersection of emotion and cognition: Aging and the positivity effect. *Current Directions in Psychological Science*, 14(3), pp. 117–121.

Cherry, K. E., Walker, E. J., Brown, J. S., Volaufova, J., Lamotte, L. R., Welsh, D. A., Su, L. J., Jazwinski, S. M., Ellis, R., Wood, R. H. and Frisard, M. I., 2013. Social engagement and health in younger, older, and oldest-old adults in the Louisiana healthy aging study (LHAS). *Journal of Applied Gerontology*, 32(1), pp. 51–75.

Chien, W. and Lin, F. R., 2012. Prevalence of hearing aid use among older adults in the United States. *Archives of Internal Medicine*, 172(3), pp. 292–293.

Cornwell, E. Y. and Waite, L. J., 2009. Social disconnectedness, perceived isolation, and health among older adults. *Journal of Health and Social Behavior*, 50(1), pp. 31–48.

Cotten, S. R., Anderson, W. A. and McCullough, B. M., 2013. Impact of Internet use on loneliness and contact with others among older adults: Cross-sectional analysis. *Journal of Medical Internet Research*, 15, pp. 1–13.

Czaja, S. J., 2005. The impact of aging on access to technology. *ACM SIGACCESS Accessibility and Computing*, 83, pp. 7–11.

Czaja, S. J. and Lee, C. C., 2006. The impact of aging on access to technology. *Universal Access in the Information Society*, 5(4), pp. 341–349.

Czaja, S. J. and Lee, C. C., 2008. Information technology and older adults. In: A. Sears and J. A. Jacko (eds), *The human–computer interaction handbook*, 2nd ed. New York: Lawrence Erlbaum, pp. 778–792.

Czaja, S. J., Charness, N., Fisk, A. D., Hertzog, C., Nair, S. N., Rogers, W. A. and Sharit, J., 2006. Factors predicting the use of technology: Findings from the Center for Research and Education on Aging and Technology Enhancement (CREATE). *Psychology and Aging*, 21(2), pp. 333–352.

Davis, F. D., Bagozzi, R. P. and Warshaw, P. R., 1992. Extrinsic and intrinsic motivation to use computers in the workplace. *Journal of Applied Social Psychology*, 22(14), pp. 1111–1132.

Donath, J. S., 2007. Signals in social supernets. *Journal of Computer-Mediated Communication*, 13(1), pp. 231–251.

Donath, J. S. and boyd, d., 2004. Public displays of connection. *BT Technology Journal*, 22(4), pp. 71–82.

Duggan, M. and Brenner, J., 2013, Feb 14. *The Demographics of Social Media Users – 2012*. Washington, DC: Pew Research Center. Available at: <http://pewinternet.org/~/media/Files/Reports/2013/PIP_SocialMediaUsers.pdf>.

Duggan, M., Ellison, N. B., Lampe, C., Lenhart, A., & Madden, M., 2014. *Social Media Update 2014*. Washington, DC: Pew Research Center. Retrieved from http://www.pewinternet.org/files/2015/01/PI_SocialMediaUpdate20144.pdf.

Dumbrell, D. and Steele, R., 2015. Privacy perceptions of older adults when using social media technologies. In: M. Tavana (ed.), *Healthcare informatics and analytics: Emerging issues and trends*. Hershey, PA: IGI Global, pp. 67–82.

Ellison, N. B. and boyd, d., 2013. Sociality through social network sites. In: W. H. Dutton (ed.), *The Oxford handbook of Internet studies*. Oxford, UK: Oxford University Press, pp. 151–172.

Ellison, N. B., Steinfield, C. and Lampe, C., 2007. The benefits of Facebook "friends:" social capital and college students' use of online social network sites. *Journal of Computer-Mediated Communication*, 12(4), pp. 1143–1168.

European Commission, 2012. *Media Use in the European Union*. Brussels, Belgium. Available at: <http://ec.europa.eu/public_opinion/archives/eb/eb78/eb78_media_en.pdf>.

Friemel, T. N., 2014. The digital divide has grown old: Determinants of a digital divide among seniors. *New Media & Society*. Available at: <http://nms.sagepub.com/cgi/doi/10.1177/1461444814538648>.

Gibson, L., Moncur, W., Forbes, P., Arnott, J., Martin, C. and Bhachu, A. S., 2010. Designing social networking sites for older adults. *Proceedings of the 24th BCS Interaction Specialist Group Conference-BCS '10*. Swinton, UK: British Computer Society, pp. 186–194.

Hargittai, E., 2008. Whose space? Differences among users and non-users of social network sites. *Journal of Computer-Mediated Communication*, 13(1), pp. 276–297.

Hendler, J. and Golbeck, J., 2008. Metcalfe's law, Web 2.0, and the semantic web. *Web Semantics*, 6(June), pp. 14–20.

Hogeboom, D. L., McDermott, R. J., Perrin, K. M., Osman, H. and Bell-Ellison, B. A., 2010. Internet use and social networking among middle aged and older adults. *Educational Gerontology*, 36(2), pp. 93–111.

Hoofnagle, C., King, J., Li, S. and Turow, J., 2010. *How Different Are Young Adults from Older Adults When It Comes to Information Privacy Attitudes and Policies?* Available at: <http://papers.ssrn.com/sol3/papers.cfm?abstract_id=1589864>.

Hope, A., Schwaba, T. and Piper, A. M., 2014. Understanding digital and material social communications for older adults. *Proceedings of the 32nd Annual ACM Conference on Human Factors in Computing Systems-CHI '14*, pp. 3903–3912.

Karahasanović, A., Brandtzæg, P. B., Heim, J., Lüders, M., Vermeir, L., Pierson, J., Lievens, B., Vanattenhoven, J. and Jans, G., 2009. Co-creation and user-generated content – elderly people's user requirements. *Computers in Human Behavior*, 25(3), pp. 655–678.

Lampe, C., Vitak, J. and Ellison, N. B., 2013. Users and nonusers: Interactions between levels of Facebook adoption and social capital. *Proceedings of the 2013 Conference on Computer Supported Cooperative Work-CSCW '13*. New York: ACM Press, pp. 809–819.

Lee, B., Chen, Y. and Hewitt, L., 2011. Age differences in constraints encountered by seniors in their use of computers and the Internet. *Computers in Human Behavior*, 27(3), pp. 1231–1237.

Lee, G., Lee, J. and Kwon, S., 2011. Use of social-networking sites and subjective well-being: A study in South Korea. *Cyberpsychology, Behavior and Social Networking*, 14(3), pp. 151–155.

Lee, K.-T., Noh, M.-J. and Koo, D.-M., 2013. Lonely people are no longer lonely on social networking sites: The mediating role of self-disclosure and social support. *Cyberpsychology, behavior and social networking*, 16(6), pp. 413–418.

Lee, P. S. N., Leung, L., Lo, V., Xiong, C. and Wu, T., 2010. Internet communication versus face-to-face interaction in quality of life. *Social Indicators Research*, 100(3), pp. 375–389.

Lehtinen, V., Näsänen, J. and Sarvas, R., 2009. "A little silly and empty headed": Older adults' understandings of social networking sites. *Proceedings of the 23rd British HCI Group Annual Conference on People and Computers*. Swinton, UK: British Computer Society, pp. 45–54.

Leist, A. K., 2013. Social media use of older adults: A mini-review. *Gerontology*, 59(4), pp. 378–384.

Leonard, V. K., Jacko, J. A. and Pizzimenti, J. J., 2005. An exploratory investigation of handheld computer interaction for older adults with visual impairments. *Proceedings of the 7th International ACM SIGACCESS Conference on Computers and Accessibility, Oct. 9–12*. Baltimore, MD: ACM Press, pp. 12–19.

Leung, L., 2010. Effects of Internet connectedness and information literacy on quality of life. *Social Indicators Research*, 98(2), pp. 273–290.

Lin, N., 1999. Building a network theory of social capital. *Connections*, 22(1), pp. 28–51.

Lin, N., 2008. A network theory of social capital. In: D. Castiglione, J. W. van Deth and G. Wolleb (eds), *The handbook of social capital*. Oxford, UK: Oxford University Press, pp. 50–69.

Luders, M. and Brandtzæg, P. B., 2014. 'My children tell me it's so simple': A mixed-methods approach to understand older non-users' perceptions of social networking sites. *New Media & Society*. Retrieved from: https://www.researchgate.net/profile/Petter_Brandtzaeg/publication/275971165_My_children_tell_me_its_so_simple_A_mixed-methods_approach_to_understand_older_non-users_perceptions_of_Social_Networking_Sites/links/554d0a260cf29752ee82a08c.pdf.

Madden, M., 2012, Feb. 24. *Privacy management on social media sites*. Pew Internet & American Life Project. Washington, DC: Pew Research Center. Available at: <http://www.pewinternet.org/2012/02/24/privacy-management-on-social-media-sites/>.

McAndrew, F. T. and Jeong, H. S., 2012. Who does what on Facebook? Age, sex, and relationship status as predictors of Facebook use. *Computers in Human Behavior*, 28(6), pp. 2359–2365.

Millward, P., 2003. The "grey digital divide": Perception, exclusion and barriers of access to the Internet for older people. *First Monday*, 8(7). Retrieved from: http://firstmonday.org/ojs/index.php/fm/article/view/1066/986%3E.

Nyqvist, F., Forsman, A. K., Giuntoli, G. and Cattan, M., 2013. Social capital as a resource for mental well-being in older people: A systematic review. *Aging & Mental Health*, 17(4), pp. 394–410.

Ofcom, 2014, Apr. *Adults' Media Use and Attitudes Report*. London: Ofcom. Available at: <http://stakeholders.ofcom.org.uk/market-data-research/other/research-publications/adults/adults-media-lit-14/>.

Quinn, K., 2013. We haven't talked in 30 years! Relationship reconnection and Internet use at midlife. *Information, Communication & Society*, 16(3), pp. 397–420.

Rogers, W. A., Fisk, A. D., McLaughlin, A. C. and Pak, R., 2005. Touch a screen or turn a knob: Choosing the best device for the job. *Human Factors: The Journal of the Human Factors and Ergonomics Society*, 47(2), pp. 271–288.

Romano Bergstrom, J. C., Olmsted-Hawala, E. L., & Jans, M. E. (2013). Age-related differences in eye tracking and usability performance: Web site usability for older adults. *International Journal of Human-Computer Interaction*, 29(8), pp. 541–548. doi:10.1080/10447318.2012.728493.

Rubin, G. S., West, S. K., Muñoz, B., Bandeen-Roche, K., Zeger, S., Schein, O. and Fried, L. P., 1997. A comprehensive assessment of visual impairment in a population of older Americans: The SEE Study. *Investigative Ophthalmology & Visual Science*, 38(3), pp. 557–68.

Sayago, S., Forbes, P. and Blat, J., 2013. Older people becoming successful ICT learners over time: Challenges and strategies through an ethnographical lens. *Educational Gerontology*, 39(7), pp. 527–544.

Sharit, J., Hernández, M. A., Czaja, S. J. and Pirolli, P., 2008. Investigating the roles of knowledge and cognitive abilities in older adult information seeking on the Web. *ACM Transactions on Computer-Human Interaction*, 15(1). Retrieved from: http://www.ncbi.nlm.nih.gov/pmc/articles/PMC2792941/.

Sheldon, P., 2012. Profiling the non-users: Examination of life-position indicators, sensation seeking, shyness, and loneliness among users and non-users of social network sites. *Computers in Human Behavior*, 28(5), pp. 1960–1965.

Slegers, K., van Boxtel, M. P. J. and Jolles, J., 2008. Effects of computer training and Internet usage on the well-being and quality of life of older adults: a randomized, controlled study. *The Journals of Gerontology, Series B*, 63(3), pp. P176–84.

Smith, A., 2014, Apr 3. *Older adults and technology use.* Washington, DC: Pew Research Center. Available at: <http://www.pewinternet.org/2014/04/03/older-adults-and-techno logy-use/>.

Smith, K. P. and Christakis, N. A., 2008. Social networks and health. *Annual Review of Sociology*, 34(1), pp. 405–429.

Sundar, S. S., Oeldorf-Hirsch, A., Nussbaum, J. and Behr, R., 2011. Retirees on Facebook: Can online social networking enhance their health and wellness? *Proceedings of the 2011 Annual Conference on Human Factors in Computing Systems, CHI-EA '11*. New York: ACM Press, pp. 2287–2292.

Van Deursen, A. J. a. M. and van Dijk, J., 2009. Improving digital skills for the use of online public information and services. *Government Information Quarterly*, 26(2), pp. 333–340.

Van Volkom, M., Stapley, J. C. and Amaturo, V., 2014. Revisiting the digital divide : Generational differences in technology use in everyday life. *North American Journal of Psychology*, 16(3), pp. 557–574.

Van Volkom, M., Stapley, J. C. and Malter, J., 2013. Use and perception of technology: Sex and generational differences in a community sample. *Educational Gerontology*, 39, pp. 729–740.

Xie, B., Watkins, I., Golbeck, J. and Huang, M., 2012. Understanding and changing older adults' perceptions and learning of social media. *Educational Gerontology*, 38(4), pp. 282–296.

Zickuhr, K. and Madden, M., 2012. *Older adults and Internet use.* Washington, DC: Pew Research Center. Available at: <http://pewinternet.org/Reports/2012/Older-adults-and-internet-use.aspx>.

11 Googling grannies

How technology use can improve health and well-being in aging populations

Elizabeth Yost, Vicki Winstead, Ronald W. Berkowsky, and Shelia R. Cotten

Introduction

Though the U.S. older adult population remains one of the youngest among developed countries, the U.S. has the largest older adult population in the developed world, with 43.1 million adults over the age of 65 in 2012. It is projected that in 2050 there will be 83.7 million adults over the age of 65 in the U.S. (Ortman, Velkoff, and Hogan 2014). Individuals in the U.S. are also living longer, and the Baby Boomer generation has begun to turn 65. As the older adult population in the U.S. continues to grow for the foreseeable future, ensuring that older adults can maintain their physical health, well-being, and quality of life is vital.

Older adults are at increased risk for social isolation, loneliness, depression, and lower overall quality of life (Cornwell, Laumann, and Schumm 2008). Many of these declines are related to the loss of social ties, increasing health concerns, and changes in living environments as people progress through older age. Using information and communication technologies (ICTs) has been effective in negating some of these declines in older adults (Cotten, Anderson, and McCullough 2013). However, in the United States the older adult population continues to lag behind other age groups in terms of Internet use. The PEW Internet and American Life Study reported that 86 per cent of all adults are currently online, yet only 59 per cent of adults age 65 and older go online (Smith 2014). When delineating among the older adult population, the lag between users and non-users continues to grow. Among the oldest old (80 years of age and older), only 37 per cent report going online compared to 74 per cent of age 65- to 69-year-olds (Smith 2014). This chapter examines how ICT use can impact well-being outcomes among older adults with both review of the literature and analysis of a 5-year longitudinal study conducted in the Deep South region of the U.S. that investigated the impact of ICT use on quality-of-life outcomes among older adults.

While significant amounts of research on ICTs have focused on how they can be used to help individuals age in place, this chapter evaluates the research on how ICTs can be used to mitigate negative health outcomes and increase well-being and quality of life. The review of the literature focuses on how ICTs can be used to increase well-being among older adults in continuing care retirement communities (CCRCs) and how ICTs overall can impact feelings of isolation, loneliness, depression, and social support.

Community and health

Simply put, where you live directly impacts your health. As individuals age, every-day environments can begin to prove difficult for activities of daily living (ADLs). Stairs, large homes, lack of mobility around communities, and other aspects of the living environment can suddenly provide new spatial barriers. They can impact social interaction, making it difficult for the older adult to maintain their social ties. When their health begins to decline, when they need assistance with ADLs, and when their spouse/partner dies and they cannot maintain their independence, some older adults choose to relocate to CCRCs. These communities offer not only meals, home maintenance, and personal care, most offer significant activity options designed to keep older adults engaged and active. In many respects, individuals in these communities are frailer than those who live independently in their homes.

When moving into these communities, the transition and subsequent socialization into these communities can both positively and negatively affect the individual's quality of life (Ball et al. 2000; Chapin and Dobbs-Kepper 2001; Dupuis-Blanchard, Neufeld, and Strang 2009; Park 2009). In an attempt to curtail the negative impact of the transition, most communities try to engage residents in activities to assist in the transition. Many aging theories and multiple researchers tout the importance of staying engaged in social networks and social situations as a way to maintain quality of life and well-being (Ball et al. 2000; Park 2009; Park et al. 2012).

While moving into these communities often shows positive health benefits for individuals, as they are able to receive care and have new options for social networks, they also offer unique social and structural barriers for the individuals (Winstead et al. 2013). CCRCs are often located in larger metropolitan areas or outside of familiar areas. This might cause the individual to have to leave their familiar city to move into one of these communities or move closer to other family. This can become a barrier to their social interaction if they are unable to visit or connect with their social ties. This often requires the individual to make new friends and new routines within the community.

ICTs and health in the older adult population

Because of their frailty, individuals in CCRCs stand to gain a significant benefit from the use of ICTs. Though much of the literature around technology and aging evaluates how technology can help individuals age in place, some of the literature is starting to evaluate how technology can benefit individuals who are no longer in their homes. ICT use can impact isolation (Winstead et al. 2013), loneliness (Cotten, Anderson, and McCullough 2013), depression (Cotten et al. 2012), and social support (Cotten, Anderson, McCullough 2013).

Social isolation is an objective measure in which the number of social relationships available is reduced or limited (Russell, Campbell, and Hughes 2008). This may occur as a result of geographic displacement and removal from former social networks (Park 2009; Winstead et al. 2013). ICTs can be one way individuals can reconnect or stay connected to their formal social networks or connect to new social networks. ICTs can help individuals overcome the spatial and social barriers (Winstead et al. 2013) that can lead to feelings of isolation.

Relocation can lead to increased feelings of loneliness as individuals are removed from their home communities. As individuals age, many worry about becoming a burden or otherwise on their family. Loneliness is a subjective state, defined as the difference between the desire for social contacts and the availability of social contacts (Perlman and Peplau 1998). Internet use has been shown to reduce loneliness among users in CCRCs (Heo et al. 2015), even after transitions into CCRCs (Cotten, Anderson, and McCullough 2013). ICTs can make accessing some social contacts easier and thus have been used to reduce feelings of loneliness.

Depression and ICT use has an interesting history. Recent research suggests that the use of ICTs can decrease depression among certain populations. Particularly among older adult populations, the use of ICTs has been shown to decrease depressive symptomatology and depression classification (Cotten et al. 2012, 2014; Shapaira, Barak, and Gal 2007; Winstead et al. 2013). Using ICTs enables individuals to connect with those they might not be able to easily connect with otherwise. Through using the Internet, individuals can also connect with others with similar interests, histories, and needs that might otherwise be difficult to access. ICTs may provide a different medium for communication not previously open to the individual, given that the majority of older adults in CCRCs have not previously used ICTs. Learning the skills required to use the Internet can also be motivational for the older adult learner. It can serve as a reminder that they are no longer excluded from the world of ICTs.

Perceived social support is a highly touted measure related to quality of life and well-being. Social support is the idea that, when in need, an individual has a person or group of people to which they can turn for emotional, tangible, informational, and other types of support. While it is clear that ICTs can be used to build social networks (Courtney 2008), more nuanced research supports the idea that older adults can use ICTs as a way to stay connected and increase their perceived social support (Winstead et al. 2013). For many older adults in CCRCs, being able to connect more easily with friends, family, past connections, and perhaps new ones is not simply fun, it is a way for them to remain connected to their social support networks.

Successful aging

Rowe and Khan (1997) defined and popularized the term "successful aging." Under their definition, successful aging includes active engagement in life. Though this definition has been expanded to more clearly define each core piece, the idea that as one ages they should remain involved and active in activities that matter to them remains important. Rowe and Khan (1997) add that maintaining interpersonal relationships is very important. In a world where technology is leading to major shifts in the ways individuals communicate and interact, learning how to navigate ICTs can help individuals remain active in their communities and their families and help them feel more connected to the greater world. Though many want to tout the adage that "old dogs can't learn new tricks" it is precisely staying in tune with the "new tricks" that proves to be part of successful aging. The remainder of this chapter provides a high-level overview of one such attempt to help older adults overcome the digital divide by teaching them how to use computers and the Internet.

Methods

The ICT and Quality of Life (QoL) Study was a randomized controlled trial investigation conducted in CCRCs located within a medium-sized metropolitan area of the Deep South region of the U.S. The purpose of the study was to investigate the relationship between ICT use and various measures of social capital and QoL over time among older adults in these communities. A total of 19 assisted and independent living communities (AICs) were randomized into one of three study arms: an ICT training group, an Activities Control (AC) intervention group, and a True Control (TC) group. Participants were primarily recruited through recruitment sessions held at each AIC, which typically involved study personnel having a brief presentation about the study and a sign-up at an AIC event (town hall meeting, social gathering, etc.). In addition to these sessions, flyers and brochures were distributed throughout each AIC, and staff of the AICs also helped drum up interest by speaking directly with residents they felt may be interested. Activities coordinators at each AIC typically were able to recruit quite a few residents into the study who were not able to attend an official recruitment session. These various methods yielded a recruitment of 324 individuals; as explained later, 314 of these recruited individuals were ultimately enrolled: 101 into the ICT arm (with an additional 8 participants who participated in a pilot group), 112 into the AC arm, and 93 into the TC arm.

The ICT arm

Five of the recruited communities were randomized into the ICT arm. Participants in this study arm underwent 8 weeks of computer and Internet training specifically designed to accommodate the learning needs of older adults in a continuing care setting, including the physical and cognitive limitations the residents may experience. Accommodations included (but were not limited to):

- *Use of large roller-ball tracking mice* for those who experienced difficulty using a traditional mouse (particularly those with dexterity limitations or those who experienced tremors that prevented smooth manoeuvring of a traditional mouse).
- *Use of large-key keyboards* to assist those with little to no typing experience and those with vision impairments that prevented easy viewing of the keyboard keys.
- *Use of higher resolution on laptop screens and an increased font size* to accommodate those with visual impairments.

- *Keeping the pace of the class slow and employing repetition in the lessons* to accommodate those with decreased cognitive processing.
- *ICT reference manual*, specifically designed for the older adult learner. Every participant was given this reference manual so they could review materials for each class session outside of class time.

A mobile lab was set up in each CCRC in a location within the CCRC that was easily accessible to residents. Conducting the interventions in the CCRC rather than transporting the residents elsewhere made participation convenient for the residents. The ICT training was designed as an introductory course to the use of both a computer and the Internet and began with the very basics of using the technology: how to turn a computer on and off, how to use a keyboard and mouse, how to access and open/close computer programs, and how to get online. Each subsequent lesson built off of the concepts and procedures of the previous class, and over the 8-week intervention a number of topics were covered (see Table 11.1). The intervention culminated in a "capstone" project on the last day of class that incorporated many of the previous lessons into one activity and involved searching for information online, copying a link to a website with the needed information, and emailing the link to a friend or neighbour.

Classes were conducted such that an instructor stood at the head of the class with an instructor's laptop projected onto a large screen for participants to follow along. Participants with difficulties in seeing or hearing were put to the front of the class whenever possible so that they could more easily see the large screen and hear the instructor. Also when possible, inexperienced users were seated next to other participants with some or high levels of experience so that, should the beginner need assistance, they could call upon their neighbour for help. In addition to the instructor, other members of the study team would attend the classes and walk around during the lesson and assist participants who requested it; the number of assistants who attended varied depending on the size of the class, but it was typical for at least two assistants to be in attendance during each training session.

Each class was 90 minutes in length and occurred twice per week over the 8 weeks of the intervention. In addition to the classes, optional office hours sessions were made available to the residents once per week. These sessions were also

Table 11.1 Topics covered in the ICT training program

Topic	Week
Computer Basics	1
Email Basics	2
Internet Basics	3
Advanced Email	4
Social Networks and the Internet	5
Searching for Health Information	6
Entertainment on the Internet	7
Final Project – Wrapup of Class	8

90 minutes in length and allowed participants to meet one-on-one with members of the study team to either (a) review what had been done in class and practice the procedures or (b) learn about something new that was not covered in the class. All participants in the ICT arm were also given a specially constructed training manual that contained outlines and step-by-step procedures from all the lessons. These manuals were for the participants to keep, and thus all were encouraged to use it as a notebook, taking notes on the pages as they saw fit.

The AC arm

As the focus of the study was to determine if ICT use had a significant relationship with social capital and QoL outcomes, a control group needed to be included to help determine if any findings from the ICT group were due to changes in ICT use *or* if it was due to participation in an AIC activity or was due to interaction with the "energetic" researchers. For comparative purposes, an Activities Control (AC) study arm was included, which seven CCRCs were randomized into. In this arm, participants took part in 8 weeks of discretionary activities that included trivia games, musical sing-alongs, and crafts, among other things. These sessions were led by members of the study team and, like the ICT arm, met twice per week. The sessions themselves lasted 90 minutes; however, the study team would stay after the conclusion of each session to speak with the participants and promote further socialization among the residents (this made it so that the amount of time the team spent with the ICT arm in class/office hours and the AC arm was the same). Like the ICT arm, the AC study arm was conducted in the CCRCs themselves out of convenience for the participants.

The TC arm

A True Control (TC) study arm was included wherein residents did not participate in any intervention over the course of the study. The only interaction the TC arm had with the study team was during data collection. The TC arm served as a baseline group for comparative purposes, and a total of seven CCRCs were randomized into this arm.

Both the AC arm and the TC arm received complimentary computer/Internet training from the study team *at the conclusion of the study*. Promising the participants in these arms that they would eventually receive training encouraged participation and retention.

Data

Over the course of the study, data was collected on each participant in both quantitative and qualitative formats. Quantitative data was collected using an in-person survey instrument administered to the participants five times over the course of the study: baseline, post-intervention (approximately 8 weeks after baseline), and at 3-, 6-, and 12-month follow-ups. The questions in the survey covered various different facets of ICT use (e.g. frequency of use, attitudes towards technology, perceived limitations to using technology), social capital, and QoL (e.g. life satisfaction, mattering, loneliness, depressive symptoms). Demographic characteristics, including education, income, and health, were also measured. The survey took approximately 45 to 60 minutes to complete in most cases. Potential participants were screened for cognitive impairment using the Mini-Mental State Examination (Folstein, Folstein, and McHugh 1975); participants were required to score at least an 18 out of 24 in order to be enrolled in the study. A total of 314 participants were successfully enrolled and surveyed at baseline. Of these, 208 were able to fully complete the study (i.e. complete the 12-month follow-up survey).

In addition to the survey data the study team collected qualitative data over the course of the interventions. The qualitative data was organized into four categories:

- *Instructor updates*, which consisted of a summary of each class session as well as notes taken by the instructor during each class regarding successes and difficulties encountered (these were compiled immediately following each class session).
- *Field notes*, which were notes taken during each class by a study team member who remained removed (when possible) from interacting with the participants and who observed/detailed class environment and the actions and general response of the participants.
- *Focus group data*, collected at the completion of each ICT and AC intervention and focused on evaluating the general attitudes the participants had towards the technology/activities and where they believed improvements could be made.
- *Observation files*, which were miscellaneous notes compiled by all study team members but did not fit under the previously designated groups.

While the qualitative data covered a number of characteristics, most notes dealt specifically with the experiences of the study team with class setup and takedown, interactions with the study participants, and "what works and what doesn't work" with regards to the interventions.

Results

UAB ICT QoL participants

Participants in the ICT and QoL Study were on average 82 years of age and were primarily white and female. Most were widowed or divorced or had never married and reported that they had enough or more than enough economic resources to get by. The demographic characteristics of this group of residents reflect AIC demographics nationally. About 43 per cent of participants lived in assisted living, with the other 57 per cent living in independent living. The ICT study arm comprised 38 per cent of the total participants, with the AC and TC arms comprising

Table 11.2 Demographic characteristics of participants
in UAB ICT and QoL Study (*N* = 306*)

Female	82%
Age	82 years
AL Resident	43%
Economic Resources	
More Than or Enough to Get By	87%
Marital Status	
Widowed/Divorced/Never Married	86%
Race/Ethnicity	
White (non-Hispanic)	96%
Study Arm	
ICT	33%
AC	37%
TC	30%

*Note: *N* presented here does not include those recruited into
the pilot group in the ICT arm.

of 33 per cent and 29 per cent respectively (see Table 11.2). Results from the study indicate that older adults in IL and AL communities can benefit from a specifically designed ICT training program that addresses the unique challenges older adults face in learning about and using technology.

Changes in attitudes and usage

Approximately 70 per cent of residents had previously used a computer. However, much of their use was associated with a job, where they only used programs applicable to the job. At baseline, only 41 per cent of residents owned a computer, with 42 per cent reporting that they used a computer at least occasionally.

Residents had initially reported having an interest in using a computer and the Internet but had worries about their ability to learn and use new technology. As described earlier, older adults face unique challenges both physically and cognitively; therefore, learning something new can prove challenging. Residents who participated in the technology training gained confidence from the training so that they were better able to engage in technology use. Greater confidence in their ability to use a computer and the Internet resulted in more positive attitudes toward using the technology. They reported feeling less intimidated by the technology and more comfortable about using a computer. After training, they reported the perception that they were able to make the computer do what they wanted it to do. Post-training, they also felt that computers were easier to understand and that they were easier to use. This was in addition to feeling that they were less likely to need help using a computer (for further detail, see Figure 11.1 from Berkowsky et al. 2013). Types of usage and time invested in using a computer and getting online also changed after training.

Further findings from the study also indicated that residents not only had more positive attitudes toward computers but also spent greater amounts of time using them after the training (post-intervention, a whopping 97 per cent of ICT arm

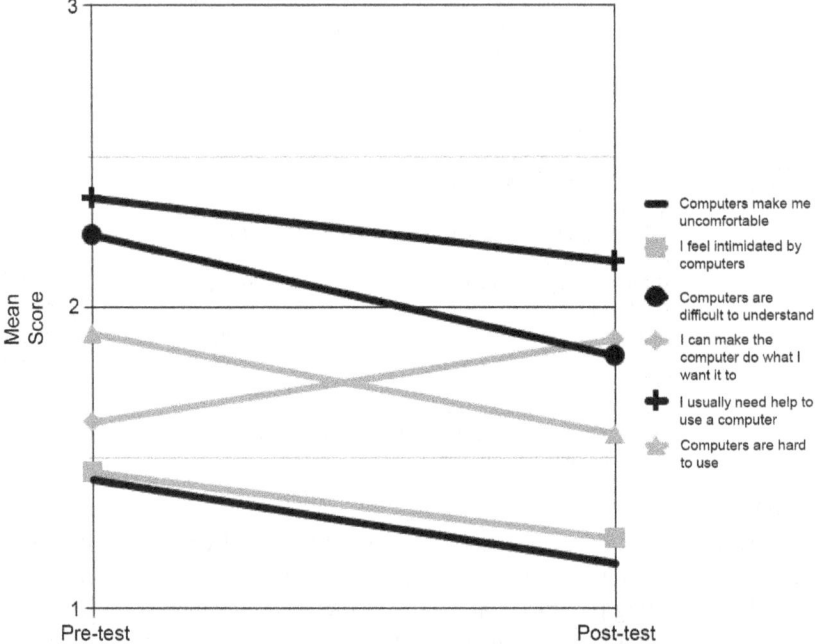

Figure 11.1 Changes in attitudes towards computers between pre- and post-intervention
(from Berkowsky et al. 2013)

participants indicated they intended to continue using a computer/the Internet).
Types of usage such as getting on the Internet, checking email, just surfing/
searching the Internet, and playing games all increased. There was not a significant difference between pre- and post-training in areas such as getting online to
get news or weather, using the Internet for entertainment, or getting on social
networking sites. There was also little or no change in other types of usage such
as getting health information, shopping, financial information, playing online
games, or using Skype or FaceTime.

There was also a reduction in perceived limitations to computer/Internet use.
As an example, the percentage of ICT arm participants who indicated that computers were too complicated or hard to use decreased from 27 per cent to 16 per
cent; the percentage that indicated they had trouble using the keyboard or mouse
dropped from 23 per cent to 3 per cent; and the percentage who indicated that
they didn't know what could be done with the Internet decreased from 40 per
cent to 10 per cent (for more results regarding changed in perceived limitations,
see Figure 11.2 from Berkowsky et al. 2013). All of these findings indicate the
efficacy of the program and manual design in enabling residents to feel confident
about being computer users, having more positive attitudes about computers, and
feeling that they have fewer limitations in becoming competent computer users.

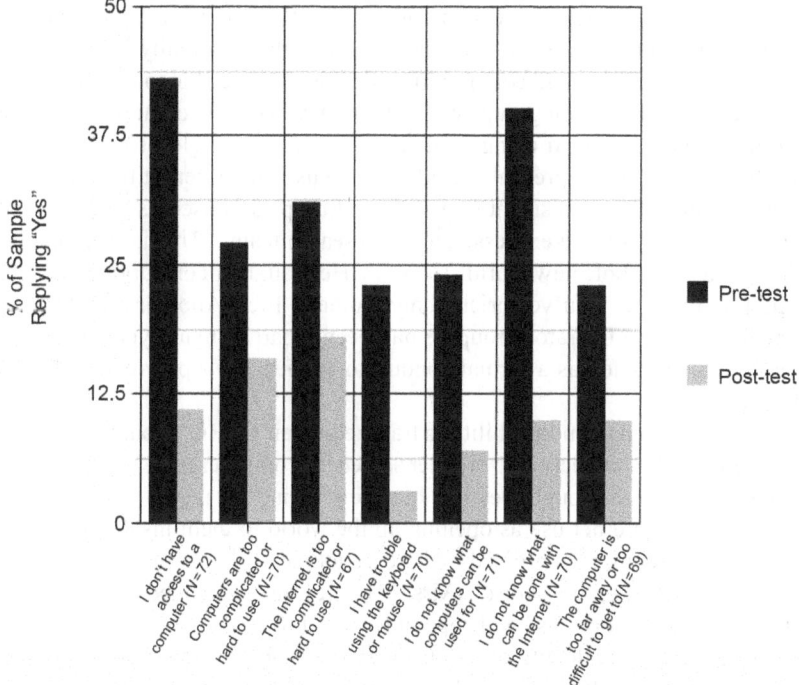

Figure 11.2 Changes in views towards what limits/prevents computer and/or Internet use (from Berkowsky et al. 2013)

Internet use and quality of life

Residents who continued using a computer and the Internet felt that both the quantity and quality of their communication was enhanced. This included feeling more connected to both family and friends. They reported being able to connect more often and felt that using the Internet to connect through avenues such as email improved the quality of the communication they had. They agreed that using the Internet had contributed to their ability to stay in touch with people they knew in addition to making it easier to meet new people. They were less bothered by not *seeing* enough of the people close to them. Internet use may have positive benefit for the mental health of socially and spatially isolated older adults in AL/IL communities. Results showed that using the Internet two or more times a week was associated with decreased feelings of depression, and they felt less lonely. These benefits, however, are associated with consistent use of the Internet.

Transcending social and spatial barriers

Internet use also enabled residents to overcome social and spatial barriers encountered from their moves into these communities and away from previous homes, social networks, and community life due to declining health and mobility. Residents often experience a compression of their social and physical world when moving into an AIC. Use of the Internet helped virtually reconnect residents to their past lives and communities. Residents were able to find old friends, organizations, and church groups with whom they had lost contact and reconnect with them. They enjoyed using applications such as Google StreetView to see their hometowns in the present. Residents also used the Internet to renew an old hobby or interest. One resident revisited the European museums she had visited as a young adult. As she expressed to the research team, "This is so fascinating. It's opened up a whole new world" (Mrs. T). Her daughter corroborated her statement in telling us, "You've enriched my mother's life." Another resident reconnected with a ham operator group he had been a part of many years previously. The technology acted as a virtual conduit to connect their previous and current lives.

ICT use allowed them the ability to transcend their CCRC through the Internet. They perceived a connection to broader society as computer users. They described no longer feeling as though they had been left behind the rest of the world. They described their Internet use as opening up the world to them inside their CCRC. As two computer users expressed, "There's another world out there" (Mrs. C) and "You have opened up our world" (Mrs. M). They also described computer use as "broadening their horizons" and "opening a window to the world."

During training, residents communicated a sense of "connectedness" in which the participants felt that they had become more assimilated into the larger world beyond their own IL or AL community. In a post-training focus group, participants from several CCRCs noted this greater sense of connection to the world at large: When asked, "Has the use of the Internet changed your life in any way? If so, how? " They described it as, "[We are] not as close to the grave as we thought." "We feel like we've joined the human race"(Mrs. W). "I may be old, but I feel like I have accomplished something" (Ms. P.). "My whole family has computers – I feel like I have accomplished something."

In follow-up interviews, residents described how using the Internet gave them not only a sense of feeling connected but also feelings of being right there with family and friends especially because they are constantly receiving pictures and messages. One resident described it as, "I feel like, you know, closer to them . . . *I feel like I'm right with them even though I'm not with them*" (Ms. N). Internet use may have positive mental health benefits for socially and spatially isolated older adults in AL/IL communities.

For CCRC residents, computer/Internet use has the potential to enrich their lives. When a training program is designed with the older adult learner in mind, and when classes are carefully constructed and carefully conducted, older adults can learn to be proficient computer and Internet users. Findings from this study have shown that there are social, psychological, and physical benefits for residents of AICs. Teaching older adults to use the Internet gives them a tool whereby they can regain control over aspects of their lives they may feel have been lost or restricted because of their change in address.

Conclusion

Although older adults, in general, are increasingly crossing the digital divide to become Internet users, those in CCRCs are less likely to be on the right side of the digital divide. Training programs, such as the one detailed in this chapter, have the potential to help older adults in CCRCs cross this digital divide. As prior research has shown and our results further illustrate, among older adults in CCRCs, getting older adults online has a range of potential positive benefits. We saw positive changes in attitudes toward and use of ICTs, as well as social connections and contact. Perhaps even more importantly, we saw the potential for using ICTs to help older adults overcome social and spatial barriers and improve their quality of life. These changes are not inconsequential; they suggest that there could be economic impacts that extend beyond the social and behavioural outcomes examined in this study. The results of this study suggest that getting older adults who live in CCRCs online can enhance their quality of life in many ways that may increase their successful aging. This may ultimately yield decreased health declines and health care utilization, not to mention cost of health care. These are issues that clearly warrant further study in more diverse older adult populations.

Given the increasing size of the demographic group of older adults in the U.S. and in other parts of the world, thinking creatively about interventions that can enhance their quality of life and well-being, as well as help them maintain independence, is vital. Initiatives such as the Apple, IBM, and Japan Postal Group collaboration may represent one such initiative. These three entities have partnered to develop apps to be put on iPads, which will be distributed to approximately 5,000,000 older adults in Japan over the next 5 to 10 years. While this project is still in development, it will be interesting to see whether a model such as this may be applicable in other parts of the world and can positively impact quality of life and independence among older adults.

Limitations and future research

This study was based in CCRCs in the Deep South region of the U.S. While the demographic characteristics of the participants in this study are reflective of those of CCRCs more generally, less is known about how the ICT use and quality-of-life impacts that were seen in the present study generalize to other older adults around the world, or even across the U.S. Having a more diverse sample in terms of race/ethnicity and socioeconomic background might also provide information on whether the patterns we identified are consistent across other groups.

Future researchers should continue to examine the pathways through which ICT use affects various aspects of quality of life for older adults in varying types of living environments. The older adult population will continue to grow, and ICTs will continue to change. The ability of ICTs to be a transformative force in the lives of older adults is well documented. Though there will likely be fewer first-time adopters, the potential impact ICTs can have for maintaining relationships and assisting in successful aging should be continuously evaluated.

Currently, research is composed of small-scale interventions. Though these types of research projects bring great understanding, repeating them in larger populations is key for greater understanding of the impacts ICTs have on this age group. Further, this research evaluates the impacts of ICT use among residents of CCRCs. Residents of CCRCs, though more frail than the general older adult population, are also wealthier, more likely to be female, and more likely to be widowed. Gathering a sample of community-based older adults or another more generalizable population would be useful in understanding the impacts of ICTs on quality of life and well-being.

In summary, our results indicate that older adults can be taught to use computers and the Internet. And ICT use can have a range of positive impacts on quality of life for residents of CCRCs. We encourage future researchers and ICT developers to think creatively about ways to engage older adults in ICT training and use, as well as interface design. As technology continues to evolve, we hope that hardware and software interfaces are designed that enable older adults, and people more generally, to quickly adopt and become skilled in the use of the new technologies. Otherwise, the digital divide will be perpetuated, and older adults will be the most likely to be on the wrong side of the divide.

References

Ball, Mary M., et al. "Quality of life in assisted living facilities: Viewpoints of residents." *Journal of Applied Gerontology* 19.3 (2000): 304–325.

Berkowsky, Ronald W., Shelia R. Cotten, Elizabeth A. Yost, and Vicki P. Winstead. "Attitudes towards and limitations to ICT use in assisted and independent living communities: Findings from a specially-designed technological intervention." *Educational Gerontology* 39.11 (2013): 797–811.

Chapin, Rosemary, and Debra Dobbs-Kepper. "Aging in place in assisted living philosophy versus policy." *The Gerontologist* 41.1 (2001): 43–50.

Cotten, Shelia R., William A. Anderson, and Brandi M. McCullough. "Impact of Internet use on loneliness and contact with others among older adults: Cross-sectional analysis." *Journal of Medical Internet Research* 15.2 (2013): e39.

Cotten, Shelia R., George Ford, Sherry Ford, and Timothy M. Hale. "Internet use and depression among retired older adults in the U.S.: A longitudinal analysis." *Journals of Gerontology, Series B: Psychological and Social Sciences* 69.5 (2014): 763–771.

Cotten, S. R., Ford, G., Ford, S., & Hale, T. M. "Internet use and depression among older adults." *Computers in Human Behavior* 28.2 (2012): 496–499.

Cornwell, Benjamin, Edward O. Laumann, and L. Philip Schumm. "The social connectedness of older adults: A national profile." *American Sociological Review* 73.2 (2008): 185–203.

Courtney, Karen L. "Privacy and senior willingness to adopt smart home information technology in residential care facilities." *Methods Inf Med* 47.1 (2008): 76–81.

Dupuis-Blanchard, Suzanne, Anne Neufeld, and Vicki R. Strang. "The significance of social engagement in relocated older adults." *Qualitative Health Research* 19.9 (2009): 1186–1195.

Folstein, Marshal F., Susan E. Folstein, and Paul R. McHugh. "Mini-mental state": A practical method for grading the cognitive state of patients for the clinician." *Journal of Psychiatric Research* 12.3 (1975): 189–198.

Heo, J., Chun, S., Lee, S., Lee, K. H., & Kim, J. "Internet use and well-being in older adults." *Cyberpsychology, Behavior, and Social Networking* 18.5 (2015): 268–272.

Ortman, Jennifer M., Victoria A. Velkoff, and Howard Hogan. (2014). *An aging nation: The older population in the United States* (pp. 25–1140). Washington, DC: US Census Bureau.

Park, N. S. "The relationship of social engagement to psychological well-being of older adults in assisted living." *Journal of Applied Gerontology* 28 (2009): 461–481.

Park, N. S., Zimmerman, S., Kinslow, K., Shin, H. J., & Roff, L. L. Social engagement in assisted living and implications for practice. *Journal of Applied Gerontology* 31.2 (2012): 215–238.

Perlman, D., and L. A. Peplau. (1998). Loneliness. In H. Friedman (ed.), *Encyclopedia of mental health* (pp. 571–581). San Diego, CA: Academic Press.

Russell, C., Campbell, A., and Hughes, I. "Ageing, social capital and the Internet: Findings from an exploratory study of Australian 'silver surfers.'" *Australasian Journal on Ageing* 27 (2008): 78–82.

Rowe, John W., and Robert L. Kahn. "Successful aging." *The Gerontologist* 37.4 (1997): 433–440.

Shapira, N., Azy Barak, and I. Gal. "Promoting older adults' well-being through Internet training and use." Aging & Mental Health, September 11.5 (2007): 477–484.

Smith, A. (2014). *Older adults and technology use: Adoption is increasing but many seniors remain isolated from digital life.* Washington, DC: Pew Research Center.

Winstead, V., W. A. Anderson, E. A. Yost, S. R. Cotten, A. Warr, and R. W. Berkowsky. "You can teach an old dog new tricks: A qualitative analysis of how residents of senior living communities may use the web to overcome spatial and social barriers." *Journal of Applied Gerontology* 32 (2013): 540–560.

12 Physical death in the digital age

Stine Gotved

In the Western world, particularly in the period characterized as Modernity, there is a certain prevalence towards hiding away dying and death. We hide the sick in hospitals and the dying in hospices, and even if the mass media are filled with reports on spectacular deaths in tragic occurrences, death and dying is not an experienced part of a normal everyday life. Death has been sanitized, purged from our involvement and devolved to specialists such as undertakers. This so-called sequestration of death in Western modernity is now being challenged by digital technologies (Christensen and Gotved, 2014), at least when we talk about the visibility and the acknowledgement of the personal loss. Increasingly, a deceased person is connected to an extended social network on different digital platforms (for example, Facebook, LinkedIn and Twitter) and furthermore, the loss is digitally shared immediately among the close family, their relatives and friends. The experiences of shock and sorrow are communicated on diverse social media, and online tributes are published, shared and commented on as part of the grieving process. In the digital age, death is no longer hidden away from everyday experience – even if the physical body is still held by institutions, the connected actions and emotions are out in the open for everybody to virtually stumble upon.

As the physical life is intrinsically connected with online services and digital social networks, so is the physical death. This chapter describes the last journey, from the reluctant planning to the digital manifestations afterwards. Using a simple timeline of antemortem, perimortem and postmortem (Gotved, 2014), that is before, just around and after the death of a human being, digital variations in the different stages are presented. They range from the need for being prepared to the intricate questions of digital assets and inheritance, from the service of online undertakers through to the shared memorials on social network sites. The truly cross-disciplinary research into death online is in the process of assembling as a field, thus producing research and results from the diverse and dynamic activity surrounding physical death in the digital age. Thus, each of the following sections starts the discussion with a trigger, a small fictional case constructed from true, real-life examples.

Antemortem

Before the physical death of an individual, there might be thoughts on how to prepare for the inevitable. As people in general are not aware of their own mortality, it depends on factors such as age, experience of loss, health and social network if the awareness is manifest. A recent study (Waagstein, 2013) concluded that even when the study's respondents were highly aware of their mortality due to their job functions, they did not include digital assets in their preparation. Quite simply, we forget these new additions to our possessions. Essentially, in the antemortem phase the possibility of physical death and a digital aftermath are double sequestered – first from the lack of everyday awareness, next from the newness of the digital add-ons. Even as offers from new digital services are abundant in the antemortem phase, they are destined to be short lived as long as their potential customers are not aware of a need for the service. Nevertheless, the antemortem phase involves certain activities, and the following subsections deal with the individual's wish for control, urge to self-perform and need for planning. In terms of legacy, these areas are overlapping and thus separated in an analytical manner: the first is about memorials, the next is about life stories and the last is about the legal aspects of digital assets and heritage.

The wish for control: planning the memorial

My grandparents wished to be buried without any marker on their grave. Born in 1904 and 1912, as kids they were dragged on endless Sunday visits to different cemeteries to attend to graves of long-gone ancestors. Unaware of each other, the children both took a serious oath: not to be such a burden to their own descendants. They did not forget the oath, and some 80 years later, within a few weeks of each other, they were buried in the cemetery's section for the anonymous. As it happened, their daughter came to feel doubly bereaved – without a physical spot as an anchor, she found the contemplative parts of mourning difficult. A few years after the funeral services, she actually had my grandparents' urns moved to a proper gravesite with their names on a headstone, thus bringing them back full circle to their childhood Sundays.

Space and location matter. This family story is ripe with questions and dilemmas found in updated versions in our digital age. If we want to decide on our last resting place, not only do we have choices about urn or casket, headstone or open scenery, but we also need to include thoughts of our potential online memorial. And as in the story above, there might be disagreements between the deceased and the descendants, disagreements about the need for grave markers or (as in a recent political discussion in the European Union) the right to be forgotten.

The Internet is a kind of parallel space in which we have placed a part of our lives, in which we are embedded in a social network and in which we leave traces behind when we die. The traces left by an individual might be viewed as 'treasure' once the person is gone, and if they are collected into a digital memorial they can serve as an accessible and convenient space for grieving. To be somewhat in control, one needs to make early decisions and preparations about a possible digital memorial – what colors to favour, what images to show, what tributes to choose. Basically, it is a whole new area connected to the planning, which is already served by companies who help us get a funeral we would like to attend (as for example MyWonderfulLife, n.d.)

Another example of control is related to Facebook, where an app for planning the inescapable is named to attract an ever-optimistic youth culture: 'IF I die'. The options are rather simple: what to write in the status update (that is, how to break the sad news of one's demise to the social network on Facebook) and whom to give the mandate of either closing down or memorializing the profile. The double sequestration of death and the digital means that only a few of Facebook's millions of users discovered this app; planning for one's mortality is not on top of the to-do list in our everyday lives.

As the initial story shows, in the end the memorial is defined by the descendants; however, the wish for control is usually intertwined with the urge to self-perform.

The urge to self-perform: setting the record straight

> *The brochure came to Khalid as personal snail-mail, in a cream, rich envelope. He was selected to try out a new online service, granted a year's VIP membership and probably expected to brag about it on his many social media profiles. Apparently, the service ensured that his own written version of his life could influence his legacy when dead, for example by setting the record straight if needed.*

Of course Khalid was curious. The service promised him the possibility of writing his own legacy, and the online space was filled with free-floating images of geniuses long gone (from da Vinci to Mozart and Einstein, with some lesser brains in the mix). At the same time, it was a promise of an audience; in the future people could just search and find his version, find Khalid. The company thus catered to a well-known tendency, as there is nothing new about the urge to tell one's story. To create a coherent narrative is to explain (and presumably understand) the choices made and the life lived. This we can see in countless autobiographies and life story workshops, and we see it, in a somewhat less organized form, in online personal profiles and weblogs. During our lives, we narrate meaning into our circumstances as a way of making sense of the passing of time. At best, a self-produced narrative will be acknowledged as part of the legacy, whereas the promise of setting the record straight (as in getting the last word) is rather hard to see fulfilled.

To make the deal even more attractive, as a customer Khalid could save his passwords in a digital locker, designate a 'named other' to be his digital executor and prepare emails to be sent out on specific dates, stretching far into the future after his demise. In short, he could be in control of his own legacy if only he acted upon the urge to self-perform. There are several varieties of services like this, focused on practicalities but somehow running the risk of reproducing the problem (a personal digital space not known by or being inaccessible to the descendants). However, the services highlight the experimental status of the connections between physical death and digital afterlife. Even if we are to overcome the double sequestration, we do not have established traditions to lean upon. The service providers might come in handy and spark the talks with our descendants on how to get a handle on our digital legacy.

The need for foresight: deciding on digital legacy

> *As a hospice nurse, she faced death on a daily basis. Thus, she was probably more aware of human mortality than most, and she did plan accordingly. She had her will sorted out, had decided on pertinent questions such as cremation or burial and felt comfortable about the low-key preparations. One day a thesis student came to the hospice to do research on the awareness of digital assets, and the nurse realized that she had never even thought about it. Despite her prepared- ness, the digital dimension had somehow escaped valuation. Family photos, social media accounts and important individual documents were password protected, and nobody but herself knew how to get access.*

The digital legacy is becoming just as important as the physical artefacts that one leaves behind, but without knowledge of them as well as access and passwords, the descendants might never be able to reach the content. In other words, getting the digital assets sorted out before the death of an individual is on par with the will distributing physical artefacts to the descendants. While part of the digital legacy might be intertwined with online social networks (as part of *their* fabric) other parts might be locked down behind different kinds of access control. For example, if doing the yearly tax reports online is a responsibility for one spouse, the other spouse might not know how to access them if bereaved. Or maybe the family photos are on an external hard disk to save the photos from theft, fire or hardware malfunction – this kind of security might also hinder the descendants in gaining access to the treasures.

Another challenge connected to the digital legacy is the realization that a lot of our digital property does not really belong to us and thus cannot be included in the will. This goes for our social media profiles, but the really sore spot is about cultural products such as books and music. The downloaded digital formats are not owned in the same way as their physical counterparts; basically, they are just paid-for check-outs from a central library. All customers in for example Apple's iTunes store have accepted (knowingly or not) the End User Licence Agreement (EULA) before downloading anything, and thus the material transfers back to the company when the account is closed. As for now, it is not possible to bequeath one's downloaded digital library to the descendants, as it does not count as a personal belonging. In 2012, there was a gossip news story about American actor Bruce Willis, who apparently was angered by the EULA conditions and willing to fight Apple for his children's right to inherit his music library. Even though the story turned out to be false, it touched a nerve in the public and made more people realize the reality of licensing issues (Wong, 2012). Thus, subsequent conditions might change, and it is probably related that in 2014 it became possible to have a shared iTunes account within a family – the terms of accessibility are more forthcoming, even if the lack of ownership is still a topic. The uproar around EULAs is not a question of format (digital or tangible) but more about a sense of unfairness – not only cultural value but also personal history is inscribed in the products. Often favorite authors or bands are seen as important vehicles for social identity formation and personality, and books and music libraries are traditionally passed on to the next generation as a kind of essence of the lived life and period in history. Losing Grandpa to EULA is bound to be an upsetting experience.

Perimortem

The perimortem phase is the time just around the death of a human being, when the chief mourners are about to lose a loved one or just did. To them falls a heavy burden, the responsibility to spread the news, deal with an abundance of practicalities and begin to sort out the estate. Perimortem is just as hard to deal with as before the advent of the Internet, and hopefully we do not get too much practice in meeting non-spectacular death in our everyday life. However, even as the digital dimensions makes the aftermath more complex it can also simplify some tasks, both in communication and in planning.

Spreading the sad news in the social network

> *The grieving family had just lost their teenage son in a traffic accident. They wrestled with the feeling of unfairness, and they wanted to share the grief and reach out to the son's network of friends. The last part was seemingly easy as they had access to the son's much-used Facebook account. However, they were faced with several dilemmas which were hard to solve in the midst of the fresh loss. If they wrote the death notice as a status update, it would seem to be sent by the son himself, which they found extra disturbing. And could they face planning the funeral as 'an event' even if they wanted the date and place of the service to be known? And what about those mourners not on the friend list (primarily family) – could they stay updated without first accepting an untimely Facebook friend request from their dead relative?*

There are many choices of communication following a physical death, and none of them are easy. The digital variations are certainly not described in Emily Post or other guides to etiquette, and faced with all the new connectedness, it is hard to navigate in a proper manner. In the end, the parents navigated these thorny issues and kept using the Facebook account in their son's name, much to the relief of the social network who would otherwise have been disconnected.

The more time the deceased individual spent online, the harder it is for the descendants to know the individuals in those social networks who are now bereaved of a participant and friend. The online activity might have involved all kinds of social interaction – from the exchange of recipes to fighting side by side in a warriors' guild – and thus the single individual might have a larger and more diverse circle of friends and acquaintances than ever expected by the closest relatives. In general, our digital society has a vast amount of 'communities of choice' that in case of physical death would appreciate being told and who are at the risk of colliding with the family (the 'community of destiny') in what counts as proper friendship or mourning. The positive effect of digital memorials (whether they are existing profiles continued or new tributes made) is the visibility of and support from fellow mourners.

In a case much like the initial story, a mother used her deceased daughter's Facebook profile-turned-into-a-memorial as comfort and solace when she needed it the most. Years after the loss, she would browse the old pictures and stories uploaded by friends and family – not as often anymore but ritualized around certain dates (birthday, funeral) and as an important part of living despite the loss (Nielsen et al., 2014). While this is more post- than perimortem it is important to recognize the long-term consequences of decisions made in the perimortem period. If for example the chief mourner's decision is to close down the social media profiles, a part of the deceased person's social network is excluded and thus, they might not be able to offer their condolences, their stories or their support in the time of loss (Pennington, 2014).

Related to these tough decisions, a service has sprung up to help the descendants with their social media management following a digitally connected person's demise (aftercloud, n.d.). Here, the pressing need for making long-term choices is boiled down to three possibilities: to have all the accounts closed down without further ado; to save the content but still close down the accounts; or to transform the profiles into memorials, frozen in time and with limited access. Even as the service seemingly has its own struggle to survive (the demand is most surely there but is presumably fulfilled by family members with digital literacy), the service's sheer existence highlights the main point of the perimortem process. In this phase, the descendants have an obligation to remember the 'hidden' social network: the friends and communities chosen by the deceased. In our digital age, the circle of mourners is bigger than what meets the eye – but the mourning might be just as valid.

Digitized services: funerals and technology

> *Amanda was sad. It was the day of her grandpa's funeral, and she missed him a lot. The day before, she had helped loading music into the iPod, to be played before and after the service. At the chapel, she was one of the people recounting a happy memory in front of the attendees, and she felt slightly grateful about avoiding feedback from the loudspeakers. Just before they left the funeral service, she found her mobile phone and took a selfie (a self-portrait) with a part of grandpa's casket visible in the background. Relieved to have a memento, she posted it online for her friends to see. They knew she was sad and that she attended the funeral, and her posting was done to ensure them that she was doing okay.*

In recent years, the practice of taking photos of oneself (dubbed *selfies*) and posting them online has spread like a wildfire (Rettberg, 2014). As we share what is emotionally important, the selfies are often from special events or celebrations, and in online services like Instagram they can be browsed by their tags – #wedding, #party or #funeral. The categories are proof of our infusion of mobile technology also into our most sacred rituals, even if the cultural negotiation of their importance is yet to be seen. More often than not, the descriptive tags are supplemented with micro-information about the sender's emotional state (for example, #sad, #ilovehimsomuch, #longday), thus creating a special kind of coded messages for the receivers to interpret. However, if these rather innocent photos with tags are taken out of the context of the digital youth culture, they might just offend somebody. That is exactly what happened when Jason Feifer sorted the photos by tags and made a selection of those with #funeral. The Tumblr-webpage *Selfies at Funerals* (Feifer, 2013) caused a media uproar in the United States, claiming the teenagers to be clueless, disrespectful and unaware of proper mourning behaviour. Even though very few of the selfies show the funeral service itself, to say nothing of caskets or deceased relatives, the sheer combination of informal photos in ritualized settings seems to provoke. Later the same year three high-profile politicians imitated the behaviour at the funeral of Nelson Mandela in South Africa. The US president, the UK prime minister, and the Danish prime minister were captured while posing for a mobile phone held by the latter. They did not tag or publish the funeral selfie, but the image of the situation with those three heads stuck together went viral anyway, causing equal amounts of amusement and outrage in its wake.

As hinted by Amanda's story, there might be a plethora of digital communication technology involved in the perimortem phase. Online undertakers are giving the more traditional businesses competition (primarily on price and convenience), and the funeral service itself might be webcasted for those not able to attend (Allen, 2014). Furthermore, if the descendants want a physical grave marker, it is possible to connect the actual stone with the Internet, using for example Quick Response codes, microchips or other near-field communication technology. No matter the access point, it can take the visitor onto a webpage of a kind – the content can be everything digital: photos, videos, text, social media profiles, online memorials and so forth. There is no way of knowing the lifetime of such technologies, but the assignment to a gravestone also points to a shift towards the digital in an otherwise physical memorial and mourning culture (Gotved, 2015).

In sum, the perimortem phase does still hold an abundance of decisions to be made despite the fresh loss. This is no different from earlier times; however, the digital era presents us with more variations and no manual to guide us. We have to somehow construct new ways of interaction around death in the perimortem phase, related to the partly invisible social network and the use of communication technology, ways that might transform into commonly acknowledged rituals with the passing of time.

Postmortem

There is no clear boundary between the perimortem and the postmortem periods, as the experience of time is highly individual. Instead of a definite marker, the difference might be in the mental state of the descendants. Still, postmortem is definitely the longest and the phase most easily recognized by many – the amount of digital tributes and memorials speaks directly to our need for remembrance and sharing the loss. On frozen Facebook profiles and webpages, blogs and dedicated memorials within 'virtual cemeteries', the expressions of loss and love are overwhelming.

Social network policy: password is the key

> *Susan and her family knew about the recently deceased aunt's social media profiles but they did not have the passwords and could not get access. All they wanted was for the accounts to be closed down, deleted for all eternity. As family, they felt entitled to decide on the aunt's legacy, but nevertheless they had a hard time figuring out the platforms the deceased had used, the regulations of each and the documentation needed to enable each of the accounts to be closed.*

This kind of story was touched upon in the perimortem section. However, often there is a longer interval before the descendant comes around to decide anything. As the immediate grief lessens they move into the postmortem phase and start to look into the least visible details of the estate.

If the deceased did not leave behind accessible profile information and passwords, and the descendants want to close down the profiles, there is no choice but to interact with the social network providers and their policies. These are updated regularly, as the service providers too seem somewhat surprised by the fact that their customers are capable of dying. Facebook first developed a policy for handling the matters connected to the death of a user in 2009. Despite updates it is still a rather manual process (based on case-to-case evaluation), and the descendants might have to wait for some time. (A different solution is offered by Google, where the digital equivalent of a dead man's switch will delete the account after a given period of inactivity – however, the account holder will have to make that choice prior to the actual need.) In 2015, Facebook is by far the world's largest online social network platform (although with regional and national differences), and the number of accounts has exceeded one billion. Despite the popular estimate that three Facebook users die every minute, we really do not know if that is the case. Even as Facebook use is spreading out to most age groups, the median age of the population on Facebook is most likely younger than in the society as a whole. Still, there must be a lot of digital ghosts in the machine – inactive profiles with no living individual behind them anymore. There are three different ways for the descendants to close down a Facebook account. First, if they have the password, they can de-activate the account themselves. Second, without the password they can report the death to Facebook and get the profile memorialized. That requires some documentation, like proof of the family relation, the death certificate and/or the obituary. Third and again without a password, the descendants can take out a petition for Facebook to permanently delete the account. In February 2015 Facebook announced another update, at first only applicable to the users living in the

United States. The main changes are geared towards more choices in the process of turning a profile page into a memorial. However, while still alive, the profile owner needs to indicate what should be done with their Facebook legacy.

Other social networks have similar possibilities, apart from the memorialization function that goes solely with Facebook's timeline structure. Getting access to the profile without a password is hitherto blocked by the privacy policy of the social networks, and even as there are more court decisions in the waiting, the chances of changing that policy are close to non-existent. Therefore, according to the news website Mashable, a lot of descendants choose not to comply with the social networks' policy on unique personal profile ownership. Instead, if they have the password they continue the account in the name of the deceased, living with the awkwardness of birthday reminders and network connections unknown to them (Buck, 2013). By doing so, they are turning the profile of a loved one into a co-constructed memorial, where the deceased did the first part of the curration work him- or herself.

Memorials and shared grief: co-constructed legacy

A few minutes after Aron's death was announced by the mass media, a memorial page came online with the first tributes. Aron had been missing for days, and his friends had used every means to search for him and spread the word. The local mass media helped by turning the search into an often-updated story, where the subsequent discovery of Aron's body in the harbour marked the closure of the story. The memorial page experienced a lot of traffic, also from strangers expressing shock and support, and it took a while for the family to realize that they did not know the person behind the website. Neither did he know Aron, but he was skilled in various ways of generating webtraffic.

There are a lot of different memorials out there, and there is no doubt that the regional and national rituals around the physical death of a person are changing towards the digital (Haverinen, 2014). On diverse online platforms we find memorials for sweethearts and spouses, for children and for parents, for pets and for pop stars, most of the memorials presumably made in the hope of coming to terms with the loss. The story above is an exception – the memorial is constructed out of something different than personal loss – but serves to frame the many ethical dilemmas found also in the postmortem phase. A digital memorial is a blessing for those connected to the deceased, especially if they are living a long distance from the other mourners and the physical cemetery or last resting place. But we have also seen different attempts of so-called trolling, for example obstructive behavior and offensive language appearing on memorial pages. Thus, though there might be many memorials hidden from public view protected from such trolling activities via passwords, we still find a huge amount of open memorials created for the benefit of social support and remembrance. Basically, three forms of online memorials can be found, with some inherent variation. First, there is the aforementioned social media profile used for commemoration, whether the profile is memorialized or just continued. Second, there are many personal webpages or blogs turned into either a digital headstone or an open memorial space for interaction (password protected or not). Last, there are huge virtual cemeteries, portals dedicated to individual memorials and a surrounding supportive community.

Many memorials have some kind of interaction possibility, and the visitors might address the dead as well as the living in the communication. Leaving a message on a memorial can feel like communicating with a kind of continued presence, and it is also an interaction into that particular community of mourning. People are able to help and support each other in the grief; they can share stories and photos and together keep alive the memory of the deceased. As with the webcasted funeral, online memorials render the actual physical distance between the mourners less important. Likewise, the location of the burial plot might lose some of the symbolic value in the mourning process, as the digital memoria are literally at hand, accessible with a few clicks on the keyboard. For the generations used to an ever-online life, this is not awkward or unnatural – keeping track of your online social network includes the invention of diverse commemorative practices for those lost to sickness, accidents or age.

Physical death in the digital age: conclusion

In our contemporary Western world, the hiding away of dying and death is challenged by a new online visibility. Most life activities are one way or another connected to online activities, at least potentially, and part of our possessions are immaterial goods. Even as the experience of dying and death is still sequestrated, with the frail bodies out of view, the digital dimension is ripe with planning tools, photos and memorials connected directly to the inescapability of our demise.

Antemortem, the level of individual planning (like writing a will) is paramount for the descendants-to-be. They can probably do without the detailed instructions for the memorial, and the personal biography is more nice than necessary, but when it comes to the digital legacy, preparation is the key. Thus, it is important to leave a list of social network profiles, passwords and other digital assets, as the descendants will have a hard time concluding the estate without that kind of information. Some digital assets are impossible to bequest (ultimately, all material downloaded under EULA acceptance), while other assets are stored in a manner where the challenge is more about getting access (for example, photos on a separate hard disc or in a cloud-based storage solution). As our immaterial possessions are accumulating in our life, so is their importance when we are dead.

Perimortem, the networked technology somehow adds a layer of complexity for the chief mourners. Not only do they have to deal with getting the message out and planning the funeral in the midst of fresh sorrow, but they need also to consider the invisible parts of the deceased's life. If they know about online activity and have access to profile accounts and the like, they can at least spread the sad words in an easy manner, but too often the online part of a social network is truly disconnected from the mourning process. The technology as such also plays a more and more significant role in the rituals that follow the death of a human being. From the loudspeakers that amplify the human voice to the small networked computers (also known as cell or mobile phones) in the hands of the funeral attendees, many if not all funerals are infused with digital technology. Photos and stories of the event find their way to the web, and the modern sequestration of death takes another blow, like small drips of water that will ultimately hollow out the stone. Our rituals around death are changing, which in itself is nothing new – even as rituals serve as connections to the past they are always negotiated and interpreted in present time.

Postmortem, we have taken the rituals concerned with the burial spot and moved them online. The accessibility of an online memorial is convenient, and the option to leave a message, light a virtual candle or offer support to other mourners might raise the sense of continued bonds to the deceased. Digital memorials are nearly as old as the Internet, and new services continue to pop up. These are not only for postmortem commemoration but also as bids for solutions to problems encountered in the ante- and perimortem phases. The website The Digital Beyond collects a lot of these services and do a nice job in keeping tabs on what is new and happening (The Digital Beyond | Insight about your digital death and afterlife, n.d.). In other words, it is a good place to start personal research into digital legacy and the possibilities of co-constructed memorials. Before you do anything else, though, please write down your profiles and passwords and store the paper in a safe place. Your descendants will strike the digital equivalent of gold when that note surfaces again.

References

aftercloud (n.d.) Available from: http://aftercloud.eu/ (accessed 17 February 2014).

Allen S (2014) *The Humanist Funeral Practitioner's Perspective.* First International Symposium on Death Online, University of Durham, England.

Buck S (2013) How 1 Billion People Are Coping with Death and Facebook. *Mashable,* Available from: http://mashable.com/2013/02/13/facebook-after-death/ (accessed 20 May 2014).

Christensen D R and Gotved S (2014) Online Memorial Culture: An Introduction. *New Review of Hypermedia and Multimedia,* 21, 1–9.

Feifer J (2013) Selfies at Funerals. Available from: http://selfiesatfunerals.tumblr.com/?og=1 (accessed 17 February 2014).

Gotved S (2014) Research Review: Death Online – Alive and Kicking! *Thanatos. Special Issue on Death, Mourning and the Internet,* 3(1), 112–126.

Gotved S (2015) Privacy with Public Access: Digital Memorials on Quick Response Codes. *Information, Communication & Society,* 18(3), 269–280.

Haverinen A (2014) *Memoria Virtualis. Death and Mourning Rituals in Online Environments.* Finland: University of Turku.

MyWonderfulLife (n.d.) *Your Own Funeral Planning Website.* Available from: https://www.mywonderfullife.com/ (accessed 14 January 2015).

Nielsen M B, Wrist J, Kragh-Petersen T (2014) Continuing Bonds and Grieving on a Facebook Memorial Page. Unpublished student article, The IT University of Copenhagen, Denmark.

Pennington N (2014) Grieving the loss of a (Facebook) friend: Understanding the impact of social media on the grieving process. In: Christensen D R and Sandvik K (eds), *Mediating and Remediating Death*. Farnham, UK: Ashgate.

Rettberg J W (2014) *Seeing Ourselves Through Technology*. Houndsmille, UK: Palgrave Macmillan.

The Digital Beyond | Insight About Your Digital Death and Afterlife (n.d.) Available from: http://www.thedigitalbeyond.com/ (accessed 15 January 2015).

Waagstein A (2013) *Døden i den digitale tidsalder (Death in the Digital Age)*. Denmark: IT University of Copenhagen.

Wong C (2012) Can Bruce Willis Leave His iTunes Collection to His Children: Inheritability of Digital Media in the Face of EULAs. *Santa Clara Computer & High Technology Law Journal*, 29, 703.

13 On deathcasting

Alone together on the edge of death

Yukari Seko

Introduction

Though relatively rare, public suicides are ubiquitous with people, taking their lives in public spaces – by setting themselves ablaze on the street,[1] jumping off buildings or bridges,[2] or committing *seppuku*, a ritual disembowelling in front of a public audience.[3] Some of these suicides were politically motivated and represented a mode of protest, while others were believed to choose public settings in a hope to engrave their last moment in the minds of witnesses.

When a 24-year-old financial clerk in northern Japan committed suicide in November 2010, he also set up a stage for a public audience. But his intended witnesses were not physically present; about 170 people who stumbled upon his last moment were behind their computers, watching the whole scene broadcast live over the Internet. Five days before hanging himself he made an announcement on a massive discussion board 2-channel (2ch) under the username Dora and invited viewers to a live-streaming website Ustream to share his final moment.

The log from the 2ch discussion forum[4] indicates that initial audience responses varied. Some responded to Dora empathetically, dissuading him by posting a phone number to a local crisis line and encouraging him to speak to mental health professionals. Others did not take him seriously and accused him of attention seeking. After four days of on-and-off dialogue with this anonymous audience on the 2ch, Dora began to broadcast his images from his apartment on Sunday November 7, disclosing that he had been on extended sick leave from work due to mental health issues (Sankei Shimbun 2010). While Dora was broadcasting on Ustream, some of the original audience continued posting on the 2ch thread and sharing their opinions toward Dora's deathcasting. The discussion log suggests that most of the posters initially took Dora seriously and offered emotional support and encouragement. However, as Dora gradually got drunk and went off topic, the audience became impatient and accused him of being a hoax. Dora went offline early morning of Monday November 8 and then resumed broadcasting at midnight of the same day. His second streaming was not as sympathetically received as the first one. Some of the audience even suggested he hurry up and complete his plan – apparently believing it a hoax. According to media reports, Dora tried to hang himself on a laundry pole on the balcony whilst broadcasting on Ustream. When his first attempt failed, the footage showed him repeating the attempt, and around 5:30 a.m. on Tuesday November 9, he eventually stopped moving. Observing Dora's body as limp and motionless, several viewers contacted Ustream around 6:00 a.m., and the broadcast was halted by 6:30 a.m. Local police confirmed his death around 8:30 a.m. (Sankei Shimbun 2010).

Dora's was not the first suicide transmitted live over the Internet. The first widely publicized suicide-casting was in 2007, when a 42-year-old British man hanged himself in front of a live-streaming Webcam (Ungoed-Thomas 2007). In 2008, a Florida teenager broadcast his suicide by overdose on a video-streaming site, Justin.tv (Kravets 2008), and in October 2010, just a month before Dora's incident, a 21-year-old Swedish man streamed his suicide live online[5] (The Local 2010). Alongside deathcasting, the Internet has also been used for organizing suicide pacts among strangers primarily in Japan, but also in South Korea, Guam, Norway, and several other countries (Ozawa-de Silva 2010). The largest online suicide pacts to date involved seven Japanese victims who met through a pro-suicide discussion board and committed joint suicides in 2004 (Seko 2008).

The increase of Internet-related suicides or so-called "cybersuicides" since the turn of the 21st century has evoked a contested debate about impacts of the Internet on people at risk. While some scholars have reported therapeutic potentials of online interaction including mitigation of social isolation and peer support (Baker and Fortune 2008; Beck 2005), others have argued that the Internet may have a detrimental effect on suicidal individuals by offering them access to detailed information on suicide methods and fostering peer pressure to die by suicide (Luxton et al. 2012; Becker et al. 2004; Baume, Rolfe and Clinton 1998). Mainstream media has blamed the Internet for enabling a disturbing trend, and Matthews's (2008) analysis of Japanese national newspaper coverage on Internet-assisted suicide pacts contended that the coverage of Internet suicide pacts spawned "a sensationalistic semantic nexus", which has reinforced a negative view of the Internet as a murky underworld.[6]

Certainly, the randomness and anonymity of the online witnesses in Dora's suicide parallel that of the crowd at public suicides. However, the fact that private suicides otherwise invisible to the public eye were broadcast live over the Internet deserves closer attention than a mere accusation of the Internet as a murky underworld. What should be recognized is that emerging cyberculture, along with its new equipment for documentation and its new ways of relating to that equipment, has introduced a new practice of self-expression whose outcome is to be instantly shared, circulated, and archived on the digital network. With the rapid growth in visual-rich social media outlets, every single moment of personal life, from the cradle to the grave, becomes visible and sharable to the public.

It is this emergent visibility of the "suicidal" self that I explore in this chapter, using online live broadcasting of private suicides, or the "deathcasting" phenomenon, as a case in point. I first provide a theoretical background by delineating the shift from Foucauldian panopticism to the emergent form of lateral monitoring among social media users. Drawing on the work by surveillance scholars

(Bauman and Lyon 2013; Andrejevic 2007, 2006), I argue that the surveiller and the surveilled are now bound together through user-friendly surveillance technologies, engaging in a social practice of "peer-to-peer surveillance" (Andrejevic 2007). In a culture of constant connectivity and online self-disclosure, a fear of being watched is replaced by a comfort of being seen and recognized, while a secret hitherto kept hidden takes on renewed life online. As a result, sensitive topics like suicide acquire new visibility and attract people with shared interests.

The focus then moves on to the demise of affinity caused by Dora's decision to switch from a text-only Web forum to a cue-rich Webcam environment. Unlike the 2ch thread where anonymous posters interact in a relatively equal power dynamic, Webcam broadcasting transformed Dora's testimonial into a one-way media spectacle that only united viewers in their isolation. Moving away from an interactive forum to a solipsistic stage of self-performance, Dora's monologue might no longer allow him to co-construct his suicidal identity with his audience, which ultimately pushed him further to the edge.

Yet the story won't end without a search for hope. The final part of this chapter explores the productive potential of the Internet, referring to three recent lines of effort in online suicide intervention: provision of online resources and self-help tools, development of online crisis lines and self-help groups, and statutory regulation over pro-suicide content. While any form of governmental intervention ought not to be imposed at the expense of the freedom of expression and the right to privacy, peer-to-peer surveillance on the Internet may represent an unprecedented opportunity for crisis intervention. Upon identifying areas for future research, this chapter concludes by calling for a more interdisciplinary approach to Internet-related suicide that offers a promising alternative to the dominant medical and public health models.

From panopticon to post-panoptic peer-to-peer surveillance

Foucault's analysis of modern panopticism, first theorized in *Discipline and Punish* (1977) and further developed throughout his career, served as an initial exploration into asymmetrical relationship between the observer and the observed. Drawing on Jeremy Bentham's architectural plan for a panoptic prison, Foucault (1977) examined modern systems of observation and the function of discipline as an apparatus of power. For Foucault, modern institutions such as prisons, hospitals, factories, and schools are architectural manifestations of disciplinary power, in which bureaucratic control over the object of surveillance is generalized to the point at which the actual act of monitoring no longer needs to be visible. Given the knowledge that they are under constant surveillance, the observed (e.g. inmates) begin to self-discipline their behaviour, even without knowing whether they are actually being watched. The successful deployment of panopticism, or what Foucault calls "a machine for creating and sustaining a power relation" (1977, p. 201), relies on this internalization of the monitoring gaze by the surveilled, who engulf themselves in a psychological straightjacket of invisible surveillance. Throughout his thesis of panopticism, Foucault puts a great emphasis on the rupture between the modern civilization of panoptic surveillance and the premodern civilization of spectacle. Modern systems of surveillance are seen by Foucault to be "the exact reverse of the spectacle" (1977, p. 216), in which public rituals of punishment (such as torture and execution) had to be "spectacular" for mass audiences in order to symbolize and reinforce the power of rulers. Contrary to medieval society governed by public observation of the few by the many, modern disciplinary society enabled the observation of a multitude of people (inmates, patients, workers, or students) by a small number of individuals (guards, doctors, managers, or teachers).

Foucauldian panopticism is still very much at play in contemporary society, as evident in the post–9/11 national security system and the massive deployment of closed-circuit television cameras in a range of urban and suburban locations. But besides such overt, state-oriented apparatus, panopticon is now extending to our everyday life in a more covert and intangible manner. Elaborating on Zygmunt Bauman's notion of liquid modernity, David Lyon (2010) employs the concept of liquidity to describe contemporary surveillance, in which institutional power no longer keeps its shape but becomes fluid and flexible, penetrating into every domain of social life. In the work of Lyon and other critical surveillance scholars such as Mark Andrejevick (2007), liquid surveillance is most salient in a consumer context. Referring to recent "digital enclosure" movement wherein every act of creativity and consumption is monitored and recorded for the purpose of marketing, Andrejevick warns that the corporate surveillance over consumer behaviour creates a regime of commercial panopticon. While interactive online tools have given an impetus to user-generated content creation and sharing, Andrejevick contends that the premise of interactivity rather "serves as an invitation to submit to the monitoring gaze of market researchers and pay for the privilege" (p. 27). Lyon (2010) echoes this, asserting that geo-tagging, location-based devices, and credit card transactions are manifestations of liquid surveillance, enabling "a reframing of surveillance as control, based on invisible, ubiquitous circuits" (p. 330).

Along with commercial and statutory monitoring, liquid surveillance also facilitates what Andrejevic (2007) calls "peer-to-peer surveillance" among ordinary users. Equipped with user-friendly monitoring and instant broadcasting tools, users had grown accustomed to a form of democratic voyeurism, in which constantly watching others becomes a tacit social norm. Social networks sites[7] (SNSs) like Facebook are among salient examples of this peer monitoring, not only among friends and family members but also acquaintances, colleagues, old classmates, and strangers who met one another in a bar. "Googling" someone before meeting them in person has become an increasingly common practice for savvy Web users on guard against the fear of deception, while relentless scrolling of Facebook and Twitter timelines symbolizes one's commitment to stay in touch with the rest of the world.

For Andrejevic, peer-to-peer surveillance essentially replicates the top-down logic of commercial and political surveillance, wherein members of the general public are spurred by the fear of deception to engage in do-it-yourself (DIY) spying, and as a result, they end up inscribing a panoptic "discipline of watching" in themselves (Andrejevic 2006). However, in a culture of constant connectivity, the urge toward watching others goes hand in hand with a desire to be seen and heard. On some level, social media users are ready to consent to reciprocal loss of privacy, because to be seen online is to be recognized, validated, and, to some extent, empowered. Zygmunt Bauman (2013), in his dialogue with David Lyon, eloquently points to this empowering potential of peer-to-peer surveillance, in which "the condition of being watched and seen has . . . been reclassified from a menace into a temptation" (Bauman and Lyon 2013, p. 23). With social media, Bauman argues, "the old panoptical nightmare ('I am never on my own')" is being "recast into the hope of 'never again being alone' . . . the fear of disclosure has been stifled by the joy of being noticed" (p. 23).

Providing users with a series of self-fabrication tools, social media platforms encourage voluntary self-disclosure and collaborative identity construction. Christine Rosen (2007) asserts that on today's social media constant revelation of personal life – through blogging, selfies, tweets, and videos – constitutes "one's entrée into the world" (p. 22) as well as rich resources for identity performance. With audience-voyeurs in mind, online self-disclosure becomes less introverted and self-absorbed, adopting instead a more interactive and exhibitionistic tone. Grounded on performative showcasing of private lives, the practice of online self-documentation no longer draws a clear line between what is "public" and what is "private" content. Instead, users increasingly employ personally customized interpretations of the word "privacy" and determine what is to be seen and shared at their own discretion. What used to be deemed by cultural norm as private is no longer stable in this context but rather varies in accordance with individual discretion and the nature of documentation platforms (boyd and Ellison 2007). A symbiotic relationship is thus formed on the Internet between voyeurism and exhibitionism, in which every single moment of life can become an object of friendly peer monitoring, even the moment of suicide.

Furthermore, with respect to the deathcasting phenomenon, peer-to-peer surveillance takes an intriguing twist with the notion of online anonymity. In the culture of online self-disclosure, a secret no longer remains in a confession chamber but extends its reach to the public forum of the Internet. Under the veil of online anonymity, a taboo topic like suicide acquires new visibility and mobilizes people with similar interests. Through online platforms, a secret kept hidden deep in one's mind gains a potential to be reclassified into social capital to be shared widely and wisely for the purpose of mitigating isolation, venting pent-up emotion, and finding similar others struggling under the burden of the same secret.[8] From this perspective, deathcasting can be seen as a form of struggle for social recognition and validation – albeit in its extreme form. Although the actual health impact of anonymous self-disclosure is difficult to estimate, the desire toward public display of the "true self" reaffirms the role confession plays in identity construction, in the sense framed by Foucault (1993) as "technology of the self." But while Foucault's conceptualization of confession was an admission of sin already committed and thus performed with humility and surrender, the present-day online confession operates in a context of interactivity, where identity becomes an open and reflexive project. The premise of ongoing interaction with (anonymous) voyeurs may motivate voyeur-exhibitionists to engage with flexible co-construction of the self – in the case of deathcasters, the suicidal self as part of an identity repertoire.

Deathcasting and the demise of mediated affinity

As a technology of real-time visuality, Webcam broadcasting constitutes a unique genre in the practice of online self-disclosure. Unlike text-only environments, a Webcam operates in a cue-rich environment where Webcammers can convey a multitude of verbal and nonverbal cues in their self-expression, including voice tone, body language, facial expressions, dress codes, and room settings. Research has shown that in mediated settings, interlocutors rely on various verbal and non-verbal communication cues in order to reduce uncertainty, feel a sense of being with others, and build mutual trust (Nowak and Biocca 2003; Walther, Slovacek and Tidwell 2001). In general, the more communicative cues available between two parties, the less uncertainty the interlocutors are likely to experience. However, when it comes to online communication, some ambivalence is discernible among researchers as to whether the presence of multiple cues contributes to the building of social attraction and affinity. For instance, Walther, Slovacek and Tidwell (2001) found that personal photographs had a positive impact on social attraction in newly formed, unacquainted groups but reduced shared affinity in long-term text-based online communities. Kear, Chetwynd and Jefferis's (2014) study also suggested both positive and negative effects of profile pictures on group interaction, in which visual cues benefited some online learners to feel in touch with others while raising privacy concern and discomfort for the others.

In the case of the Japanese deathcaster Dora, added communicational cues seemed to dampen the potential for empathetic interaction. As aforementioned, on the 2ch message board where he originally announced his plan for suicide, Dora engaged in active dialogue with others, some of whom offered him sympathy and support. However, after he started broadcasting on Ustream, some viewers expressed disappointment on the 2ch thread that Dora appeared drunk and started an uninterrupted monologue of self-praise and self-mockery. After Dora's first webcasting, the viewers who had initially approached him with empathy began expressing strong distrust and started calling him 'an attention whore'. It seems as though Dora's decision to switch from a cue-impoverished asynchronous forum to a cue-rich livestreaming website did not contribute to the reduction of uncertainty but instead increased viewers' skepticism toward the sincerity and authenticity of Dora's testimonial. The irony here is that while the cue-impoverished textual dialogue helped Dora establish a rapport with anonymous interlocutors and come out from the veil of anonymity, his self-performance on the cue-rich Webcam environment turned out to be a one-way broadcast, wherein the death-caster Dora exercised exclusive control over information flow, while few opportunities were provided for the audience to be seen and heard. Although the 2ch log indicates that Dora occasionally answered questions posed by his viewers via chat on Ustream, he nonetheless exercised ultimate control over which questions were answered and which were not.

In this sense, Dora's Webcam testimonial resembled what Guy Debord (1976) called the mediated spectacle that sets a clear division between the spectacle and the spectators. When consuming the spectacle, viewers are connected "only by a one-way relationship to the very center that maintains their isolation from one another" (p. 22). Mediated events provide isolated viewers with shared experience, but only through the screen and under the condition of separateness. Moving away from the 2ch message board to Ustream, Dora might have stopped inhabiting the same narrative universe with his audience: broadcast from a less anonymous and solipsistic stage for self-performance, Dora's self-disclosure might have yielded an asymmetry between Dora and his audience, who, unlike on the 2ch thread, possessed little control over the fate of the spectacle.

In addition to the demise of potential affinity, Dora's deathcasting also highlighted an essential gap between Webcammers and viewers with respect to the promise of reality. Central to the popularity of lifestreaming is the promise of unscripted and unedited reality – in the sense heralded by reality TV. For the most part images broadcasted via private Webcam are destined for real-time documentations of unscripted drama happening in front of the camera, often situated in private locations like one's apartment. However, although some aspects of a Webcammer's personality are identifiable through live footage, audio, and textual chat with the viewers, there is yet little way to verify who the Webcammer really is and where his apartment is. This lack of shared context makes it extremely difficult for viewers to verify the verisimilitude of the footage, particularly in a case of deathcasting that may involve some moral issues. Even looking at his attempt to hang himself, some witnesses of Dora's suicide were uncertain of the seriousness of the incident until he stopped moving and his body became limp. The irony of this line is that, no matter how realistic and genuine Dora's suicide attempt seemed to be, viewers were still sceptical and unable to determine what was really happening on the other side of the screen. Unlike crowds standing beneath a potential jumper in a real-life situation, the viewers had little way to accurately judge and contextualize the seriousness and urgency of Dora's action.

The gap between Dora and his audience also indicates a tendency among viewers to consider mediated events as a source of sheer entertainment. Underneath sceptical and irresponsible attitudes of the witnesses of Dora's suicide lies a tacit recognition of the Webcam as a medium to plug in and play for fun rather than to assess actual risk. While the realness and authenticity of the content did matter – and indeed Dora's viewers were obsessed with reality to the extent that some of them egged him on to prove he was not a hoax – what the viewers expected seems to be a glimpse at what appears to be a true suicide. For whimsical Web surfers, taboo topics like suicide might be too serious to be true, but at the same time, those who publicize deathcasting plans must be "suicidal enough" to keep the promise of reality. In their discursive analysis of suicide discussion forums, Horne and Wiggins (2009) point to this dilemma of presenting oneself as "too" suicidal versus "not suicidal enough." The authors assert that members of the forums went to great lengths to establish their "authentically suicidal" self and seek validation from others. If one is deemed not being authentically "on the edge" of life and death, then that person is "likely to be excluded from further participation or discussion in the interaction" (p. 182).

Online media here not only works to connect the deathcaster and his audience but also creates and even stabilizes the boundary between them. Sherry Turkle once famously embraced the Internet's ability to fulfil human desire to be someone else, calling cyberspace a "social laboratory for experimenting with the constructions and reconstructions of self" (1995, p. 180). However, in her 2011 book *Alone Together* Turkle takes a much more critical tone and raises concern as to how we, due to our anxiety about intimacy, use "digital technology for ways to be in relationships and protect ourselves from them at the same time" (2011, p. xii). In Dora's case, both the deathcaster and the viewers used technology to keep in touch while keeping at bay the risk that such intimacy entails. On the one side of the screen, the premise of anonymity and savvy scepticism protected the viewers from bearing moral responsibility. On the other side of the screen, the deathcaster took advantage of the one-way broadcasting and constructed a suicidal self – alone at his own discretion. Through deathcasting, Dora's testimonial seems to be flattened into a spectacle that connected viewers only in their solitude while pushing the deathcaster further to the edge of death.

Suicide intervention via the Internet: a glimpse of hope

Though there is no way to verify the truth, Dora's deathcasting might be the flip side of his desperate cry for help. When he decided to broadcast his suicide, Dora's inner pain might have become so unbearable that the prospect of death and relief might have effaced his biological imperative for life. Yet, when he turned on the Webcam and invited others to witness his last moment, he might have looked for reasons for giving up his plan. At least, the Internet has provided Dora with an opportunity to share otherwise hidden suicidal thoughts and gain social recognition by anonymous online viewers. Although in Dora's deathcasting this opportunity has led to a tragic outcome, it nonetheless shows a glimpse of hope for constructive potential of the Internet for suicide prevention.

Over the past two decades there has been an increasing number of attempts made by mental health experts and public health professionals to employ online tools for suicide intervention. Among the most prominent is the effort toward the provision of online resources and self-help tools. For example, the National Suicide Prevention Lifeline (NSPL) in the United States (www.suicidepreventionlifeline. org) provides several resources including suicide prevention toolkit, safety plans, and coping tips, as well as survivors' video testimonies to raise social awareness. There is also a series of suicide intervention initiatives to provide online DIY aids to people with suicidal thoughts. Online tools are expected to offer a cost-effective means to reach suicidal people who do not seek or receive professional help due to attitudinal barriers like shame and fear of stigma, as well as the lack of access to face-to-face services. DIY programs based on cognitive behavioral therapy (CBT) have reportedly produced significant decreases in suicidal ideation among the intervention group in Australia (Christensen et al. 2013), Japan (Sueki 2013), and the Netherlands (Kerkhor, van Spijker and Mokkenstorm 2013). In addition to resource provision, researchers point to the importance of improving suicide literacy and access to evidence-based knowledge. Westerlund and Wasserman (2009) recommend search engines like Google use optimization strategies to increase the probability of suicidal people finding reliable information and self-help resources.

Another effort has focused on harnessing the interactive capacity of the Internet in crisis intervention. One of the earliest online interventions dates back to 1994, when the Samaritans of the UK and Ireland started email support for people suffering suicidal thoughts. According to their website, the organization now receives 600 emails a day, and nearly half of the emails express the feeling of suicide (The Samaritans 2014). These messages are forwarded to trained volunteers and answered within 12 hours. Compared to phone conversation, email messages to the Samaritans are reportedly "more direct, raw and intense" and often clearly express suicidal ideation (Armson 1997, p. 105). Since 1994, diverse interactive channels have been used for crisis intervention and prevention, including texting via mobile phone (Chen, Mishara and Liu 2010), mobile apps (Aguirre, McCoy and Roan 2013), and an online virtual reality, Second Life (Luxton, June and Kinn 2011). Particularly, the use of social media is becoming essential for the established crisis intervention programs. In 2011, the National Suicide Prevention Lifeline (NSPL) extended its partnership with Facebook to provide crisis intervention to American and Canadian users. The service enables Facebook users to report suicidal comments or content that evoked safety concern to Facebook through the *Report Suicidal Content* link. The Facebook safety team reviews the report and, if appropriate, sends the at-risk user an email encouraging them to call the NSPL or to click on a link to begin a confidential chat session with a crisis worker (Facebook 2011).

Alongside expert-driven eHealth initiatives, there are numerous online self-help groups organized by suicide survivors and people with suicidal thoughts. However, most researchers to date have taken an ambivalent position as to whether such groups pose a risk or an opportunity. On the one hand, peer-driven online forums have been reported to create a relatively safe space for venting suicidal worries and existential distress, finding similar others, and exchanging emotional support (Horne and Wiggins 2009; Eichenberg 2008, Baker and Fortune 2008; Seko 2008). Most self-help groups studied are operating on anonymous message boards or chat rooms, in which cue-impoverished textual communication allows members to act out their suicidal thoughts with little fear of any socially binding consequences. In their research on suicide and self-harm message boards Baker and Fortune (2008) found that participation in these online groups helped members reduce feelings of social isolation, offered access to practical advice from similar others, and provided a sense of belonging to a community.

On the other hand, concerns have been raised over detrimental effects of the Internet on vulnerable populations. One recent large-scale cohort study in Japan with more than 5,000 participants found a positive correlation between suicidal ideation and suicide-related Internet use. People who had searched for suicide methods on the Internet increased suicidal ideation, while those who had mental health consultation with anonymous others showed worsening depression and anxiety. The authors concluded that online self-disclosure of suicidal ideation has a potential harm on people at risk of suicide and mental illness (Sueki et al. 2014). The tendency observed among "pro-suicide" websites to normalize or promote suicide as a problem-solving strategy has also been identified as a risk factor. Becker and Schmidt (2005) note that on the pro-suicide websites suicide is often advocated as a problem-solving strategy for problems in life, while psychiatric and other professional sources of help are deemed as worse than helpful. The authors argue that this "antipsychiatric attitude" may justify suicide as a deliberate decision and, at the same time, marginalize the voice for alternative plans. Peer pressure to carry out suicide might also be heightened in a community setting. In a study on a pro-suicide discussion board Baume, Rolfe and Clinton (1998) reported a case in which one poster made a clear announcement of his suicide plan and wrote "I'm gonna do it any day now. Really, I promise!" (p. 139). Though his fate was unknown, the authors surmise that he might have felt obliged to proceed with his plan in order to avoid losing face. Ethnographer Chikako Ozawa-de Silva (2008) makes a similar line of observation in her work on Japanese pro-suicide websites, illuminating a group mindset shared among members. She revealed that site users often expressed a distinctive kind of existential suffering to the extent of feeling too lonely to die alone, which made the choice to die with strangers seem more justifiable than living.

With the rise of pro-suicide content online, some countries have increased vigilance over websites that promote or instigate suicide. To reduce potential risks, various measures have been proposed, including content self-regulation by internet service providers (ISPs) and filtering of websites at home, school, and other environments where vulnerable people have access to the Internet (Westerlund and Wasserman 2009). While legal bans on websites have been generally considered difficult due to the borderless nature of the Internet and public concern over unwarranted censorship, some countries have taken a stringent approach against pro-suicide websites. In 2005 Australia enacted amendments to its Criminal Code and outlawed not only promotion and incitement of suicide on the Internet with method descriptions but also the receipt and possession of such material (Pirkis et al. 2009). Although the actual impact of regulation is yet unknown, Pirkis et al. (2009) assert that the law has at least deterred individuals who might otherwise have posted or retrieved pro-suicide content on domestic websites.

In Japan, where the increase of online suicide pacts became a significant social issue since 2003, suicide intervention by the police has been promoted as a public health policy. In 2005, the Japanese National Police Agency (NPA) compiled guidelines that oblige ISPs to provide police with users' personal information when finding content suggestive of suicidal intent, such as death notes and calls for suicide pacts. According to the guidelines, police can place an emergency request to ISPs to disclose personal information when posted messages indicate the writer's explicit intention to die by specifying place, motive, method, or other

Table 13.1 Persons who reported to the police about suicidal message on the Internet

Informant/Year	2009	2010	2011	2012	2013	Total
Suicidal person him-/herself	13	13	16	10	16	68
General Internet user	99	140	193	127	131	690
Website moderator	74	101	100	63	65	403
Internet hotline center	4	5	1	7	3	20
Other	33	21	19	22	28	123
Total (case)	223	280	329	229	243	**1,304**

Source: Japan National Police Agency Cybercrime Project (2013)

details, or when the date of the proposed suicide (or suicide pact) is imminent (Telecommunications Carriers Association et al. 2005). In 2013, the NPA Cybercrime Project released a brief report about the cases in which police made such requests to ISPs for the purpose of crisis intervention. During the period from 2009 to 2013, the NPA recorded a total of 1,304 cases involving 1,335 individuals and a range of people who have reported to the police of online suicidal messages. As Table 13.1 presents, in more than a half of the cases ($n = 690$) informants were general Internet users who stumbled across suicide announcements. This can be seen as the result of increasing social awareness around Internet-related suicides and the knowledge that it requires intervention. It is also worth noting that about 5 per cent of reports ($n = 68$) were made by suicidal individuals themselves, which suggests the potential of the Internet serving as a crisis line for individuals with acute needs.

A breakdown of the outcome of police intervention is presented in Table 13.2. From 2009 to 2013, there have been 26 completed suicides and 49 suicide attempts recorded, while 395 people were identified as at high risk for suicide. For those at risk, the local police performed crisis intervention by directly dissuading them from carrying out the plan, referring them to mental health services, or requesting their family members to look after them (Japan National Police Agency Cybercrime Project 2013).

While the Japanese experience with legislation is yet unfolding, the police report indicates that collaboration between the government and ISPs may benefit some online users in need of crisis intervention. On some level, the culture of

Table 13.2 The outcome of police intervention

Outcome/Year	2009	2010	2011	2012	2013	Total
Suicide completed	2	11	5	6	2	26
Suicide attempted but survived	9	14	15	4	7	49
No attempt but high suicidal risk	78	89	81	63	84	395
No risk (incl. suicide hoax)	104	129	167	130	128	658
Unable to identify the person	35	46	65	29	33	308
Total (person)	228	288	333	232	254	**1,335**

Source: Japan National Police Agency Cybercrime Project (2013)

peer-to-peer surveillance seems to have positive potential for increasing public awareness and encouraging general Web users to take action and contact local authorities. While statutory prohibition of suicide-related content and ISPs' self-regulation must be accompanied by a considerate discussion about the freedom of speech and the right to privacy, governmental intervention of this kind may raise awareness and mobilize community efforts toward grassroots suicide prevention. Given the double-edged potential of suicidal communication online, there is a pressing need for research to better understand what draws people to suicide-themed websites and how interactions with cyber peers influence suicidal thoughts and behaviours. Understanding the perceived impacts of peer-driven web communities may enable the identification of mental health needs in suicidal individuals who are not satisfied with conventional, professional-oriented services.

Along with the need for empirical research, deathcasting illuminated the scarcity of knowledge about the impact of the *visibility* suicide has gained over the Internet. To date, little has been explored about the role visual communication plays in the practice of suicide and how the real-time or delayed participation in mediated suicides would influence public understanding of suicidal behaviour. As the demise of potential affinity between Dora and his audience implies, the visibility may have a particular impact on mutual trust established among cyber peers in regard especially to authenticity and acuteness of one's suicidal risk. Moreover, once broadcast live online, one's deathcasting can be archived, reposted, and consumed over and over by countless spectators at any time, at any place, and on any medium. In archived footage the victims repeatedly commit suicides beyond their original intention, and it is largely unknown how such posthumous digital traces would impact the witnesses. Given the burgeoning growth of visual technology and the epistemological role images play in our society, exploring cybersuicides from a critical, visual communication perspective adds enrichment to the field of suicide prevention traditionally dominated by medical and public health discourses. It is therefore necessary to take a shift from an exclusively pathological approach toward a more interdisciplinary and nuanced understanding of suicide and call into question how exactly suicide is represented online, what the potential implications of taking part in the mediated spectacle are, and how such an understanding would help us prevent tragedies like Dora's.

Conclusion

The phenomenon of deathcasting illuminated the potential of hitherto taboo, private events, being live broadcast over the Internet, consumed, archived, and re-circulated by anonymous voyeur-spectators. With its shocking and harrowing impact, one may call deathcasting a symptom of social malaise in the era of mass voyeurism, in which people's relentless quest for entertainment goes further till goading one to commit suicide. However, to fully grasp this phenomenon requires the understanding of the current era of online self-disclosure and constant connectivity, wherein the act of confession has taken on a renewed meaning with the promise of online anonymity and the practice of peer-to-peer surveillance.

Arguably, the relative anonymity of online communication has lowered psychological and attitudinal barriers for people suffering suicidal thoughts, allowing them to disclose pent-up emotions and find similar others. For better or worse, the topic of suicide has entered into the public discourse via the multitude of online voices and acquired an unprecedented global visibility, especially through live broadcasting via Webcam. For Japanese deathcaster Dora, however, the excessive visibility might have created a rupture with his audience, who became increasingly skeptical of the verisimilitude and acuteness of the deathcasting. Captured through Webcam, Dora's suicide became a tragic media spectacle in which he, the victim of self-murder, became both the solitary actor *and* lone member of an audience being "alone together" with technology.

Dora's tragedy suggests a pressing need to update our understanding of suicide with respect to the ever-expanding visual culture. Recent efforts in suicide prevention by medical and public health professionals seem promising but ought to be complemented by a critical analysis of the role images play within our society and the way visuals shape our understanding of suicide. More research is therefore required as to how the "suicidal self" is visually constructed and performed over the Internet and how such media representations would impact the suicidal actors and the spectators behind their screens. An interdisciplinary approach will not only enrich the scope for suicide prevention but will also allow us to see suicide in a more nuanced and potentially beneficial manner.

Notes

1 One of the most publicized self-immolations was that of Thích Quảng Đức in 1963. The Vietnamese Buddhist monk sat himself on fire in the middle of a Saigon street to protest alleged persecution of Buddhists by South Vietnam's government. Malcolm Browne at the Associated Press photographed Quảng Đức's suicide and his work was featured on newspapers across the world (Associated Press 2013). Self-immolation still continues as a form of political protest particularly in Tibet. According to International Campaign for Tibet (2014), since 2009, 132 Tibetans have self-immolated to protest against the Chinese government.
2 As for public suicides at bridges, see very thought-provoking and controversial documentary film *The Bridge* (directed by Eric Steel in 2006) which pictures the people jumping off the Golden Gate Bridge in San Francisco and investigates narratives of the survivors and the bereaved.
3 For example, Yukio Mishima's suicide in 1970 that sent a shock wave across Japan. The writer committed *seppuku* at the Japanese Self-Defense Forces headquarters after a failed coup d'état to restore the power of the emperor. Fox (2014) states that Mishima's longing for a traditional ritual suicide was rather aesthetically motivated than politically inspired, carried out in a hope to atone for the loss of Japanese identity in the post-war era.
4 The original thread on which Dora announced his suicide plan was no longer accessible. However, copied logs are still available at the time of writing (October 2014) on log storage sites such as *mimizun* (http://mimizun.com/log/2ch/campus/1288804461/). References to the 2ch thread in this chapter are based on the copied log retrieved from *mimizun.*
5 While most deathcasting videos, including Dora's Ustream footage, were deleted almost immediately after the incident by the site moderators, this Swedish deathcasting by Marcus Jennes is still viewable online in many formats at the time of writing (October 2014). The video was archived online and extensively distributed over YouTube and

other online depositories, later being reproduced as short motion pictures and gif images. A time lapse of the whole footage is available on Liveleak.com as of October 2014.

6 While blaming the Internet, Japanese mass media have enthusiastically reported on online suicide pacts with detailed descriptions about the methods and pro-suicide websites where people with suicidal thoughts can meet and even arrange group suicides. Since the first suicide pacts occurred in February 2003, there were 599 articles in five national newspapers and 156 incidents of television coverage on online suicide pacts (Ozawa de-Silva, 2010). Researchers have expressed concern that such media coverage could cause a contagion effect.

7 boyd and Ellison (2007) define social network sites as "web-based services that allows individuals to (1) construct a public or semi-public profile within a bounded system, (2) articulate a list of other users with whom they share a connection, and (3) view and traverse their list of connections and those made by others within the system".

8 The online art project PostSecret (http://postsecret.com/) manifests this desire to disclose secrets on the Internet. This weblog posts images of homemade postcards sent in by anonymous creators on which they reveal a secret that they had never disclosed, ranging from humorous anecdotes ("I bought my wife stockings. She won't wear them so I do!") to poignant confession ("The only man who ever loved me back has a wife and a daughter he named after me"). According to Frank Warren, the founder of PostSecret, the site often receives postcards revealing suicidal thoughts. In April 2008, Warren partnered with 1-800-suicide (a national crisis hotline) to launch a peer-run crisis hotline on university campuses (Holahan, 2008).

References

Aguirre, R., McCoy, M., and Roan, M., 2013. Development Guidelines from a Study of Suicide Prevention Mobile Applications (Apps). *Journal of Technology in Human Services*, 31, pp. 269–293.

Andrejevic, M., 2006. The Discipline of Watching: Detection, Risk, and Lateral Surveillance. *Critical Studies in Media Communication*, 23(5), pp. 391–407.

Andrejevic, M., 2007. *iSpy: Surveillance and Power in the Interactive Era*. Lawrence: University of Kansas Press.

Armson, S., 1997. Suicide and Cyberspace – Befriending by E-mail. *Crisis*, 18(3), pp. 103–106.

Associated Press, 2013. The Burning Monk 50th Anniversary: A Defining Moment Photographed by AP's Malcolm Brown. *Associated Press*. [online] Available at: http://www.ap.org/explore/the-burning-monk/ [Accessed 30 September, 2014].

Baker D., and Fortune, S., 2008. Understanding Self-harm and Suicide Websites. *Crisis: The Journal of Crisis Intervention and Suicide Prevention*, 29(3), pp. 118–122.

Bauman, Z., & Lyon, D. (2013). *Liquid Surveillance: A Conversation*. Cambridge, UK: Polity Press.

Baume, P., Rolfe, A., and Clinton, M., 1998. Suicide on the Internet: A Focus for Nursing Intervention? *The Australian and New Zealand Journal of Mental Health Nursing*, 7, pp. 134–141.

Beck, C. T., 2005. Benefits of Participating in Internet Interviews: Women Helping Women. *Qualitative Health Research*, 15(3), pp. 411–422.

Becker, K., Mayer, M., Negaenborg, M., El-Faddagh, M., and Schmidt, M. H. 2004. Parasuicide Online: Can Suicide Website Trigger Suicidal Behavior in Predisposed Adolescents? *Nordic Journal of Psychiatry*, 58(2), pp. 111–114.

Becker, K., and Schmidt, M. 2005. When Kids Seek Help On-line: Internet Chat Room and Suicide. *Reclaiming Children & Youth*, 13(4), pp. 229–230.

boyd, d., and Ellison, N. B., 2007. Social Network Sites: Definition, History, and Scholarship. *Journal of Computer-Mediated Communication*, 13(1), article 11. [online] Available at: http://jcmc.indiana.edu/vol12/issue1/boyd.ellison.html.

Chen, H., Mishara, B. L., and Liu, X. X., 2010. A Pilot Study of Mobile Telephone Message Interventions with Suicide Attempters in China. *Crisis*, 31(2), pp. 109–112.

Christensen, H., Farrer, L., Batterham, P. J., Mackinnon, A., Griffiths, K. M., and Donker, T. 2013. The Effect of a Web-Based Depression Intervention on Suicide Ideation: Secondary Outcome From a Randomised Controlled Trial in a Helpline. *BMJ Open*, 3(6), e.002886.

Debord, G., 1976. *The Society of the Spectacle*. Translated from French by D. Nicholson-Smith, 1995. New York: Zone Books.

Eichenberg, C., 2008. Internet Message Boards for Suicidal People: A Typology of Users. *Cyberpsychology and Behavior*, 11, pp. 101–113.

Facebook, 2011. New Partnership Between Facebook and the National Suicide Prevention Lifeline. Available at: https://www.facebook.com/notes/facebook-safety/new-partner ship-between-facebook-and-the-national-suicide-prevention-lifeline/310287485658707 [Accessed 27 October, 2014].

Foucault, M., 1977. *Discipline and Punish: The Birth of the Prison*. Translated from French by S. Sheridan, 1977. New York: Vintage.

Foucault, M., 1993. About the Beginnings of the Hermeneutics of the Self: Two Lectures at Dartmouth. *Political Theory*, 21(2), pp. 198–227.

Fox, S., 2014. Yukio Mishima – 'The Lost Samurai.' *Japan Today*. [online] 12 January. Available at: http://www.japantoday.com/category/opinions/view/yukio-mishima-the-lost-samurai [Accessed 30 September, 2014].

Holahan, C., 2008. Post Secret Founder Trying to Save Lives. *BusinessWeek*. [online] 02 April. Available at: http://www.businessweek.com/the_thread/techbeat/archives/2008/04/post_secret_fou.html [Accessed 15 October, 2014].

Horne, J., & Wiggins, S. (2009). Doing Being 'On the Edge': Managing the Dilemma of Being Authentically Suicidal in an Online Forum. *Sociology of Health & Illness*, 31(2), pp. 170–184.

International Campaign for Tibet, 2014. Self-Immolation by Tibetans. *International Campaign for Tibet*. [online] 22 September. Available at: http://www.savetibet.org/resources/fact-sheets/self-immolations-by-tibetans/ [Accessed 30 September, 2014].

Japan National Police Agency Cybercrime Project, 2013. *Internet jō no Jisatsu Yokoku Jian heno Taiō Jyokyō ni tusite* [Brief report: Dealing with suicide announcement on the Internet], 27 March. Available at: http://www.npa.go.jp/cyber/statics/h25/pdf01–3.pdf [Accessed 08 August, 2014].

Kear, K., Chetwynd, F., and Jefferis, H., 2014. Social Presence in Online Learning Communities: The Role of Personal Profiles. *Research in Learning Technology*, 22:19710 [online] Available at: http://dx.doi.org/10.3402/rlt.v22.19710.

Kerkhor, A., van Spijker, B., and Mokkenstorm, J., 2013. Reducing the Burden of Suicidal Thoughts through Online Cognitive Behavioural Therapy Self Help, in B. Mishara & A. Kerkhof (eds), *Suicide Prevention and New Technologies: Evidence Based Practice*. Hampshire: Palgrave Macmillan, pp. 1–23.

Kravets, D., 2008. Teen Kills Self on Justin.tv – Update. *Wired*. [online] 20 November. Available at: http://www.wired.com/2008/11/teen-kills-self/ [Accessed 27 September, 2014].

The Local – Swedish News in English, 2010. Swedish Man Dies in Live 'Cyber Suicide' Broadcast. [online] 12 October. Available at: http://www.thelocal.se/20101012/29566 [Accessed 03 October, 2014].

Ludwig, A. M., 1997. *How Do We Know Who We Are? A Biography of the Self*. Oxford: Oxford University Press.

Luxton, D., June, J. and Kinn, J., 2011. Technology-Based Suicide Prevention: Current Applications and Future Directions. *Telemedicine and e-Health*, 17, pp. 50–54.

Luxton, D., June, J., and Fairall, J., 2012. Social Media and Suicide: A Public Health Perspective. *American Journal of Public Health*, 102, pp. S195–S200.

Lyon, D., 2010. Liquid Surveillance: The Contribution of Zygmunt Bauman to Surveillance Studies. *International Political Sociology*, 4(4), pp. 325–338.

Matthews, J., 2008. Suicide and the Japanese Media: On the Hunt for Blame. *Electronic Journal of Contemporary Japanese Studies*. [online] Available at: http://www.japanese studies.org.uk/discussionpapers/2008/Matthews.html [Accessed 30 September, 2014].

Nowak, K., and Biocca, F., 2003. The Effect of the Agency and Anthropomorphism on Users' Sense of Telepresence, Copresence and Social Presence in Virtual Environments. *Presence*, 12(5), pp. 481–494.

Ozawa-de Silva, C., 2008. Too Lonely to Die Alone: Internet Suicide Pacts and Existential Suffering in Japan. *Culture, Medicine, and Psychiatry*, 32, pp. 516–551.

Ozawa-de Silva, C., 2010. Shared Death: Self, Sociality and Internet Group Suicide in Japan. *Transcultural Psychiatry*, 47, pp. 392–418.

Pirkis, J., Neal, L., Dare, A., Blood, R., and Studdert, D. 2009. Legal Bans on Pro-Suicide Web Sites: An Early Retrospective from Australia. *Suicide and Life-Threatening Behavior*, 39(2), pp. 190–193.

Rosen, C., 2007. Virtual Friendship and the New Narcissism. *The New Atlantis*. 17, pp. 15–31.

The Samaritans, 2014. *Email Samaritans*. Available at: http://www.samaritans.org/ how-we-can-help-you/different-ways-you-can-get-touch/what-happens-when-i-email [Accessed 15 October, 2014].

Sankei Shimbun, 2010. *Douga saito de Jisatsu Chūkei*. [Man broadcasted suicide on livestreaming site]. 10 November. Available at: http://sankei.jp.msn.com/affairs/ news/110111/crm11011120590218-n1.htm[Accessed 27 September, 2014].

Seko, Y., 2008. 'Suicide Machine' Seekers: Transgressing Suicidal Taboos Online. *Learning Inquiry*, 2(3), pp. 181–199.

Sueki, H., 2013. Web-Based Suicide Prevention Using the Concepts of Cognitive Behavioral Therapy. *Bulletin of the Faculty of Human Studies* (Wako University), 6(1), pp. 35–45.

Sueki, H., Yonemoto, N., Takeshima, T., and Inagaki, M., 2014. The Impact of Suicidality-Related Internet Use: A Prospective Large Cohort Study with Young and Middle-Aged Internet Users. *PLoS ONE*, 9(4), e94841.

Telecommunications Carriers Association, Telecom Services Association, Japan Internet Providers Association, and Japan Cable and Telecommunications Association, 2005. *Internet jō no Jisatsu Yokoku Jian heno Taiō ni kansuru Guideline*. [Guidelines for dealing with suicide threats on the Internet] 05 October. Available at: http://www.telesa.or.jp/ consortium/suicide/pdf/guideline_suicide_051005.pdf [Accessed 09 September, 2014].

Turkle, S., 1995. *Life on the Screen: Identity in the Age of the Internet*. New York: Simon and Schuster.

Turkle, S., 2011. *Alone Together: Why We Expect More From Technology and Less From Each Other*. New York: Basic Books.

Ungoed-Thomas, J., 2007. Police Hunt Chatroom Users Over Web Suicide 'Goading.' *Sunday Times*. [online] 25 March. Available at: http://www.thesundaytimes.co.uk/sto/news/ uk_news/article62066.ece [Accessed 27 September, 2014].

Walther, J. B., Slovacek, C. L., and Tidwell, L. C., 2001. Is a Picture Worth a Thousand Words? Photographic Images in Long-Term and Short-Term Computer-Mediated Communication. *Communication Research*, 28(1), pp. 105–134.

Westerlund, M., and Wasserman, D., 2009, The Role of the Internet in Suicide Prevention, in D. Wasserman & C. Wasserman (eds), *Oxford Textbook of Suicidology and Suicide Prevention: A Global Perspective*. Oxford: Oxford University Press, pp. 525–532.

Index